READING *THE LORD OF THE RINGS*

READING *THE LORD OF THE RINGS*

NEW WRITINGS ON TOLKIEN'S CLASSIC

EDITED BY ROBERT EAGLESTONE

continuum
LONDON • NEW YORK

Continuum

The Tower Building   15 East 26th Street
11 York Road   New York
London SE1 7NX   NY 10010

www.continuumbooks.com

British Library Cataloguing-in-Publication Data
A catalogue record for this book is available from the British Library.

ISBN HB: 0–8264–8459–X
ISBN PB: 0–8264–8460–3

Library of Congress Cataloging-in-Publication Data
Reading The Lord of the Rings : new writings on Tolkien's
trilogy / edited by Robert Eaglestone.
    p. cm.
    Includes bibliographical references and index.
    ISBN 0–8264–8459–X—ISBN 0–8264–8460–3 (pbk.)
    1. Tolkien, J.R.R. (John Ronald Reuel), 1892–1973.
Lord of the rings.   2. Fantasy fiction, English—history
and criticism.   3. Middle Earth (Imaginary place)
I. Eaglestone, Robert, 1968–
PR6039.032L63713   2006
823′.912—dc22   2005018695

Typeset by RefineCatch Limited, Bungay, Suffolk
Printed and bound in Great Britain by
MPG Books Ltd, Bodmin, Cornwall

CONTENTS

INTRODUCTION

Robert Eaglestone

OLD BATTLES

Writing critical work on Tolkien and *The Lord of the Rings* often involves drawing battle lines, between, for example, advocates of the popular and guardians of high culture, between academic scholarship and 'fan' writing, between admiration for a text and a fear of murdering it by dissection, between Old English experts and critics of modern writing, and so on. This volume will not be drawn explicitly into these conflicts, not least, simply, because many of these debates are, or ought to be, done with. One can admire and study both Joyce and Tolkien. *The Lord of the Rings* is clearly an important book with no little literary value, a significant film trilogy, a social and cultural phenomenon and is, for all these reasons, the subject of this volume and wider resurgent critical interest.

However, there is one 'battle' with which this book is involved. The most notable scholars of Tolkien make clear their opposition to what is called 'theory'. Patrick Curry writes that he 'has too much respect for Tolkien's work ... to sacrifice it on the altar of theory' (Curry 1998: 18). Even Tolkien's best critic, Tom Shippey, equates theory with Saurman's evil and Vietnam generals ('with their body bags') when he writes that 'literary theorists with their différances and ratures' (Shippey 2000: 126) are trapped in a belief-draining jargon. Of course, much – but not all – of this is simply academic knockabout: both Curry and Shippey have 'theories' of how literature in general and Tolkien in particular work. Curry pays tribute to postmodernism and to eco-criticism in his book as enabling sets of ideas; Shippey, with more complexity and drawing on Tolkien's valedictory address, argues that the world, literature and language, diachronically understood, are inextricably woven together, and that the meaning of Tolkien's text lies through the reconstruction of this through philology. By attacking other theories as 'theory' in general, these and many other writers cover up their own unavoidable presuppositions in reading. And indeed, this is one of the things that 'theory' – a poor word, binding together a huge range of different ideas and discourses – can be seen to be: simply, the often-unacknowledged presuppositions that one takes into reading. Nobody, not even an eleven-year-old boy reading Tolkien for the first time, is a blank slate: each of us has predispositions, ideas and pre-existing prejudices that shape our reactions to a text. But 'theory' has another meaning: it names the way that literary studies changes and develops. To tell an often-repeated story: from the 1970s to the present, a huge range of new ideas have been reshaping the study of literature. Some of these ideas come from other disciplines (from politics, from the study of sexuality, from philosophy, from history); some from rapid social change, especially over issues of gender, race and social difference, and from the collapse of the European empires and from globalization; some developed from different interweavings and new conjunctions of literary texts. All of these ideas have and are still transforming how we read, as well as revealing that what 'we used to believe' (say, that literature simply embodied 'good values') was theoretical too.

However, these sorts of approaches – not understood in the way they are often taught, as simple mechanical filters through which to read literature or see films, but as a changing and developing intellectual contexts – have rarely been clearly engaged with Tolkien's work. Indeed, the resistance to this has been quite strong. The study of this major novelist has been, as it were, cut off from the main, and in general, those that study his work have preferred this. Oddly, much Tolkien criticism has isolated Tolkien's work in a way that unwittingly supports those who would rather not see it studied and explored for other reasons.

This book, then, seeks to reintegrate *The Lord of the Rings* into the broad sweep of current literary critical and theoretical interests, and in this way to save it from the very many woolly-minded positive, often naively apologetic, sometimes psychoanalytical readings of the novel which see it simply as the triumph of Good over Evil, or a psychological journey: these – despite their shrill protests of its worth – actually reduce the literary achievement of *The Lord of the Rings* to that of a simple fairy tale or children's story. The book is no such thing: it is a meditation on what the very nature of community and evil might be in the twentieth century, traumatized by two World Wars, mass death and totalitarian disaster. The book is – could only be – a mid-twentieth-century novel: Middle-earth is better compared to Orwell's Air Strip One or Margaret Atwood's Gilead than to Narnia or Earthsea. This, in a way, is to reiterate the points made by Tom Shippey, when he places Tolkien's work into the mainstream of British modernist literature in the twentieth century (Shippey 2000: 312).

READING THE TEXT OF *THE LORD OF THE RINGS*

One of the most important things that literary theory does is to focus attention on the text and the language of the text itself. In the case of *The Lord of the Rings*, this is extremely important because the book has been the victim of too many readings that seek to show it as a mythopoetic journey, or archetypal process or some such: all these, precisely, do not to read the text itself, but see it as a symptom of some other mythical, religious or psychological process. This is not to deny these outright, but to say that these sorts of reading are always interpretations and are read in tension with the text. Indeed, they often ignore the complexities of the text and the plot in their eagerness to make some wider claim. In contrast, paying attention to both the text and its language produces all sorts of significant results. Shippey's monumental and insightful readings and knowledge of Tolkien's intellectual background have, of course, taught us a great deal about the construction of the text through what he calls 'calquing' (though it's noticeable that some of Shippey's most insightful assessments – his discussion of evil, his contextualizing of Tolkien as a modernist writer – diverge from this). However, this is only one way of paying attention to the language.

For example, it is widely asserted that Tolkien is a 'traumatized' author although little evidence – apart from the moments of horror in his writings and the rather patronizing assumption that as a veteran of World War One he simply was traumatized, or the (clearly incorrect) idea that he escaped from the world into his fantasy world – is marshalled for this assumption. However, attention to the text of *The Lord of the Rings*, and recent work in trauma theory might offer an insight into this, and into its importance as a novel and success in British and Anglophone cultural life. One of the unusual things about *The Lord of the Rings*, and something that certainly sets it apart from much twentieth-century British literature, while tying it into the cultural fabric of the century as remembered more broadly, is that it reflects the experience of both World Wars. Unlike World War Two, refracted in Orwell's *1984* or Waugh's 'Arms and the Man' trilogy, or World War One, retold by Siegfried Sassoon or Robert Graves, and in the poetry so often taught and cited, *The Lord of the Rings* represents the personal and cultural trauma of both wars together, each with its own rhetorics or discourses. It is in this, perhaps, that its centrality and historical context as an English novel lies: a literary equivalent of the way that war memorials were rewritten after 1945, with a mixture of tragedy, courageous assertion and resigned melancholy, to take account of the War after the War to End Wars.

Paul Fussell, perhaps the most significant critic of the psychological and emotional culture of the two great 'hot' wars of the twentieth century, describes the rhetoric of war in the following ways. In a celebrated pair of columns in *The Great War and Modern Memory*, Fussell highlights the 'raised' rhetoric used in discussions of World War One:

A friend is a	Comrade
Friendship is	Comradeship, or fellowship . . .
The enemy is	the foe, or the host
Danger is	peril . . .
The Dead on the battlefield are	the fallen . . .
The front is	the field . . .
One's chest is one's	breast
Dead bodies constitute	ashes or dust
(Fussell 1975: 20–21)	

This rhetoric – call it 'inflationary' – was taught and developed in the adventure stories of 'Henty; the male-romances of Rider Haggard; the poems of Robert Bridges; and especially the Arthurian poems of Tennyson and the pseudo-mediaeval Romances of William Morris' (Fussell 1975: 20): all influences on Tolkien. *The Lord of the Rings*, too, abounds in echoes of these conscious heroic archaisms: *The Fellowship of the Ring*, the Field of Cormallen. This discourse is also one explanation for the very use of a fantastic idiom: it is only in a fantasy world that is untouched by 'our' world that this heroic rhetoric is not immediately and simultaneously subverted just as it stands. That is, to our ears just these words are immediately ironic. But Tolkien's work does not let this irony happen in and of its own accord. Of course, this World War One inflationary rhetoric was soured by the actual experience the troops underwent and much of Fussell's study is about the ironic division between this high language and actual experience, and how literary texts described and exploited this with what one could call 'deflationary rhetoric'. In *The Lord of the Rings*, while maintaining the heroic discourse unironically, there is also this strong counter-rhetorical strand of deflationary ironic subversion. This rhetoric is enacted in a number of ways: constantly by the perspective of the (literally) little people, rather than the great, and also, for example, by the war-torn environment outside and inside Mordor ('a land defiled, diseased beyond all healing', *TT*, IV, ii, 294). Frodo, too, is a figure of this ('I am wounded . . . it will never really heal') (*RK*, VI, ix, 371).

But Tolkien's book, and its rhetoric, is neither an exculpation or an evasion in its 'inflationary' raised tone nor is it a 'deflationary' condemnation. Instead these two discourses are tempered by a third, laconic language.

> The Second World War was silent . . . silence ranging from the embarrassed to the sullen. It's as if both the ironic and the elegiac conventions for making some literary sense of modern war had been exhausted earlier. Result: a new laconic style . . . Second World War poetry is . . . notably an art of litotes.
> (Fussell 1988: 128, 130)

For Fussell, the rhetoric of World War Two was not one of a crusade nor subversion. Instead it reflected the thoughts of those on the Allied side, that the war was simply a task to be undertaken: not a noble quest but, as Sam sees his task, a pragmatic 'errand' (*TT*, IV, x, 425). World War Two, inconceivable as 'romantic', was 'indescribably cruel and insane': indeed, it

> was not until the Second World War had enacted all its madness that one could realize how near Victorian social and ethical norms the First World War really was . . . [the Second World War] was a

savage affair, barely conceivable to the well-conducted imagination (the main reason there's so little good writing about it) and
hardly approachable without some unfashionable theory of
human mass insanity and inbuilt inherited corruption.
(Fussell 1989: 132)

At its heart, for Fussell, World War Two was characterized by an
ideological vacuum, by the simple need for the Allies not to lose:
victory not for King and Country, but for survival. 'Why we fight'
was not so much *for* something as against fascism, and against
destruction. In this sense, the Allies mirrored Hitler's rhetoric and
mindset: for the Nazis, the war was a total 'race war' for survival and
domination. And this, as the characters repeatedly say, is what faces
the West in the war of the Ring. Not victory for Gondor or Rohan,
but simply survival, and even this at no little cost. Throughout *The
Lord of the Rings* both the 'inflationary' tone proclaiming (a perhaps
vacuous) ideological security and the subversion of this in the
horror of war and its damages are diffracted by a simple understated
language that invokes the need to 'get the job done'. 'What am I
to do then?' Sam asks himself, stranded and alone with Frodo's
seeming corpse: 'See it through' (*TT*, IV, x, 425).

Like the threads that make up a rope, these three rhetorics are
constantly interwoven and shifting. For example, what could
embody understatement more than the name 'Strider' for the
returning king. Yet, in the end, it becomes a royal name: in 'the
High Tongue, it will not sound so ill, and *Telcontar* I will be' (*RK*, V,
viii, 158–9). These shifts in tone can take place at the smallest level:
Merry (though here the more heroic Meriadoc) slung his shield
heroically 'at his back' (*RK*, V, vi, 133), not the more prosaically 'on
his back': the choice of preposition marks the discourse. Later he
asks (deflationary) 'Are you going to bury me?' (*RK*, V, viii, 152).
The response to this contains all three modes:

'No indeed!' said Pippin, trying to sound cheerful [laconic],
though his heart was wrung [heroic, inflationary] with fear and
pity [deflationary, unheroic]. 'No [the repetition itself is unheroic,
responding to the suffering not the heroic glamour of Merry's
state], we are going [laconic, matter of fact] to the Houses of
Healing [heroic].'
(*RK*, V, viii, 152)

Or, again, Frodo's explanation of his leave-taking to Sam:

It must often be so [inflationary in its syntax], Sam, when things are in danger [laconic, pragmatic]: someone has to give them up [laconic], lose them, so that others may keep them [deflationary, with contrast between loss and keeping, and the hint of a Christ-like sacrifice].
(*RK*, VI, ix, 376)

Thus, one of Tolkien's greatest strengths as a novelist is precisely to use these (usually very separate) rhetorics, and to mix and play them off as a counter point to each other.

More than this, the discourses themselves reflect on each other. Sam, in Mordor carrying the Ring, looks around and in an exemplary 'laconic'/getting the job done discourse moment he realizes that Mordor's defences are to keep people in (the laconic/'getting the job done' question is: how does it work? not how will it sound? Then he is besieged by the vision of 'Samwise the Strong, Hero of the Age' (*RK*, VI, i, 206) but the fullness of his 'plain hobbit sense' (*RK*, VI, i, 206) stops this inflation, and he begins to plan what to do. Here, the one discourse has, effectively, critiqued the other. Again, when Merry attacks the Nazgûl, the deflationary rhetoric ('Merry crawled on all fours like a dazed beast, and such a horror was on him that he was blind and sick' (*RK*, V, vi, 128) – shades of the gas attack casualty in that most deflationary of poems, Owen's 'Dulce et Decorum est' – is countered by the heroic, complete with heroic, archaic syntax ('King's man! King's man! . . . Pity filled his heart, and suddenly the slow-kindled courage of his race awoke', *RK*, V, vi, 128). Indeed, the book offers inside itself various retellings of its own story in different discourses: 'Nine-Fingered Frodo and the Ring of Doom' as heroic/inflationary; Bilbo's book as comically deflation-ary (trying to find the right title, Bilbo's inevitable failure to complete it); and laconic and successfully pragmatic: Frodo's com-pletion and titling of the book, in his 'firm flowing script' (*RK*, VI, ix, 373).

But these three rhetorics are more than simply ways of telling the story: each has its own internal logic which does not simply embody the plot but determines it. Shippey argues that Tolkien believed that

beneath all this there might be a 'true language', one 'isomorphic with reality' and that in any case there might often be a close connection between thing-signified, person-signifying and language signified-in.
(Shippey 2003: 114)

This is to imply not only that the world shapes language, as Shippey argues, but also that, in turn too, language shapes the world. Aragorn and Theoden, for example, as to some lesser extent the Hobbits who transform from Pippin and Merry to Peregrine and Meriadoc, inhabit this heroic world, and cannot but be, live and die heroically. This heroic discourse, except where inverted (in, for example, Pope or in places in Chaucer and Joyce), simply can't do mundane realities or even (Fussell again) US marines

sliding under fire down a shell-pocked ridge slimy with mud and liquid dysentery shit into the maggoty Japanese and USMC corpses at the bottom, vomiting as the maggots burrowed into their own foul clothing.
(Fussell 1988: 30)

Likewise, the character closest to the deflationary ironic discourse, Frodo, simply can't live happily ever after, nor be traditionally heroic: it is the deflationary discourse itself that forces this. And the laconic discourse is simply matter of fact in a 'life goes on' way: Sam's 'I'm back' (*RK*, VI, ix, 378). In this way the discourses themselves shape the plot and the action, they shape the events of the novel.

Many readings of the novel, even those that discuss it as a work of 'trauma' miss this interplay of rhetorics. However, it is precisely in the interplay, the interweaving of these rhetorics that the 'trauma' is made apparent. The 'wound' of the trauma of the two wars is simply that there can be no one choice of a unifying, final rhetoric. No one of these three languages – the heroic inflationary, the ironic deflationary and the laconic pragmatic – is a 'master language'. There is no 'final' language in which to speak. In this, *The Lord of the Rings* avoids even the closure of (for example) *The Waste Land*. Each rhetoric, and each rhetoric's plot (the heroic king returned, the traumatized victim, the pragmatic toiler), winds around the other, sometimes supportive, sometimes distracting: this explains the three endings of the novel (heroic, traumatized, pragmatic) and its length. However, it is perhaps precisely the 'traumatized' mixture of these different discourses, from the level of vocabulary, style and syntax, and up to the level of plot and character, that gives the book not only its literary strength but also opens it to polyvalent ideological interpretations which have, in part, ensured its popularity. Indeed, as the films show, different discourses – different threads from the rope – are taken up in different times and places. One might, for example, be tempted to find Jackson's films a good reflection of that odd mixture of victimized self-pity and arrogance, rather than the more laconic pragmatism of Stud Terkel's oral history of the 'Good War', that characterizes much contemporary American culture.

Finally, the inconclusive mixture of discourses, too, serves to locate the novel as a response to the personal, social and cultural traumas of both World Wars. This complex and doubled historical context – one written for all to see in the language of public memory in the UK, in museums like the Imperial War Museum and public monuments, but rarely discussed in the literature for which the gulf between the wars is too great – perhaps allows *The Lord of the Rings* uniquely to enunciate something about British collective memory. *The Lord of the Rings* does not offer or create a mythology for England – as if England (Arthur, Robin Hood, Alfred, Joseph of Arimatheia, even Brutus of Troy for who 'Britain' is supposedly named) lacked such a thing: instead, like any modern novel, it is intimately interwoven with, but as art not simply reducible to, its time and historical context. As the celebrated letter 131 reads, Tolkien wanted to *dedicate* his mythology to England, because it came from the cultural context.

DIFFERENT READINGS

This book, then, explores a heterogeneous range of critical themes drawing from a range of discourses that might be categorized as theoretical. There is not one overall programme or view among the contributors, except a sense that a 'rereading' of this very significant text needs to take place.

The first chapter, 'Towards a better Tolkien criticism' by Michael Drout, a leading North American Tolkien specialist, takes an overview of the analysis of Tolkien's works, and argues that debates over authorship – especially Foucault's essay on this subject – are extremely illuminating for *The Lord of the Rings* and are more widely liberating for Tolkien criticism in general: moreover, work on Tolkien also nuances these critical/theoretical debates. In Chapter 2 screen-writer and literary and film critic Barry Langford, in his account of the differences between the film trilogy and the novel, focuses on the use of time in both texts. In her chapter, 'Gothic echoes', Sue Zlosnik offers a different literary genealogy and context for Tolkien's work as a gothic work, which serves to fix the text in a different tradition, both contemporary and modern. The novelist and critic Adam Roberts asks the question: why a ring? The answer to this seeming basic question turns out to shape the work, its values and meaning. In contrast, Robert Eaglestone's chapter focuses on the significance of the invisibility the Ring confers, and finds in this, following the work of Emmanuel Levinas and contrasting with Shippey's celebrated account, the root of evil in the novel, as well as its relationship to modernity. Simon Malpas turns to Martin Heidegger to analyse the significance of modernity and the idea of home in *The Lord of the Rings*. Jennifer Neville, in Chapter 7, con-trasts Tolkien's understanding of the representation of women, drawn from Old English texts, to contemporary readings of the same material, and finds the two dissonant. Drawing on *Beowulf*, she argues that Tolkien underestimates the role of women in Old English culture and then brings this underestimation forward to his novel. Following on from this, Holly Crocker explores the ways that the construction of masculinity orders the text, and carries a pro-found ideological charge. Esther Saxey's chapter focuses on the homoeroticism in both the novel and the films, and explores both the celebration of this and the very strong cultural forces that would rather silence this aspect of the text and its interpretation. Scott Kleinman sees the novel as a meditation on the nature of service, and finds a series of overlapping models of service in the text. The final two chapters explore Tolkien's legacy outside the book and film texts. Barry Atkins looks at the ways in which Middle-earth figures in video games, and finds interesting paradoxes in their development. Finally, novelist and writer Roz Kaveney offers an insightful overview into the ways that Tolkien's model of fantasy has been used, reacted against and adopted by a range of contemporary writers.

A note on citation: Michael Drout has suggested that

because there are so many editions of *The Hobbit* and *The Lord of the Rings*, citations will be by book and chapter as well as by page-number . . . Thus a citation from *The Fellowship of the Ring*, book two, chapter four, page 318 is written '*FR*, II, iv, 318'.

I have followed this advice and this book will use the widely available HarperCollins 1994 three-volume edition.

PART I

CONTEXT AND CRITICISM

CHAPTER I

TOWARDS A BETTER TOLKIEN CRITICISM

Michael D. C. Drout

The literary works of J. R. R. Tolkien present some challenging theoretical and interpretive problems that have not, to this point, been engaged by Tolkien scholarship. This lack of engagement represents a series of missed opportunities: Tolkien criticism would benefit from grappling with these theoretical issues, and literary studies would stand to gain by testing some widely held theories against the complexities of Tolkien's works. But cultural, intellectual and even political divides have thus far hindered what could be a fertile interchange of ideas.

Although there is no agreement as to the cause of the chasm between mainstream literary and cultural studies and the specialized world of Tolkien scholarship, there is no denying that it exists and rather closely matches larger divides in contemporary criticism between medievalists and specialists in later (particularly twentieth-century) literatures (see also Shippey 2000 vii–ix, xxi–xxvi, 305–18). Even within the specialization of Tolkien criticism there is a significant divide between 'Tolkien Studies' (scholarship about Tolkien the author and his works of literature) and, to use John Ellison and Patricia Reynolds' terminology, 'Middle-earth Studies' (analysis of Tolkien's invented worlds, histories, languages, creatures, etc.), a disjunction that to some degree mirrors the separation between the scholarship and Tolkien fandom. The boundaries between each of these interpretive communities – mainstream literary scholars, Tolkien scholars, Tolkien fans – are porous, poorly marked and difficult to negotiate, with many individual scholars and works of criticism not fitting neatly into any one category. Furthermore, although critics do not always acknowledge the fact, each category is to a great extent dependent upon the others. Without Middle-earth Studies to explicate the internal relationships in Tolkien's works, particularly the connections between Tolkien's invented languages and his literature, Tolkien Studies would be immeasurably impoverished. Without Tolkien Studies to generate 'clean' texts, explain connections between Tolkien's works and other literature, and link the author's life and scholarship to his writing, Middle-earth Studies would be missing evidence with great explanatory power. For example, it makes no sense to speak of the language of the Rohirrim without acknowledging that it is Old English and can thus be translated. 'Pure' Middle-earth Studies (if such a monstrosity actually existed) would be unable to translate. A 'pure' Tolkien Studies that did not attempt to understand Middle-earth Studies is almost impossible to imagine. Without the interdependent Tolkien Studies and Middle-earth Studies, mainstream criticism almost immediately goes wrong in discussing Tolkien, such as the embarrassingly bad piece 'Fantasy is the Opium of the Ignorant and Indolent' by historian Felipe Fernandez-Armesto (2002) or the even worse 'Arms and the Men and Hobbits' by Salman Rushdie (2003).

Most of the above will not be terribly controversial among those who have devoted significant intellectual energy to the study of Tolkien. Although some scholars are more focused on Tolkien Studies and others on Middle-earth Studies, and both sides defend the primacy of their chosen fields of study, neither side really thinks that the other can be completely ignored. The same is sadly not the case for mainstream literary scholarship. And likewise – and to the equal detriment of the field – Tolkien scholarship of both categories has in general been signally uninterested in mainstream literary theory and criticism (beyond taking great and justified enjoyment in demonstrating the errors, logical fallacies, bad predictions and simple stupidity in the works of those critics who have most vocally and intemperately attacked Tolkien).[1] This chapter is in part a plea for all sides to take each other's work into account. In what follows, I hope to demonstrate both that Tolkien scholarship can effectively challenge some of the most fundamental theoretical constructs of mainstream literary criticism and that some of the theoretical tools of that criticism can be profitably applied to Tolkien's works.

Michel Foucault's 'What is an Author?' (1984) is one of the *loci classici* for theoretical engagement with the problems of authorship. Foucault's major contribution here is the idea that '. . . there are a certain number of discourses that are endowed with the "author function", while others are deprived of it' (107). The 'author-function' designates ownership (and all the social and cultural powers that go with ownership), and in interpretive terms is a projection upon a persona of the 'operations that we force texts to undergo, the connections that we make, the traits that we establish as pertinent, the continuities that we recognize or the exclusions that we practice' (110). Thus the texts create the author.

Immediately many readers are objecting that this is a nonsensical inversion. People write texts: a man named J. R. R. Tolkien, a unique and identifiable individual human, put pen to page and wrote the words that are now printed as *The Lord of the Rings*. Not exactly, as we shall see. A man named J. R. R. Tolkien did indeed write a great number of texts. We can see his autograph manuscripts in the archives at Marquette University Library and Oxford's Bodleian Library. But the words on those pages were changed and re-worked in a variety of encounters: Tolkien read chapters of *The Lord of the Rings* to C. S. Lewis, Charles Williams and others; he sent some of the chapters as a serial to his son Christopher when Christopher was serving in South Africa with the RAF.[2] He presumably received commentary on them from Lewis, Williams, Christopher Tolkien and others and may have adjusted his material based on these comments (see *War* 144). Tolkien also revised the story – in major and minor ways – a number of times.[3] Then there was the typing process, the editing process, the printing, the editing of galleys and so forth. At each stage words were changed, eliminated and inserted. Not all of these actions were taken by Tolkien in splendid isolation. Some of the editor's suggestions he may have used, thus changing, adding or eliminating words. Others he would have ignored. Still others he would have chosen to engage, but perhaps also made changes other than those suggested. Still more might have been missed by him and entered in the textual tradition. This whole complex mess is made even more difficult when the problems of revising *The Lord of the Rings* to challenge the legality of the Ace Paperback edition are noted (Carpenter 1977: 226–9). Do these changes have equivalent sources in the same 'author-function' as the changes discussed above? Are they 'artistic' in the same sense the originals were? Given that Tolkien was continually revising, what are the 'originals' of any one published text? What are the 'completed' versions, given that nearly 40 years after the publication of *The Lord of the Rings* and after the creation of a 'clean text', Christopher Tolkien can note apparently intended lines and passages that did not make it into the final published version?[4]

It is important to separate genuine insight from critical huffing and puffing; however, here Foucault's insight is quite compelling: our idea of Tolkien the 'author' is produced by our social discourses and allows us to pull together this dizzying complexity of different materials and their relations both to individual writers and to the social, cultural and economic processes of book production and distribution – 'the author is the principle of thrift in the proliferation of meaning' (118). Foucault does not think that this is a good thing. Certainly the invocation of 'J. R. R. Tolkien' as the source for all the words published under his name does serve to simplify matters, and just as clearly it is not entirely correct. Nevertheless it would be very useful for Tolkien Studies to apply a bit of Foucault's author-skepticism to the persona and author-function of J. R. R. Tolkien, in part to counteract the effects of Tolkien's own abilities as a critic to channel interpretation in certain, author-focused directions. The immense influence of '*Beowulf*: The Monsters and the Critics' and 'On Fairy-Stories', both of which are seen as origins for, respectively, modern *Beowulf* criticism and the criticism of fantasy literature, have served to turn Tolkien into his own leading critic, to the possible detriment of effective analysis. The very fact that I have hesitated many times before writing the next sentence demonstrates the extent of the problem. Not everything Tolkien wrote was correct.

This is not to deny the importance of Tolkien's scholarship or its quality. But it is simply unreasonable to expect that every element of every piece of scholarship in a difficult and contentious field like Anglo-Saxon can stand the test of time. So, at the micro-level, we have Tolkien asserting that Beowulf predicts hell as the destiny of Unferth (41). *Beowulf and the Critics* shows that this assertion is based on *Beowulf* lines 588b–589, 'þaes þu in helle scealt / werðo dreogan, þeah þin wit duge' ('for which you must endure punishment in hell though your wit be strong' (author translation)). The *Beowulf* manuscript is defective at this point, and both of the Thorkelin transcripts read 'helle', which was used by Klaeber (1950) and which Tolkien must have accepted. Contemporary scholarship, however, reads the defective word as 'healle' (in the hall), making Beowulf's comment not a prophesy, but a statement of fact, particularly since 'werðo' could be read as 'social punishment' or even 'humiliation', and Unferth, as is shown by his interaction with Beowulf, is in fact humiliated in the hall (by Beowulf in their flyting) for his kin-slaying (Tolkien 2002: 69, 135), and see Klaeber (1950: 23), Robinson (1974: 119–37), Orchard (2003: 253 n. 54). Of course the above does not necessarily obviate the larger point Tolkien was arguing, that in *Beowulf* there is mention of hell as a destination for individuals, but heaven is never spoken of by the characters (and may not even be spoken of by the poet if Tolkien was correct and lines 175–88 are later interpolation). But it nevertheless goes to show that Tolkien was not infallible in matters of Anglo-Saxon or even matters of philology, as recent work on Chaucer's 'The Reeve's Tale' may show (Horobin 2001: 97–105). Tolkien's infallibility in his larger claims, both in medieval studies and in discussion of his own work, is not subject to refutation in the same way, since matters of interpretation operate according to different standards of proof. But Tolkien's interpretation of *The Battle of Maldon* has found few scholars to support it (for a discussion, see Shippey 1991: 5–16). Likewise, Tolkien's assertions about his dislike of allegory and Shakespeare have both been shown to be not entirely correct (Carpenter 1977: 27; Shippey 1992: 39–46, 159–73; Drout 2004c: 137–45). Even his denial of a lack of connection between the words 'hobbit' and 'rabbit' is, as Shippey has argued, questionable at the very least (1992: 60–4).

I do not intend to mount an attack on Tolkien in the same way that George Clark (1990) does, and both my experience in Anglo-Saxon studies and my work with Tolkien's unpublished scholarship has convinced me that Tolkien was far more often right than he was wrong. But the practically hagiographic treatment given to Tolkien's persona, 'The Professor' in the words of fandom, is problematic not only in theoretical terms, but also for the practical reasons given above: he was not always correct, and his opinion, even of his own books, should not be given the status of holy writ.

The reader who thinks I am exaggerating need only examine the influence of *The Letters of J. R. R. Tolkien* (Carpenter 1981) in a few recent works of Tolkien criticism. The *Letters*, which were first published in 1981, appeared long enough after the publication and first criticism of *The Lord of the Rings* so that they appeared to challenge or to vindicate certain critical arguments. For example, Jane Chance, in the revised edition of her *Tolkien's Art: A Mythology for England*, writes:

The first point made by [the first edition of her] *Tolkien's Art* –
that Tolkien wished to construct an overarching mythology that
was embedded in all his published fiction except for the fairy-
stories and his medieval parodies – has been legitimized by
Tolkien's letter 131, to Milton Waldman at Collins. That Tolkien
wished to create the mythology *for England*, a nation he believed
lacked any coherent mythology comparable to the Germanic or
Finnish mythologies, is also attested in that important letter.
Thus the title of this monograph – *Tolkien's Art: A Mythology for
England* – can be seen in its first edition to have anticipated the
publication of letter 131 and, with it, Tolkien's own analysis of
how his corpus of creative writing fits into a discernible schema.
(2001: vii)

The *Letters* have also been mercilessly invoked as evidence not only
of Tolkien's plans for his 'secondary world', but also his interpretations of his literary works. Joseph Pearce's *Tolkien: Man and Myth*,
for instance, quotes the *Letters* at excruciating length, and it is only a
slight exaggeration to note that his quotations from the *Letters* carry
more of the weight of his argument than his citations from Tolkien's
literary works. Likewise Patrick Curry (1997) is heavily invested in
the truth of the *Letters*, as are many other critics. Specific quotes
from the *Letters*, most particularly Tolkien's assertion that *The Lord
of the Rings* is 'of course a fundamentally religious and Catholic
work; unconsciously so at first, but consciously in the revision'
(no.142; *Letters* 172), have been quoted *ad infinitum*, as have
Tolkien's letters in which he discusses his plans for a mythology for
England (although Tolkien never used that specific phrase).[5] We
are, of course, fortunate to have the *Letters* and the posthumously
published works of Tolkien's scholarship, and no real scholar would
ever wish for *less* information about an important author and his
works. But in their zeal to find the interpretation of Tolkien's literature in his letters, critics ignore the problem that the *Letters* are not a
transparent, unambiguous guide to the 'real meaning' of Tolkien's
literature or, for that matter, his scholarship.

Roland Barthes' 'The Death of the Author' is one of the old
chestnuts of literary theory, typically imposed upon undergraduate
English majors in their mandatory 'methods' or 'theory' courses
(1977). Barthes argues that a practice of interpretation that takes
for its telos the discovery of what the author really meant by his or

her text is epistemologically flawed. 'Writing,' Barthes asserts, 'is the destruction of every voice, of every point of origin. Writing is that neutral, composite, oblique space where our subject slips away, the negative where all identity is lost, starting with the very identity of the body writing.' We can never know what the author really meant if our only evidence is that author's text: the logic is circular. Tolkien himself recognized this same kind of circularity with regard to *Beowulf*: 'But the Beowulf critic, *as such*, must go first to the evidence for the period outside his poem. The process must not for him be a vicious circle in which the poem is used to depict a period, and that picture is then used to explain the poem' (Tolkien 2002: 39). Meaning in a text exists not only because an author has consciously put it there, but also due to factors outside the author's control. Unexpected resonances, double-meanings, unconsciously constructed and unintentional images may be found in the text, and all questions about the presence or absence of these elements cannot be answered by invoking authorial intention. For Barthes, the focus of criticism should be turned from invocation of the intents of the author to the effects produced on the reader.

Texts, even letters, do not present their meaning transparently; they must be interpreted by readers. By assuming the transparency of Tolkien's *Letters*, critics assume first of all (and most problematically) that the *Letters* do not need to be interpreted, and second, that Tolkien's evaluation of his own work is correct. My admiration for Tolkien's intellect and scholarship is enormous, but *all* authors can be tendentious in their self-criticism, and all have various blind spots and biases. Surely Tolkien is no exception. He may be (in my view, he is) a very good critic of his own work, but, as Barthes argues, '... a text is not a line of words releasing a single "theological" meaning (the "message" of the Author-God) but a multidimensional space in which a variety of writings, none of them original, blend and clash. The text is a tissue of quotations drawn from the innumerable centres of culture.' The over-reliance of critics upon the *Letters* guides Tolkien scholarship down the narrow channel of finding a single, 'theological' meaning for Tolkien's works, more often than not a meaning found in the *Letters*.

Barthes and Foucault are often read together and interpreted as saying much of the same thing, but I think that the problems raised by Tolkien show that their arguments are in fact different. That is, there is a *differentiation* to be made between the ontological status of autograph manuscripts, revised texts, and possibly collaborative or partially collaborative works. Barthes' exhortation to look at the text and its apparent effects on the reader would have us discard interesting information and merge into a seamless mass the very complexities of ownership and authorship that Foucault articulates. When Foucault says that the 'author' is used as a principle of thrift, he is being descriptive, not normative. A reasonable critic may choose to stop at this point, not to accept the extreme form of Foucault's call for a form of culture 'in which fiction would not be limited by the figure of the author' (1984: 119), and instead follow Foucault in attempting to disambiguate the different layers of discourse in a particular text, all of which 'belong' to the person, the persona, the author and the author-function of J. R. R. Tolkien in different ways.

Using Tolkien's works in this way allows us to use a practice founded in Foucault's critique to challenge some of Barthes' assertions. Barthes writes: 'a text is made of multiple writings, drawn from many cultures and entering into mutual relations of dialogue, parody, contestation, but there is one place where this multiplicity is focused and that place is the reader, not, as was hitherto said, the author' (1977). But Barthes' description of a text and its *reader* seems to describe Tolkien as *author*, perfectly. As Tom Shippey and so many other critics have shown, Tolkien indeed constructed his literature from an enormous variety of medieval and classical stories, traditions and discourses.[6] Not only did Tolkien incorporate disparate source materials into his work, but he also arranged these and other materials into an invented tradition with the same sorts of complexities, blind alleys, conflicting sources and incomplete materials as the real historical record. Tolkien thus *deliberately* alters the function of his authorship by pretending to be a translator (*The Lord of the Rings* from Frodo's and Bilbo's diaries, and *The Silmarillion* from Bilbo's *Translations from the Elvish by B.B.*, preserved in the *Red Book of Westmarch*;[7] the complex and everchanging series of tales and annals ascribed variously to Eriol/ Ælfwine, Rúmil, Heorrenda, Pengolod, Ælfwine and other chroniclers),[8] or finder of long-lost manuscripts (*The Notion Club Papers*).[9]

Christopher Tolkien's editing of *The Silmarillion*, *Unfinished Tales* and *The History of Middle-earth* to different ends also introduces interpretive problems that are not solved by following Barthes and simply ignoring the author(s) in favor of the text(s). For example,

The Silmarillion was edited to produce a coherent narrative out of multiple and contradictory materials; *Unfinished Tales* accepted the incomplete nature of different texts but in the end clarified them according to the editor's judgement; *The History of Middle-earth* presented material in as unmediated a fashion as possible. Who is the author of these texts? J. R. R. Tolkien? Christopher Tolkien? What about the Map of Middle-earth, drawn by Christopher Tolkien at his father's direction? (*Treason*: 295–343). Are we really to ascribe every wiggle of every river and the precise shape of the coastline to the god-like presence of J. R. R. Tolkien, or should Christopher Tolkien be credited (and what does such credit do to the interpretation of the 'text' of the Map)? From a cultural-production point of view, we can always follow the money, and note that the words and the map are owned by the Tolkien Estate (and thus de facto by Christopher Tolkien, the literary executor), and that the Estate has defended not only its copyrights, but also its ability to influence Tolkien Studies (by controlling access to and publication of texts), with legal ferocity. We might also note that the title pages of volumes I–VI and X–XII of *The History of Middle-earth* read 'edited by Christopher Tolkien', while volumes VI–IX, which are subtitled 'The History of the Lord of the Rings', read simply 'Christopher Tolkien'.

Further interpretive problems are raised by the instability of the text of *The Lord of the Rings* and even more of *The Hobbit*. The 1937 first edition of *The Hobbit* contains a 'significantly different' version of the chapter 'Riddles in the Dark'. When Tolkien was writing *The Lord of the Rings*, he realized that he could not harmonize the new storyline with *The Hobbit* without revising this chapter, which he did in the 1951 edition of *The Hobbit* (Anderson, *Annotated Hobbit*, 123–36). But Tolkien also recognized that many of the pre-1951 copies of *The Hobbit* would be read as the prolegomenon to *The Lord of the Rings*, so he introduced the idea that Bilbo had invented a false story (in which Gollum intended to *give* Bilbo the Ring) for the benefit of the dwarves. Thus in 'A Long Expected Party' Gandalf asks Frodo which version of the story Bilbo had told him, and Frodo replies 'Oh, not what he told the dwarves and put in his book', but rather the true story (*FR*, I, i, 52). Likewise at the Council of Elrond, Bilbo says 'I will now tell the true story, and if some here have heard me tell it otherwise . . . I ask them to forget it and forgive me. I only wished to claim the treasure as my very own in those days, and to be rid of the name of thief that was put on me' (*FR*, II, ii, 326).

As a reader of *The Hobbit* and *The Lord of the Rings* I was, for many years, completely confused by these statements. I had only read post-1951 versions of 'Riddles in the Dark', and so Frodo's and Bilbo's statements about another version of the story did not really make sense. It is obvious from *The Lord of the Rings* that Bilbo told a different story at one point, but only the bare outlines of that story – 'inventing all that about a "present"' (*FR*, I, i, 53) could be deduced from the actual text. I do not think that Stanley Fish was thinking of *The Hobbit* when he made his various assertions about the 'instability of the text', but the multiple versions of 'Riddles in the Dark' illustrate his point far better than any examples actually chosen. In fact, there can be *no* consistent and stable text of *The Hobbit* and *The Lord of the Rings*: the pre-1951 *Hobbit* text is inconsistent with the story of *The Lord of the Rings* (although that inconsistency is explained away, later), but the post-1951 *Hobbit* is also inconsistent, since it does not contain the version of 'Riddles in the Dark' that is referred to in *The Lord of the Rings*. Faced with the above complexities, Barthes would have us ignore the author or authors, and concentrate on the reader, attempting to understand what the effects of the text are upon the reader. This approach is not necessarily wrong. There are in fact some readers, many readers, even, for whom *The Lord of the Rings* does manifest itself simply as a text (perhaps even an error-filled Ballentine paperback edition), or merely as a film, and does not carry with it the complex back-story that a really knowledgeable reader will have learned from Tolkien's other texts and his sources.

This is not to excuse shoddy, shallow criticism, the weak efforts of media-seeking opportunists like Rushdie or Shulevitz who make a quick hit upon the text without even good close reading, much less the laborious acquisition of background knowledge, both in Tolkien's works themselves and in his many sources. Barthes' injunction to read only the text has been accepted so frequently not only because it challenged the ossified author-focused critical practice of his time, but also because in many ways it is *easy*. Taken to extremes, Barthesian text- and reader-criticism allows the critic to avoid engagement with the complexities of the production of the text. Nevertheless, the reading experiences of readers who are not Tolkienists (and those, among Tolkienists, who are not medievalists) are not unworthy of analysis. If critics are careful to specify the readers whom they have constructed (via imagination, intuition, or at best deduction), then their criticism works to establish, in a roundabout way, the 'horizon of expectations' that reader-response criticism uses to limit the otherwise free-play of possible interpretations of a text (Iser 1981: xii). The difficulty in avoiding solipsism when constructing the reading experience of this imagined audience, however, is not an easy problem to solve. Of course one can simply embrace the solipsism, as is done in the *Meditations on Middle-earth* collection of essays, in which famous writers discuss their personal impressions of reading Tolkien (Haber 2001). This sort of belletristic criticism can be enjoyable to read, and it certainly can be seen as the logical extension of a focus on the reader, but in the end its very epistemological safety (one cannot very well argue with the critic who says that 'my experience of reading *The Lord of the Rings* is X') also ensures that it is unsatisfying.

A more subtle approach to the analysis of the naive reader of Tolkien's works might focus on those aspects of, say, *The Lord of the Rings* as text that can be reasonably argued to produce certain effects in most naive readers. For instance, the reference to the cats of Queen Berúthiel (*FR*, II, iv, 325) can only be understood by those readers as an enigmatic figure of speech, part of a pseudo-traditional or pseudo-proverbial statement that can be interpreted as meaning 'having good vision in the dark' but cannot be linked up with other materials within *The Lord of the Rings* itself in the same way that references to Beren, Eärendil or even Túrin can. Such analysis could then attempt to explain how, for example, Tolkien's works give the famous 'impression of depth' without directly engaging the materials from which Tolkien drew that depth. This eschewal of the posthumously published materials is not as perverse at it first might appear. If the posthumously published materials had never appeared, or had been lost, or were unknown, the phenomenon of the perception of depth (or of mythic power) would still require some explanation.

I have taken some time to justify, *arguendo*, the eschewal of background both in Tolkien Studies and in Middle-earth Studies, but I do not think that this is the best approach to the production of good criticism. The complicated and possibly contradictory relationships between author, editor, author-function, editor-function, sources, analogues and texts can to some degree be teased apart by careful scholarship. Reading *The Lord of the Rings*, *The Silmarillion*, *Unfinished Tales* and *The History of Middle-earth* simply as words on the page is a refusal to engage with important and potentially useful information that can go a long way towards explaining those very words. Mainstream literary scholars who would use Barthes to justify approaching *The Lord of the Rings* simply as a text miss an enormous amount of valuable data that could make their analysis far more penetrating. For example, Gergely Nagy (2003) has demonstrated the 'Great Chain of Reading' that links various versions and back-stories of Tolkien's Túrin legends, showing in the process that there are recursive characteristics of texts that can be shown to generate what has been called 'mythopoesis', the successful imitation of myth (whatever that term may mean) by invented traditions. (In my opinion this article is the single most important essay published on Tolkien in the past decade.) Further work in this vein, building upon the archive of *The History of Middle-earth*, would serve to greatly enrich Tolkien criticism.

Using a term like 'enrich', of course, could be seen as falling into the fallacy of *petitio principii*. The real question, which I have thus far been avoiding, is the philosophical problem of enumerating formal criteria by which a particular criticism could be deemed 'enriched' or, more broadly, if a particular interpretation is correct or not. This is a subset of the problem of determining the 'meaning' of a work, phrase or word.

Obviously this is one of the central philosophical problems of literary studies. Barthes, Foucault, Derrida and the host of other contemporary critics who have followed them have argued that there is no way to determine if a particular interpretation is correct. And yet criticism proceeds apace. Stanley Fish attempts to solve this conundrum without contradicting the French post-structuralists by arguing that meaning is determined by 'interpretive communities', groups of individuals who are socially and culturally authorized to confer 'meaning' upon utterances, interpretations and literary works. Fish's argument can be regarded as sophism but, if one is feeling charitable, it can be accepted as a kind of anthropology of interpretation. That is, Fish explains the social process by which meaning is conferred: 'interpretive communities' with varying memberships and degrees of political power determine meaning to varying degrees. Unfortunately, Fish's argument does not account for the differing formal characteristics of texts that might serve to limit the flexibility of interpretive communities. For instance, no matter how powerful an interpretive community might be, it is hard to imagine a meaning being conferred upon *Beowulf* that interprets the poem as an allegory for the making and eating of bratwurst. The free-floating meaning that Fish accepts is limited not only by the power of the interpretive community, but also by the text itself – within limits, and to my mind these limits are far more interesting than the assertion of free-floating meaning. (I conceptualize this as the problem of 'word to world "fit"' in much greater detail in my *How Tradition Works*.)

Be that as it may, Fish's idea of 'interpretive communities' can be fruitfully applied to Tolkien criticism. Rather than adopting an invented reader and intuiting that reader's 'horizon of expectations', I propose that Tolkien critics be specific about the audience that they have in mind. If they are interpreting Tolkien's work in light of a presumed audience that is ignorant of back-story, medieval references or linguistic complexities, they should say so. If they are assuming an audience who has read the appendices and *The History of Middle-earth*, they should also say so. The same article could even move between the different audiences, arguing, perhaps that a naive film audience would see only an interesting visual with a Winged Beast and Nazgûl hovering in front of a ruin while an educated audience would guess at some reference to the fallen Tower of the Dome (and its Dome of Stars, which housed the palantír) at Osgiliath and thus a more detailed reference to the lost glory of Gondor (for the significance of the Dome of Stars and the Tower of the Dome, see *TT*, III, ix, 248 and Appendix A).

Such specificity of audience would do at least some work to make Tolkien criticism by those outside of Tolkien- or Middle-earth Studies more reasonable and less easy to ignore. But it will not solve all problems. Perhaps nothing will, and mainstream critics and Tolkien scholars will continue to talk past each other. But if both sides would borrow a bit from each other, they might find that their work would be improved. For instance, a critic might want to discuss the vexed topic of race in Tolkien. Such a critic would be wise not to ignore the gigantic discourse on race and literature that has been developed over the past 30 or so years (that is, the critic should approach the mainstream criticism of race and literature and, perhaps, postcolonial studies). But if one wants to discuss Tolkien and race intelligently, it is not wise to ignore the various kinds of race in Tolkien, not only the various 'races' of men (the Rohirrim, the Númenoreans, the men of Dale, the Beornings, the Southrons/Haradrim, the

Variags of Khand, etc.), but also the other intelligent 'species' in Middle-earth (Elves, Men, Dwarves, Ents, Orcs, Trolls, Hobbits, etc.) and their ontologies. One must be well-versed in Middle-earth Studies to understand the differing kindreds of the elves (the differences between Vanyar, Noldor and Teleri, or between Grey Elves and Silvan Elves, for instance, are extremely significant). But to really produce an intelligent criticism, the putative critic must not only understand both mainstream theory on race and the details of 'race' in Middle-earth, but must also recognize and understand the interconnections between, for example, the Anglo-Saxon 'Sigelhearwan', Old Norse fire giants, and Tolkien's balrogs – and their conceptual evolution from Tolkien's earliest writings such as 'The Fall of Gondolin' – and medieval concepts of the Ethiopians and other dark-skinned peoples. The critic who pulled together all of these strands of material would be able to write an article on race and Tolkien that might actually explain (and perhaps critique) Tolkien's works in a nuanced and intelligent manner. Such a critic would perhaps discover that his or her work would end up having more influence than critical approaches that leave out literary theory, or Middle-earth Studies, or Tolkien Studies. For Tolkien's works are texts that speak to readers who learn, and thus the best way to approach them is to learn more.

CHAPTER 2

TIME

Barry Langford

Louis Menand was disappointed with Peter Jackson's *The Lord of the Rings: The Fellowship of the Ring* (2002).[1] As he explained in the *New York Review of Books*, somewhere in the F/X-laden, action-packed, breathless kineticism of the Hollywood blockbuster, whatever caused his childhood reading of the novel to linger in his memory as 'an eleven year-old's-Proust' was lost (Menand 2002: 8). Kristin Thompson (2003: 47) agrees that 'a book about imaginatively conceived characters on a lengthy journey with occasional skirmishes has been turned into what might . . . seem to some a gallery of battles and monsters'. For Thompson, however, Proust is a step too far: she suggests Walter Scott or Dickens as more appropriate comparisons, on the apparent presumption that what Tolkien and these High Victorians share – powerful narrative drive on a very large scale and an extensive gallery of boldly-drawn, perhaps larger-than-life characters – also categorically distinguishes them all from the interiority, psychologism and complex narrative schemata that characterize a modernist writer such as Proust.

One need not share all Thompson's preconceptions of the classic realist novel to agree that a counter-argument aimed solely at recovering a 'modernist' Tolkien would appear a barren prospect. Partly because the job has already been done: Tom Shippey (2000) and Brian Roseberry (1992), amongst many others, have persuasively placed Tolkien's worldview firmly and recognizably in the mid-twentieth-century. Menand himself does not go on to elaborate on what strikes him now, or struck him when a child, as Tolkien's Proustian qualities – perhaps it was sheer length. Yet in its loosest application – the centrality of time and memory, and the problem of situating the self in relation to them – there is indeed something in *The Lord of the Rings* that can be characterized as 'Proustian'. I propose that understanding the novel's distinctive treatment of time, in both its *lisible* and *scriptible* aspects, also helps illuminate just what, beyond the important yet superficial factors of narrative compression and acceleration, makes the story-world of Jackson's *Lord of the Rings* so different to that of Tolkien's novel. Developing this argument requires in the first instance a summary narratological analysis showing how Tolkien's novel importantly exploits a sense of 'deep', and dimensional, time which operates for the reader in ways that are both structurally comparable and as sensuously palpable as its celebrated creation of a wholly fictitious, yet mimetically plausible, cultural and physical geography.

NARRATIVE EXTENSION IN MIDDLE-EARTH

It was written slowly and with great care for detail, & finally emerged as a Frameless Picture: a searchlight, as it were, on a brief episode in History, and on a small part of our Middle-earth, surrounded by the glimmer of limitless extensions in time and space.
(*Letters* 412)

As we all know, *The Lord of the Rings* is as furiously detested as it is passionately loved. Admirers and detractors however tend to concur on at least one source of its enduring appeal: the unusual density of Tolkien's wholly imaginary fictive world. C. S. Lewis, among the completed manuscript's first readers, remarked admiringly on its profusion of 'sheer sub-creation – Bombadil, Barrow Wights, Elves, Ents – as if from inexhaustible resources and construction' (quoted in Carpenter 1977: 207). For Tolkien's critics, conversely, it is precisely the elaborate realization of an entirely imaginary world that solicits an uncritical, even regressive, immersion in fantasy and a retreat from reality. (Tolkien himself was not unconscious of this criticism: cf. a 1955 letter to Rayner Unwin: 'I am not now at all sure that the tendency to treat the whole thing as a kind of vast game is really good – certainly not for me, who find that kind of thing only too fatally attractive' [*Letters* 210].) The narrative technique upon whose exceptionally effective exploitation this appearance of density relies is narrative *extension* – here denoting the supplement and enhancement of novelistic verisimilitude by the declaration or suggestion of a much broader diegetic world, continuous with and in effect sustaining the main narrative action, which nonetheless is only briefly or tangentially present.

Such narrative extension is a necessary feature of any narrative, but it exists in what might be called 'remarked' and 'unremarked' forms. Generally speaking, extension becomes more remarked in direct proportion to the distance between the immediate experience, hence knowledge, of the reader and the matter of the narrative; in effect, proportionate to the extent of the reader's reliance upon the writer for the fundamental elements of the diegesis and their orientation within and towards it. Thus narratives with a contemporary setting can rely on largely unremarked narrative extension – the real-world geography of modern urban locales like London or New York, or the cultural and social mores of contemporary life are all present in any contemporary narrative as both enabling and validating narrative contexts. The narrative extension of historical narratives such as *War and Peace* or *Regeneration* is more remarked insofar as the reader relies to a greater (though of course varying) degree on the knowledge supplied by the text itself to chart pathways through historical settings of greater or lesser familiarity. Finally, most fantasy and many science-fiction narratives include a heavily remarked element of narrative extension inasmuch as the story-world's imaginative extension is wholly dependent on the writer's suasive capability. On this last count, of course, *The Lord of the Rings* is famously successful. Tolkien himself was fully conscious of his use of extension as an effective narrative device and noted succinctly shortly after the publication of *The Fellowship of the Ring* in 1954 that 'a part of the [novel's] "fascination" consists in the vistas of yet more legend and history, to which this work does not contain a clue' (*Letters* 185).

Narrative extension in *The Lord of the Rings* may be conceived as operating along two principal axes, the cultural and the temporal. Since most critical attention has focused on the former, its operation need only be briefly summarized. The main subdivisions of the cultural axis are the *linguistic* and the *geographical*. *Linguistic* extension is effected through the presence of proper names and untranslated interpolated fragments in the various languages of Middle-earth – the Elvish tongues Sindarín and Quenya, the Black Speech of Mordor, the dwarvish tongue, Entish, and so on – all of which of course 'existed' for Tolkien (in the sense of having, to varying degrees, a developed grammar and morphology, most thoroughly in the case of Elvish, though even here as Tolkien confessed not a fully comprehensive vocabulary or idiom). Indeed, as Tolkien frequently explained, his philologist's hobby of creating imaginary linguistic structures predated the elaboration of the histories/mythologies in which they were eventually embedded. Tolkien could be quite categorical that his mythology served essentially to provide a chamber in which his languages might germinate and amplify: 'my long book is an attempt to create a world in which a form of language agreeable to my personal aesthetic might seem true' (*Letters* 264).[2] Thus the derivation from Quenya or Sindarín, the most completely worked-out of his languages, of the majority of the names in Tolkien's legendarium, as he himself noted lends 'a certain character (a cohesion, a consistency of linguistic style, and an illusion of historicity) to the nomenclature, or so I believe, that is markedly lacking in other comparable things' (*Letters* 143). Beyond that, the philological substance of *The Lord of the Rings*' languages undoubtedly empowers them in offering the reader, when s/he encounters them at first hand, with the impression of a briefly intensified intimacy with cultures otherwise known only through their representative characters.

Given this imaginative centrality, it follows that the *geographical* dimension – encompassing both Middle-earth's topography and its diverse cultures – of the cultural axis of extension is itself heavily bound up with the linguistic dimension: as often noted, the character of Tolkien's languages tends to corroborate the ethnic and cultural attributes lent to their respective races. Tolkien's insistence on providing maps has allowed most readers the opportunity at some stage to pore over them and wonder about those locations marked but never journeyed to or in some cases even mentioned in the text (for example, Forlinden, the Sea of Rhûn, or the Ice Bay of Forochel, whose absence from the action Tolkien himself regretfully noted [*Letters* 199]). The maps also tantalizingly provide habitations for some of the many races and cultures who make passing appearances on the pages of *The Lord of the Rings* – the Haradrim, the 'Easterlings' who besiege the Dwarves in Dale, the Corsairs of Umbar. These fleeting encounters all aid the reader's sense that this sizeable text is nonetheless merely skimming a vast and barely-glimpsed hinterland, an effect that powerfully enables the conviction of Middle-earth's realization (and one partly warranted: 'there is hardly any reference in *The Lord of the Rings* to things that do not actually *exist* on its own plane (of secondary or sub-creational reality): sc. have been written' [*Letters* 231, emphasis original]).[3]

> Part of the attraction of *The Lord of the Rings*, is, I think, due to the glimpses of a large history in the background: an attraction like that of viewing far off an unvisited island, or seeing the towers of a distant city gleaming in a sunlit mist. To go there is to destroy the magic, unless new unattainable vistas are again revealed.
> (*Letters* 333)

Much of this effect relies importantly on Tolkien's modulation of what Mieke Bal (1985) terms 'focalization': the manipulation of the narrative perspective(s) from and through which knowledge of the diegesis is brought to the reader. *The Lord of the Rings* for the most part communicates its sense of the wonderful elaboration of a world by relying on the perception of those to whom these wonders are almost as new as they are to the reader, pre-eminently of course the Hobbits. This interestingly highlights the specific narrative satisfactions of perspectival withholding: the perhaps paradoxical experience that an embedded and proximate – hence necessarily partial, even fallacious – perception of an invented reality may provide a far more persuasive rendition of the imagined world than a more holistic one. This is a truth to which, one suspects, many readers of the chronicle-like *The Silmarillion*, dissatisfied by its synoptic austerity, can testify. Yet for Tolkien the crucial contrast of narrative perspective between the two works was not one of completeness (omniscience) versus incompleteness (relativity), but rather of different *types* of partial perspective. The term 'deixis' in narratology usually denotes the gestural immediacy of an actually speaking or named narrator, but stretching usage slightly – given Tolkien's own stress on this point – one might say that *The Silmarillion* and *The Lord of the Rings*, nominally part of the same saga, are differentiated by their distinct deictic centres,[4] respectively Elvish and mortal; that Elvish deixis nonetheless remains a prominent feature in the later work; and that in the absence of a personal narrator, the key to distinguishing the two modes can be found in their differing temporalities. Moreover, it is in the dialectical relationship of these temporalities and their triangulation by a temporal perspective posited but not realized in the novel itself that the heart of Tolkien's mythos is to be found.

TEMPORAL EXTENSION IN *THE LORD OF THE RINGS*

For Tolkien, time and space were equally important dimensions in supplying both the effect and the themes of *The Lord of the Rings*. Given Tolkien's conception of the War of the Ring as the effective culmination of the epochal narrative whose archaic passages he had recounted in *The Silmarillion*, the cultural axis of extension – especially its linguistic division – necessarily includes a strong temporal dimension: that is, it opens up to the characters, as usual in varying degrees of totality and comprehensibility depending on their respective competences (most for Gandalf and Elrond, least for Pippin and Merry), the vastly larger narrative arc within which their own actions are situated. Thus the novel was, Tolkien explained, underpinned by 'very elaborate and detailed workings of geography, *chronology*, and language' (*Letters* 210, emphasis added). Yet by comparison with language and geography, which as we have seen principally comprise the cultural axis of narrative extension, the temporal axis has received much less critical attention. Despite extensive discussion of the importance of time to Tolkien, particularly in relation to the theological underpinnings of his mythology (see most notably Flieger 1997; also Aldrich 1988), the ways in which the reader is significantly interpellated, and his/her active participation in meaning construction solicited, by the modes of temporal extension present in the novel, have gone largely undiscussed.

Temporal extension in *The Lord of the Rings* can be straightforwardly enough modelled as three layers, or levels, around the principal action (taking in not only the 18 months between Gandalf's last visit to Hobbiton and the Scouring of the Shire, but the 20-year period from Bilbo's farewell feast to Sam's return to Bag End from the Grey Havens): in order of their progressive distance from the main narrative, we may for convenience's sake label these the 'contextual', the 'archaic' and the 'contemporary'. It is important to distinguish all of these from the kind of temporal effects (analepsis and prolepsis) that in conventional narratological terms typify modernist (and postmodern) texts: although there are of course large overlapping 'rewinds' and occasional flashbacks (for example, Legolas and Gimli's account of their journey through the Paths of the Dead) to take in the different fields of action after the sundering of the Fellowship, in general *The Lord of the Rings* limits and contains the impact of such devices within a homogeneous narrative frame.

The contextual extension, enfolding the narrative proper both before and after, principally includes *The Hobbit* ('retrofitted' as a kind of prequel to *The Lord of the Rings*) and the later landmarks concerning the surviving members of the Fellowship, summarized in the Appendix and culminating in Aragorn's death and the passing of Legolas and Gimli over Sea. The references to *The Hobbit* (anterior contextual extension), apart from of course the story of Bilbo's acquisition of the Ring (whose existence in two versions interestingly problematizes the relationship of past, and of memory recalled, falsified, and reinscribed, to present), mostly lend a satisfying sense of continuity and community linking reader and protagonists (as when Aragorn and the Hobbits chance upon the petrified trolls). The posterior contextual extension provides an unusually complete rounding-off of the (earthly) narratives of the remaining principal characters. Combined, this period covers 189 years – longer than the comparable narrative hinterland in most large-scale dynastic sagas, but not without precedent.[5] The contemporary extension, beyond the Prologue, is largely suppressed in *The Lord of the Rings* and may be said to consist only in such fleeting observations as that modern-day elephants are 'but memories of [the] girth and majesty' (*TT*, IV, iv, 332) of the Mûmakil of Harad. Whereas a novel such as John Fowles' *The French Lieutenant's Woman* employs contemporary extension as a consistent structural device (subjecting the sexual politics of the novel's Victorian setting to the sceptical interrogation of the 1970s), *The Lord of the Rings* by and large forgoes addressing the reader in his/her 'own' time.[6]

At once the novel's most distinctive and by far its most important form of temporal extension is into the archaic domain of the Second and Third Ages of Tolkien's mythology (epochs that in their entirety span some 6,400 years) and back still further into the primeval First Age. The reader's sense of the vast expanse of the archaic period, once again importantly focalized by the Hobbits, also evolves through brief, not always fully explained, references, all of which develop an expanded sense of unguessable antiquity bearing upon present action. At the simplest level, Tolkien again registers the fascination for the reader of the occult reaches of time past, and their capacity to effect a mysterious yet compelling extension of his narrative. Tolkien's descriptions of the Balrog and Shelob, the novel's two principal out-and-out monsters, exploits their archaic, almost atavistic aspect to transform and enlarge their threat, raising mere horror to terror and awe. The apparition in Moria, which overwhelms even Aragorn, is 'an evil of the Ancient World' and is confirmed by Legolas as a creature created by Morgoth. More than two decades before the posthumous publication of *The Silmarillion*, the name 'Morgoth' could only strike *The Lord of the Rings*' first readers as darkly resonant in an unspecific, indeed unspecifiable way, evoking a threat literally inconceivable in present-day terms and the transgressive intrusion into that present of a primal avatar: cthonic deities such as the Furies in the *Oresteia* carry a similar charge. As another embodiment of this primal evil, once again Shelob's great age significantly intensifies her vileness and raises the frightening yet simple peril of outsized spiders (which Tolkien had previously exploited in *The Hobbit*) to a positively elemental level:

> [O]ther potencies there are in Middle-earth, powers of night, and they are old and strong. And She that walked in the darkness had heard the Elves cry that cry [Frodo's cry: '*Aiya Eärendil Elenion Ancalima!*'] far back in the deeps of time, and it did not daunt her now . . .
>
> There agelong she had dwelt, an evil thing in spider-form, even such as once of old had lived in the Land of the Elves in the West that is now under the sea, such as Beren fought in the Mountains of Terror in Doriath, and so came to Lúthien upon the green sward amid the hemlocks in the moonlight long ago. How Shelob came there, flying from ruin, no tale tells, for out of the Dark Years few tales have come. But still she was there, who was there before Sauron, and before the first stone of Barad-dûr . . . none could rival her, Shelob the Great, last child of Ungoliant to trouble the unhappy world.
>
> (*TT*, IV, ix, 411, 414–15)

As the spawn of Melkor/Morgoth's spider-ally Ungoliant, Shelob is like the Balrog, a creature of the Elder Days of the First Age. Again, the proliferation of resonant but to most readers inscrutable names – Doriath, Lúthien, Ungoliant – and the invocation of unknown or half-understood events underscores the primeval nature of the threat. (Sauron himself, of course, Morgoth's sometime lieutenant, also originates in this dim anteriority.)

The distant past is however dynamically central to *The Lord of the Rings* in ways that go beyond simple atmospherics or 'fascination'. Tolkien ensured this by identifying the Ring – now recast as a baleful heirloom of the Second Age – as the unexploited element from the earlier story on which to centre his 'new *Hobbit*': the chapter in which Gandalf reveals the Ring's true nature to Frodo is appropriately entitled 'The Shadow of the Past'. But the relationship between the narrative present of *The Lord of the Rings* – the final years of the Third Age – and the remote or even primeval past is neither straightforwardly linear nor simply causal. The powerful immediacy and linear momentum of the quest narrative are at once offset and informed by the unfolding historical context, solely within which Frodo's mission acquires meaning. It can indeed be argued that the moral and ethical landscape of *The Lord of the Rings* is to a significant degree constituted across the different perspectives on, and relationships to, the distant past – thence to time itself – articulated by and through different characters.

Although narratively peripheral in *The Lord of the Rings*, as both chronicler of the long prior history of the Rings of Power (*FR*, II, ii, 317ff) and himself a major participant in that history, Elrond is perhaps the most important of the several speaking characters who, by virtue of their extreme age, connect the events of the narrative of *The Lord of the Rings* directly to the archaic period. (These are – in rough order of ancientness – Bombadil, the Elves, Shelob, the Ents and the Wizards. Certain artefacts also connect the ages, notably the *Palantíri*, Narsil/Anduril, and of course the Ring itself.) Indeed, the revelation of his age throws Frodo into confusion at the Council of Elrond. Elrond's response to Frodo's surprise – 'I have seen three ages in the West of the world, and many defeats, and many fruitless victories' (*FR*, II, ii, 318) – opens up an unusual, but characteristically Tolkienesque, perspective: a vast reach of time to which the present is not only inheritor or successor, but to which it is bound in active and conscious relation. It is this sense of epochal time as forcefully present and, as a direct consequence, ethically compelling that constitutes the most distinctive aspect of the novel's temporal extension, a perspective summed up in Gandalf's admonition that they need to act not for one time but to 'seek a final end of this menace' (*FR*, II, ii, 349). Gandalf's judgement clarifies that the function of the Council's extended narrative preambles – which in the case of Elrond's chronicle of the Elder Days (only summarized in the text) lasted an entire morning – has been to restore to the assembled representatives of the Free Peoples precisely that sense of connectedness and obligation from age to age with which the Wise are empowered, but which the abbreviated perspectives of mortal life inevitably overlook. (Boromir's bridling rejoinder to Galdor soon afterwards that, even if Gondor's power is decreasing, it is still very strong might be seen as his attempt both to embrace this impossibly large arc of time, to redress its diminishing perspective, and in so doing unwittingly but tellingly to confess the partiality and limitations of his own.) Consciousness of the unity of created time carries with it as a consequence an obligation not only to the present but to the future.

This understanding of time and of the individual's ineluctable implication therein, although universally available to the Elves by virtue of their immortality, is apparently not embraced by all of them: not, for instance, by those Elves glimpsed early in the novel passing through the Shire on their way to the Havens, who are no longer concerned with Middle-earth. Indeed, according to Tolkien such recognition was the exception rather than the rule for most Elves, who

> ... wanted to have their cake and eat it: to live in the mortal historical Middle-earth because they had become fond of it ... and so tried to stop its change and history, stop its growth, keep it as a pleasaunce (*sic*), even largely a desert, where they could be 'artists' – and they were overburdened with sadness and nostalgic regret.
>
> (*Letters* 197)

There are, it would seem, many different ways in which historical subjects can mistake their relationship to history, and accordingly different outcomes. For Elvish immortals, the chronic attachment to the past may breed melancholic stasis. Conversely, for a mortal, history's crushing mass may engender mortal despair – as besets Denethor, for whom, in Marx's famous words in the *Eighteenth Brumaire*, 'the tradition of all the dead generations weighs like a nightmare upon the mind of the living'. Saruman, by complete contrast, applies a willed obliviousness to his relationship to the (his own) past. His speech is marked by an insistent presentness – compatible, one might say, with his role as the novel's representative of cautionary modernism – that invokes the past merely to exploit it in the rhetorical service of the self (indeed, in Gandalf's account it is marked as, precisely, rhetoric):

> [Saruman] drew himself up then and began to declaim, as if he were making a speech long rehearsed. 'The Elder Days are gone. The Middle Days are passing. The Younger Days are beginning. The time of the Elves is over, but our time is at hand: the world of Men, which we must rule.'
> (*FR*, II, ii, 339–40)

Then there are those who 'opt-out' of history altogether – a stance Tolkien depicts as morally as well as practically unsustainable. Some characters in *The Lord of the Rings* – like Butterbur, or Gaffer Gamgee – are simply ignorant of history and hence of their own historical situation. But the price they pay is to be placed (however indulgently or fondly) as the objects, not the subjects, of a history they can have no part in shaping. Outright refusal of one's proper orientation in and to time, so to speak a conscious forgetting, is a more serious matter whose appeal and dangers are both embodied in Tom Bombadil. In Tom's hi/stories, to begin with time unfolds in linear fashion but at an accelerated pace, a kind of time-lapse:

> There were fortresses on the heights. Kings of little kingdoms fought together, and the young Sun shone like fire on the red metal of their new and greedy swords. There was victory and defeat; and towers fell.
> (*FR*, I, vii, 172)

Subsequently his narrative roams further still, dispensing altogether with comprehensible narrative sequence or apprehensible relation:

> When they caught his words again they found that he had now wandered into strange regions beyond their memory and beyond their waking thought, into times when the world was wider, and the seas flowed straight to the Western shore; and still on and back Tom went singing into the starlight, when only the Elf-sires were awake.
> (*FR*, I, vii, 172)

But as all-embracing as Tom's perspective is, it is also almost wholly unhistorical (exemplified in the abandonment of chronology or recognizable temporal landmarks as his recitation proceeds) and devoid of any meaningful sense of relationality – as the recursiveness of his (and Goldberry's) answers to Frodo's queries about his identity implies. Yet Tolkien suggests strongly that Bombadil's animistic self-sufficiency is ultimately flawed or at least limited. As a primal nature spirit, Bombadil is beyond good and evil: moral categories are irrelevant to him and he is indifferent to them (when Elrond wonders whether he should have invited Bombadil to the Council, Gandalf replies that he would not have come). Ultimately, however, this dislocation from the social – expressed through indifference to temporality – renders Bombadil not only irrelevant but vulnerable to those who are motivated (as is even Sauron, albeit in an entirely destructive way) by the claims of the social and temporal. (Gandalf too wanders 'out of thought and time' after defeating the Balrog (*TT*, III, v, 123), but of course returns to complete his assigned task.) Moreover, according to Glorfindel, Bombadil is not ultimately immune to the powers Sauron can muster. Significantly, the Hobbits do not visit Bombadil upon their return to the Shire: Gandalf judges him to be 'As well as ever . . . Quite untroubled; and, I should guess, not much interested in anything that we have done or see, unless perhaps in our visits to the Ents' (*RT*, VI, vii, 332). Yet at this late stage of the narrative, after all we have seen and shared with Frodo and his companions, can we share or even approve of Bombadil's indifference to the world of social relations ('anything we have done or seen')? Gandalf's reference to the Ents is telling since, though not as ageless as Bombadil, the Ents too belong to the novel's category of beings whose immense age runs directly counter to the limited perspectives of mortals, and feel a similar inclination to opt out of the political struggles of Middle-earth: as Treebeard comments, '. . . I do not like worrying about the future. I am not altogether on anybody's *side*, because nobody is altogether on my *side*, if you understand me . . .' (*TT*, III, iv, 83). Yet, ultimately, the Ents do recognize their own unavoidable implication in the social and commit themselves to a side, even at the cost of their own existence: 'likely enough . . . we are going to *our* doom: the last march of the Ents. But . . . we may help the other peoples before we pass away' (*TT*, III, iv, 102).

As ancient as they are, the Ents do not possess foresight as such, but Treebeard intuits what the Elves know, as does Théoden after meeting the Ent: that, win or lose, 'much that was fair and wonderful shall pass for ever out of Middle-earth'. This insight, first clearly stated in Lórien when Galadriel chooses to 'diminish . . . and remain Galadriel' (*FR*, II, vii, 480), becomes the dominant motif of the novel's later stages. The novel's extended winding-down makes it very clear not only that, as Gandalf had replied to Théoden 'to such days we are doomed' but that even 'remaining Galadriel' may be denied as myth supersedes memory. In a memorable passage, Tolkien describes the Elves, Elrond and Gandalf reflecting silently as the Hobbits sleep – 'recalling the ages that were gone and all their joys and labours in the world' – and the future – 'holding council, concerning the days to come'. Yet whatever their accumulated and collective wisdom or insight, it seems doomed to oblivion. The Hobbits encounter a superficially similar temporal disorientation in the house of Bombadil – 'whether the morning and evening of one day or of many days had passed Frodo could not tell' (*FR*, I, vii, 173) – and later, intensified, in Lórien:

> 'Anyone would think that time did not count in there!' [says Sam, his reckoning of the duration of the Fellowship's sojourn in Lórien confused by the new moon he sees rising over Anduin after their departure] . . .
> Legolas stirred in his boat. 'Nay, time does not tarry ever', he said, 'but change and growth is not in all things and places alike. For the Elves the world moves, and it moves both very swift and very slow. Swift, because they themselves change little, and all else fleets by: it is a grief to them. Slow, because they do not count the running years, not for themselves. The passing seasons are but ripples ever repeated in the long long stream.'
> (*FR*, II, ix, 510)

The significance of Legolas' gnomic account of the immortal's melancholic sense of time is that he, like Elrond and the other Elves who have not yet departed from the Havens, has taken the measure of the Elves' own past implication in (and partial responsibility for) Sauron's power and uses his knowledge of the past as their spur to engagement with the present. With fairly obvious if understated symbolism, Legolas' disquisition on time is delivered from a skiff borne swiftly on the currents of the Great River, where he finds himself as a member of the Fellowship, compelled by the ineluctable materiality of the Ring.

As Elrond suggests at the Council, however, awareness of the larger temporal arc within which the present narrative moment is con-stellated entails the concomitant recognition of that arc's inexorable trend towards extinction and final defeat. The painful lesson Elrond derives from all the defeats and empty victories he has seen, first enforced in the First Age when Melkor's/Morgoth's stronghold Thangorodrim was overthrown, is that evil may be defeated for a season or many seasons but inevitably recurs. This is a 'long view' that only a few – including Gandalf, Aragorn (who, although a mere stripling at 87 compared to Elrond, shares his perspective) and, by the end of the novel, Frodo – are able to adopt, and it makes their choice to act for the good notwithstanding the likelihood or even inevitability of ultimate failure significantly more meaningful than the essentially reactive bravery (Shippey [2000: 187] nicely characterizes it as 'mere furious heroic dauntlessness') of a man like Boromir. Bound up with their consciousness of the abyss of time subtending the present moment is a doubled awareness of defeat, encompassing both the invariable transience of victory and an awareness that even success in destroying the Ring will necessarily entail consigning the elder peoples of Middle-earth themselves to that same archaic history. It is a history, moreover, which – because its inheritors and bearers will not be the first-born or even in the long run men like Aragorn, in whose veins 'the blood of Numenor runs true', but fatally limited and historically oblivious contemporary men and women – in short order will become not history at all but rather the timeless, unplaceable, half-believed and at best half-understood domain of legend.

In this sense, of course, the experience of reading *The Lord of the Rings*, with its 'unattainable vistas' and half-understood histories, itself enacts the posterity of its own telling. In the quite complex folded temporality of Tolkien's narrative, final integration of the different timeframes of Tolkien's narrative articulates at a structural level the trilogy's central premise of an ultimate unity transcending the purely phenomenal: the reader who works to synthesize these disunities is thereby encouraged into an ethical stance through the act of reading itself. The reader – like the Hobbits – is caught between an original unknowing and an unfolding knowing that remains inadequate to full understanding but at some stage must become sufficient for action. This is what Tolkien characterized as 'the complexity of any given situation in Time, in which an absolute ideal is enmeshed' (*Letters* 326). Thus what is ultimately at stake in *The Lord of the Rings*, for the reader as for the protagonists, is the nature of moral and ethical decision.

HOLLYWOOD TIME

The canons of narrative art in any medium cannot be wholly different.
(*Letters* 270)

Self-evidently, Peter Jackson's *The Lord of the Rings* treats time very differently indeed from Tolkien's novel. Since the compressions, deviations, omissions and inventions wherein the film departs from its literary source have been exhaustively explored and debated elsewhere, both in print (e.g., Smith and Matthews 2004) and particularly online, in this concluding section of this chapter I will confine myself to some general observations and selected examples that illustrate the temporality of the film trilogy.

If, as we have seen, the unique narrative temporality of *The Lord of the Rings* develops out of the tension between the 'mortal' – propulsive narrative drive – and 'Elvish' – primally nostalgic – dynamics, *LOTR* replaces this dialectical relationship with a dominating linearity. Far from the novel's compacted, almost fractal encounter of the present and the archaic, Jackson's film is relentlessly present-tense and ruthlessly goal-oriented. Such archaic narrative matter as survives is largely condensed into the Prologue depicting Sauron's defeat by the Last Alliance, with Elrond (present at the battle) and Galadriel (as narrator) supplying the links to the narrative proper. Thereafter the film never deviates from the present moment (with the exception of Gollum's 'origin story' that opens *LOTR: Return*), nor does the narrative 'open up' to 'deep time' after the manner of the novel: neither the Balrog nor Shelob – first-rate movie monsters both – are threatening principally for their primeval aspects, as emphasized in the novel.

Amongst *LOTR*'s most striking modifications of Tolkien is the ruthless compression of Tolkien's stately but precise time-scheme, collapsing for example the five months that elapse between Gandalf's last visit to Frodo in Hobbiton (to say nothing of the 17 years since Bilbo's leaving-party, which in *LOTR* seems to take place just days beforehand) and the latter's departure from Bag End to (at best) a fortnight. Tolkien had encountered – and complained about – precisely such dramaturgic compressions in the script for the abortive Ackerman-Zimmerman-Brodax adaptation in 1958: 'I may say that I fail to see why the time-scheme should be deliberately *contracted*' (*Letters* 271). Tolkien felt that through the over-use of such labour-saving devices as the eagles, time was again and again 'contracted and hurried, with the effect of reducing the importance of the Quest' (*Letters* 273). As the quotation at the head of this section indicates, Tolkien saw no inherent clash between the narrative practices of dramatic (film) and prose narratives. In stark contrast, Peter Jackson and his co-screenwriters Philippa Boyens and Fran Walsh have justified these changes repeatedly (notably in the audio commentaries to the extended DVD releases) as the essential, substantive and (apparently) unchallengeable medium-specific differences of film and prose. The most important of these concerns the comprehension – both the filmmakers' own, and that attributed by them to the audience – of individual action. Essentially, according to Jackson action consists, precisely, in *activity*: thus he remarks (one instance amongst many) even Aragorn's brief period of apparent inactivity at Edoras awaiting the summons of the beacons as a regrettable dramatic lacuna.[7] Film narrative thus conceived is organized around action, understood in the most literal sense as dynamic action, or simply movement – from which contemplation, meditation or even deliberation is by definition excluded.

It is unsurprising in this light that the novel's most extended deliberative sequence, the Council of Elrond, is foreshortened in *LOTR*. Not only are the participants fewer, but their discussions a great deal more casually constituted (the Council seems a much more *ad hoc* affair than the novel's formally convened meeting). Whereas the Council in the novel, as we have seen, is as important for the operative mode of temporal relation it proposes for characters and readers alike as for the bald information it relays, the filmic version follows the films' general pattern by reducing exposition and debate ('talk') to a minimum, transforming discussion into dramatic conflict and constructing a new arc for the scene with the Council's (invented) collapse into rivalry and recrimination and Frodo's decisive intervention. Elrond's role undergoes a correspondent transformation, from temporal-ethical cynosure in the novel to the film's ambivalent facilitator, freighted with a marked patriarchal frostiness towards Aragorn.

In this regard *LOTR* embodies the tendency in the contemporary Hollywood blockbuster to revert to earlier cinematic modes: notably (and notwithstanding contemporaneous experiments with complex time-schemes in such independent productions as *Pulp Fiction* [1994], *Memento* [2000] and *24 Grams* [2003]) the reassertion of the primacy of what Deleuze calls the 'movement-image', in which continuity editing reduces time to an indirect result of movement and effaces the constructed temporality of the narrative. In this regard, the extended parallel montage through which both *LOTR: Towers* and *LOTR: Return* are organized (cross-cutting between the separate but simultaneous planes of action of the members of the dispersed Fellowship, eventually to be reintegrated at Aragorn's coronation) might be said to exemplify Hollywood's domestication of the much more radical experiments in parallel montage undertaken by Griffith in *Intolerance* (1916), whose cuts leap across not only space but vast passages of time to link present, recent past and remote past (ancient Babylon) in dialectical and didactic fashion.[8] This foregrounded narrative temporality approaches the more complex and irrational manipulations of time and space that Deleuze associates primarily with the postwar European art cinema and terms the 'time-image'. With the time-image, time is liberated from its subordination to movement and acquires an autonomous status that exercises a new and more stringent compulsion on the spectator: 'aberrant [narrative] movement speaks up for an anteriority of time that it presents to us directly' (Deleuze 1989: 37). In somewhat domesticated form, the time-image entered commercial US cinema during the New Wave-influenced 'Hollywood Renaissance' period of the late 1960s and 1970s – a period of critical modernistic experimentation with film form in Hollywood to which the spectacular success of simplified, highly linear narrative forms in *Star Wars* and its blockbuster descendants is generally regarded to have ended (on the Hollywood blockbuster, see Stringer 2003). It is noteworthy that Gollum's 'origin story', which at one stage was to have been included in *LOTR: Towers* as Gollum's own memory-trace, triggered when Frodo addresses him as 'Sméagol', and thus introducing a clear time-image element into *LOTR*'s dominant movement-image, was eventually normalized into a sequential, if compressed and elliptical, narrative relation at the start of *LOTR: Return*.

Once the Fellowship leave Rivendell, the quest presumably unfolds at approximately the same pace as in the novel: one has to say 'presumably' since Tolkien's precise chronology is displaced by conventional filmic markers of elapsed time – notably montage sequences in which the characters are framed, often in sweeping aerial shots, against various scenic New Zealand wilderness terrains. Whether such shots effectively communicate either the distance or the duration of the journeys undertaken is rather a matter of personal taste. One inevitable and important consequence, in any case, is to jettison the anagogic precision of Tolkien's time-scheme. Tolkien's assignment of key narrative events to central dates in the Christian calendar (the Fellowship's departure from Rivendell on Christmas Day; the destruction of the Ring on 25 March, as Shippey [2000: 208] notes the date assigned in old English tradition to the Crucifixion) cannot easily be assigned to any one part of the matrix of temporal extension discussed above: it extends the meaningfulness of the action into a dimension which – being, as Tolkien believed eternally contemporary – ultimately stands outside time altogether. It opens, that is, into exactly that eternity to which the immortal (but only within the circles of the world) terrestrial Elves are prohibited; of which the pre-Christian mortals of Middle-earth (whom Shippey compares to Dante's virtuous pagans, locked forever in Limbo) can have no knowledge; but which the reader of *The Lord of the Rings* is spurred to understand as the true (a)temporality that alone can provide restitution to the apparently inexorable decline of earthly things. The contemporary Hollywood blockbuster, by contrast, in its apparently breathless linear momentum towards narrative resolution in fact masks a compulsive fragmentation into an insistent and inescapable present-tense, a realm of pure phenomena that closes down any space or possibility for critical reflection or ethical engagement by the spectator.

CHAPTER 3

GOTHIC ECHOES

Sue Zlosnik

The title of this collection invites some personal musings. I first read *The Lord of the Rings* as a post-war baby boomer in the psychedelic and politically charged 1960s; the years between then and my recent rereadings have witnessed a transformation in English Studies. I have not, I should add, been a serial reader of the text over this period; I remembered Tolkien's major work as a lengthy piece of entertaining whimsy, which I had enjoyed at the time but had no desire to revisit. However, the spectacle of the Peter Jackson films and the series of polls hailing *The Lord of the Rings* as 'the book of the century' (leading Tom Shippey to sub-title his new study of Tolkien's work 'author of the century') suggested that it was time to return to a text frequently dismissed even by those who had been busy firing the canon over the last quarter of a century. Given that I had thought Che Guevara more important than Frodo Baggins in an era when graffiti regularly claimed that both 'lived', I suspected that I would now read differently and perhaps more wisely. In returning to *The Lord of the Rings*, I have found a text more rooted in its recent history than I might have imagined. What I remembered as archetypal evil forces, I found represented through the discourses of late Victorian Gothic fiction. This perception has been enabled by the emergence of a wealth of scholarship in Gothic studies over the last 25 years. The work of Gothic scholars has established critical paradigms that enable us to read *The Lord of the Rings* as a text that, although set in a mythical past, is preoccupied with the fears of a twentieth century still haunted by a legacy of late nineteenth-century anxieties.

While generally respecting Tolkien's dislike of allegory, a number of critics have embraced the 'freedom of the reader' to find 'applicability', which he endorsed in his foreword to the second edition of

The Lord of the Rings (*FR*, xviii). Most have identified the traumas of twentieth-century history in the text. Some see Tolkien's own experiences in the trenches of the Great War as providing the powerful imagery for the hellish journey into Mordor and its outcome (see, e.g., Barton Friedman's 1982 essay 'Tolkien and David Jones: The Great War and the War of the Ring' which compares Tolkien's text with World War One writings). He himself acknowledged that the figure of Samwise Gamgee was inspired by his admiration for qualities of courage, endurance and loyalty that he saw in the enlisted soldiers who acted as officers' batmen in the battlefield (Carpenter 1977: 81). Most persuasively, the prospect of the 'Shadow' engulfing Middle-earth even into the sequestered rustic Shire mirrors the threats of a shrinking world in which there are no hiding places, not only from the ravages of war but also from the evil effects of corrupt power. The latter point is reinforced by the book's coda, 'The Scouring of the Shire', in which the returning Hobbits find their homeland despoiled by Gandalf's old adversary Saruman, now know as 'Sharkey'. Saruman is shown as behaving as a petty tyrant aided and abetted by 'ruffians' who are now 'on top, gathering, robbing and bullying, and running or ruining things as they like, in his name' (*RK*, VI, viii, 344). Tom Shippey sees Saruman as the most contemporary figure in *The Lord of the Rings*, 'both politically and linguistically', one who is 'on the road to "doublethink"' (Shippey 2000: 76). The despoliation is characterized by a creeping industrialization with its attendant pollution, the old mill having been replaced with one that is 'always a-hammering and a-letting out a smoke and a stench' (*RK*, VI, viii, 354), and environmental damage of fouled waters and lopped trees. Frodo asserts that 'this is Mordor . . . just one of its works'. The influence of the great eye of Sauron manifests itself here in more mundane methods of surveillance and oppression: rules, enforcers, spies, and those who 'like minding other folk's business and talking big' (*RK*, VI, viii, 340).[1]

In response to what he saw as his dark and debased century, Tolkien's acknowledged project was to create a mythology for England (Carpenter 1977: 89–90). His debt to the literature and languages of the first millennium has been well documented. The zeal with which he created his mythological world means that the appendices to the second edition of *The Lord of the Rings* constitute an extensive paratext that creates an elaborate, detailed and entirely fake history. Here the reader can find calendars, maps, family trees, linguistic guides and ancillary 'historical' material. In shoring up an illusion of reality created by his fantasy world in this way, Tolkien's work seems to indulge in a practice that has been characteristic of Gothic texts since Horace Walpole's 1764 novel *The Castle of Otranto*. The preface to the first edition of this text claimed that it had been found in 'the library of an ancient Catholic family in the North of England', and, relating events that had happened in 'the darkest ages of christianity', possibly dated from that era (Fairclough 1968: 39). In the preface to the second edition, following the success of his novel, Walpole confessed to the authorship of what he was now calling his 'gothick story'. Lest there be any confusion, it is in the sense of the tradition of 'gothick stories' following Walpole that I use the term 'Gothic' in this essay, rather than the language and lore of the ancient Goths that Tolkien drew on.[2] Jerrold E. Hogle has suggested that the binary of 'fakery'/'authenticity' that helps structure the Gothic novel is indicative of a specifically modern and fractured subjectivity. For Hogle, the modern condition finds expression in the Gothic text through fakery and simulacra.[3] He argues that:

> The Gothic refaking of fakery becomes a major repository of the newest contradictions and anxieties in western life that most need to be abjected by those who face them so that middle-class westerners can keep constructing a distinct sense of identity. The progress of abjection in the Gothic is inseparable from the progress of the ghost of the counterfeit, particularly as that symbolic mode and the ideologies at war within it keep employing each other – and acting out abjections – both to conceal and to confront some of the basic conflicts in western culture.
> (Punter 2000, 297)

Hogle thus suggests that the rise of modernity, from the Renaissance onwards, has resulted in a crisis of identity in the western world. Inflecting this perception with his reading of Jean Baudrillard's *Symbolic Exchange and Death*, Hogle goes on to argue that the stability of the feudal world has been replaced by the social mobility and geographical displacements/relocations characteristic of a post-Renaissance world. The resulting psychological instability has manifested itself in a breakdown between the sign and its referent: 'Educated Europeans felt that they were leaving behind the age of the "obligatory sign", the notion of signifiers as always referring to an ordained status in people and things where "assignation is absolute and there is no class mobility"' (Punter 2000: 297).

Tolkien's mythology for England is fake; his extended exercise in creating the language of Elvish, for example, constitutes the creation of a simulacrum, designed to look and feel like a retrieval of something ancient. Humphrey Carpenter's biography gives an account of his painstaking crafting of ' "The Book of Mazarbul", a burnt and tattered volume that . . . is found in the Mines of Moria', and his disappointment that it had proved too expensive to include a facsimile of this in the first edition of *The Fellowship of the Ring* (Carpenter 1977: 217). The detail with which the fantasy world is constructed in Tolkien's work encourages a willing suspension of disbelief in its readers that appears to have been carried to extremes by some of its devotees, as a cursory glance at material on the Internet will confirm. This precarious boundary between the authentic and the fake makes reading *The Lord of the Rings* a Gothic experience in the sense that Hogle indicates.[4] The dismissal of Tolkien's fiction by many in the literary world parallels the reception of Gothic in the academy until recent decades. *The Lord of the Rings* is, I suggest, best read like a Gothic novel: to expect the realism of psychological complexity in its characters is to be disappointed for, as in the Gothic novel, we find representative figures and no shortage of grotesques; to expect conformity to a critical paradigm of 'the marvellous' is to find the book 'weighed down by the mechanisms of the realistic novel' (Brooke-Rose 1980: 67). Gothic since its inception has been a hybrid and protean form, shifting its focus to adapt to the conditions of the time in which it is produced.

Since Walpole's location of supernatural and shocking events in a distant past that he inaccurately identified as 'gothick', Gothic writing has persisted as a form of discourse capable of giving shape to the unspeakables of post-enlightenment modernity. While (as critics broadly agree), the Gothic novel as a genre (however diverse its examples) can be located in the period from *The Castle of Otranto* (1764) to *Melmoth the Wanderer* (1820), Gothic as a mode of writing pervaded the fiction (and, indeed, other kinds of writing) of the nineteenth century as a kind of textual haunting. Similarly, the settings of Gothic became no longer confined to those of the earlier genre. As Julian Wolfreys suggests, 'Escaping from the tomb and the castle, the gothic in the Victorian period becomes arguably even more potentially terrifying because of its ability to manifest itself anywhere' (Robbins and Wolfreys 2000: xiv). In the last decades of the nineteenth century, Gothic writing gave expression to a range of contemporary anxieties in texts such as Stevenson's *The Strange Case of Dr Jekyll and Mr Hyde* (1864) and Bram Stoker's *Dracula* (1897) as well as a host of less-remembered works, which provoked horror or terror or both. Gothic elements are also apparent in the popular fictional form of the time known as 'Victorian quest romance', of which Stevenson, Haggard, Kipling and Conan Doyle were the major exponents. Several critics have drawn attention to Tolkien's debt to this form of fiction in the structuring of the narrative of *The Lord of the Rings*[5] but less attention has been paid to the Gothic aspects of Victorian quest romance in Tolkien's text.[6]

The quartet of Hobbits who set out from the Shire do so to defend a way of life readily identifiable as rooted in an English countryside already lost by the time the book was written. The portrait of an innocent rustic way of life under threat is not unfamiliar to the English reader. Thomas Hardy's early fiction paints a similar portrait of a passing world: Tolkien's Hobbits are not so different from Dick Dewey and the other villagers of Mellstock in *Under the Greenwood Tree* (1872), whose traditional customs are threatened by the appearance of a pert young schoolmistress who will play the organ that will supplant the old choir and its instruments in Mellstock Church. Hardy's symbolism is here more mundane than Tolkien's and his elegiac text remains firmly within the bounds of realism. Tolkien's Hobbits are the 'little people' of this world, literally miniaturized and with strong, hairy feet that make them close to the earth and also, like Frodo's Uncle Bilbo in *The Hobbit*, equipped for travelling when necessary. A mixture of Victorian gentlemen, with their liking for hearth, home and pipe (Shippey 2000: 5) and 'ordinary boys' (Carpenter 1977: 223), they make unlikely heroes. The journey undertaken by Frodo and his companions, however, is a journey of necessity rather than a search for adventure; for this is a quest narrative in which the aim is not to find something, an equivalent of the holy grail, but to be rid of something: the most powerful Ring of all with its destructive power to corrupt. As Gandalf tells Frodo, 'It would be a grievous blow to the world if the Dark Power overcame the Shire; if all your kind, jolly, stupid Bolgers, Hornblowers, Boffins, Bracegirdles and the rest, not to mention the ridiculous Bagginses, became enslaved' (*FR*, I, ii, 64).

The pervasive threat of the Ring's power is one that manifests itself not simply at the level of brute, or even monstrous, force but, more disturbingly, at the level of the individual psyche. It infects the bearer with the will to power in a manner that is destructive to him (always a him) as well as to others. Frodo's quest takes him into a world characterized by entropy and decay. This is a world in which creatures are fading or in decline: early in the story, Bilbo tells Gandalf that he feels 'thin, sort of *stretched* . . . like butter that has been scraped over too much bread' (*FR*, I, i, 42); the Elves are a remnant, most of their kindred having 'long departed' and 'only tarrying here a while, ere [they] return over the Great Sea' (*FR*, I, iii, 106); and Aragorn, revealed as heir to the decayed kingdom of Gondor, appears at first as 'Strider', an enigmatic figure reminiscent of the Gothic wanderer.[7] Moreover, Middle-earth is a place in which the uncanny is ever present. Hardly out of the Shire, Frodo and his companions are imprisoned by a Barrow-wight, the undead inhabitant of a burial site, 'a tall dark figure like a shadow against the stars' with 'two eyes, very cold though lit with a pale light that seemed to come from a remote distance' (*FR*, I, viii, 184) until they are rescued by the benevolent forest-dweller Tom Bombadil. The Freudian sense of the uncanny is evoked by the description of Rivendell as 'The Last Homely House east of the Sea' (*FR*, II, i, 295). Indeed, the world of Middle-earth is one in which the last corners of civilization are threatened by the creeping Shadow from the East. In late Victorian Gothic fiction, the East is habitually represented as the locus of threat and often the source of demonic Gothic figures. Dracula comes out of the far reaches of Romania and Svengali, in George du Maurier's *Trilby* (1894), is described as originating from 'the poisonous East – birthplace and home of an ill wind that blows nobody good' (du Maurier 1992: 239).

Figures such as Dracula and Svengali exemplify the way in which late Victorian Gothic fiction is not only haunted by the uncanny but also pervaded by the anxieties of degenerationism. Daniel Pick identifies degenerationism as a complex phenomenon, the discursive descent of which cannot be tied to the roots of one ideology, but sees it as extending into many theories and fictions of the first 40 years of the twentieth century (Pick 1989: 234). Although slightly out of this time-frame, it is clear that Tolkien's epic is underpinned by the discourse of degenerationism and draws on those Gothic tropes of the popular fiction of the later Victorian period that expressed the multiplicity of anxieties to which it gave rise. Saruman's Orcs, for example, are 'foul folk', according to Treebeard, who suggests that he has 'been doing something to them' and that he has possibly 'blended the races of Orcs and Men', to produce, he implies, a degenerated creature that embodies the worst of both (*TT*, III, iv, 84). Kelly Hurley sees degenerationism as 'a "gothic" discourse, and as such ... a crucial imaginative and narrative source for the *fin de siècle* Gothic' (Hurley, 65). This is, she claims:

> a genre thoroughly imbricated with biology and social medicine: sometimes borrowing conceptual remodellings of human physical identity, as it did from criminal anthropology; sometimes borrowing narrative remodellings of heredity and culture, as it did from the interrelated discourses of evolutionism, degeneration, and entropy; sometimes borrowing spatial remodellings of the human subject, as it did from the psychologies of the unconscious.
> (Hurley, 5)

The Victorian preoccupation with degenerationism often manifests itself in the fiction of the period in the form of the term 'abhuman' (a term that Hurley borrows from a popular Gothic writer of the time, William Hope Hodgson). Hurley recognizes that the concept of the abhuman resonates strongly with Julia Kristeva's concept of 'the abject', a concept that has proved useful in Gothic criticism (1982). Identifying 'the abject' as a psychic state deriving from our earliest experiences of being 'betwixt and between' in the process of birth, Kristeva applies the term to that which 'disturbs identity, system, order. What does not respect borders, positions, rules. The in-between, the ambiguous, the composite' (Kristeva 1982: 4). The abject has been seen as manifested in Gothic bodies and used as a way of understanding that which society itself has 'thrown down'. Culture is shored up by what it abjects; in the Gothic, in the words of Jerrold E. Hogle, 'struggles for cultural definition are what haunt the Gothic most in its anomalous monsters and spectres, as well as in the desires of its heroes and its heroines' (Hogle 1996: 826).

The Gothic fiction of the late nineteenth century abounds in monstrous figures, including the monstrous female. Studies such as those of Elaine Showalter (1987 and 1991) have built on the work of Foucault to point to the pathologization of women's bodies in that period; Eve Kosofsky Sedgwick's work (1985) identifies a prominent homosociality among men in response to a perception of the 'otherness' of women. The prevalence of anxiety about female corporeality finds expression in some memorable examples of female monstrosity in the fiction of the period: in the monstrous women of Rider Haggard, in the morphic beetle in Richard Marsh's story of the same name and in Arthur Machen's *The Great God Pan*, to take three examples. The polarity of nineteenth-century sexual ideology in the form of Madonna and whore figures so extensively uncovered by second-wave feminism is clearly demonstrated in *The Lord of the Rings*. Displaying the characteristic homosociality of the Victorian quest narrative in the bonding of its male characters, the story presents female figures who are representative of different forms of purity: the Elf, Arwen (eventually to become a fit queen to Aragorn's king), the powerful and demonstrably incorruptible Galadriel who resists the Ring and, to those inclined to read from a Catholic perspective, represents the Immaculate[8], the fierce and frosty shield maiden Éowyn, who is thawed by the love of Faramir, and the domestic ideal of Rosie Cotton to whom Sam eventually returns. There is, however, one memorably monstrous female figure in the form of Shelob, ancient spider of gigantic proportions and 'soft squelching body' which lives in the earth and feeds off men, 'the most loathly shape he [Sam] had ever beheld, horrible beyond the horror of an evil dream' (*TT*, IV, ix, 417). The episode in which Frodo is captured by Shelob and fought off by Sam using the phial of light given to the Hobbits by Galadriel has been persuasively examined from a feminist perspective by Brenda Partridge. Partridge concludes that 'the female linked with sexuality is seen as evil, paganism' (Giddings 1983: 191). Her analysis is best contextualized by seeing the abject figure of Shelob as representative of an anxiety that had become particularly acute in the late Victorian era.

Gollum is clearly an abject figure of a different kind, to all intents and purposes abhuman. Frodo and Sam's first sight of him presents him as a repulsive creature, behaving in a most un-Hobbit-like way:

> Down the face of a precipice, sheer and almost smooth it seemed in the pale moonlight, a small black shape was moving with its thin limbs splayed out. Maybe its soft clinging hands and toes were finding crevices and holds that no Hobbit could ever have seen or used, but it looked as if it was just creeping down on sticky pads, like some large prowling thing of insect-kind. And it was

coming down head first, as if it was smelling its way. Now and again it lifted its head slowly, turning it right back on its skinny neck, and the Hobbits caught a glimpse of two small pale gleaming lights, its eyes that blinked at the moon for a moment and then were quickly lidded again.
(*TT*, IV, i, 268)

It is worth comparing this with Jonathan Harker's account of watching Count Dracula:

> ... my feelings changed to repulsion and terror when I saw the whole man slowly emerge from the window and begin to crawl down the castle wall over that dreadful abyss, *face down*, with his cloak spreading out about him like great wings. At first I could not believe my eyes. I thought it was some trick of the moonlight, some weird effect of shadow ... I saw the fingers and toes grasp the stones, worm clear of mortar by the stress of years, and by thus using every projection and inequality move downwards with considerable speed, just as a lizard moves along a wall.
> (Stoker 1996, 34)

There is a striking similarity of rhetoric here in the evocation of 'repulsion and terror' occasioned by these abhuman figures.

For Hurley, the abhuman subject is 'a not-quite-human subject, characterized by its morphic variability, continually in danger of becoming not-itself, becoming other' (Hurley 1996, 3–4). The transgression of boundaries characteristic of Gothic manifests itself most clearly in the late Victorian period as a preoccupation with the boundaries of the self. Gandalf tells Frodo the story of how Gollum had long ago been Sméagol, a member of a 'clever-handed and quiet-footed little people' (*FR*, I, ii, 69) who had killed his cousin Déagol for possession of the Ring that he had found. Under the influence of the Ring, he had degenerated into Gollum (so named because of 'the gurgling in his throat' [*FR*, I, ii, 71]) whom Bilbo had encountered deep inside the Misty Mountains, where he had been for an age having 'wormed his way [there] like a maggot' (*FR*, I, ii, 71). Frodo responds to the idea that Gollum had come from a people connected with Hobbits with the exclamation 'what an abominable notion' (*FR*, I, ii, 72).[9] When he later encounters Gollum, his appeal to the Sméagol he once was causes that buried identity to surface and

fight out a battle for consciousness with the monstrous and corrupted figure that he has become under the influence of the Ring. As
Frodo observes, 'when Gollum used *I* . . . that usually seemed to be a
sign, on its rare appearances, that some remnants of old truth and
sincerity were for the moment on top' (*TT*, IV, iii, 309). In many
respects, Gollum resembles Stevenson's Dr Jekyll with Mr Hyde in
the ascendancy (himself a descendant of other *doppelgänger*
haunted selves such as Hogg's Robert Wringhim in the much earlier
Confessions of a Justified Sinner). As Hurley points out, 'Freud's hint
that a doubling relationship, which on the surface accomplishes a
simple bi-furcation of the self, gestures towards a more radical fis-
sioning of the self – towards an amorphous version of the self which
is a non-self, because it has forfeited all the boundaries that enabled
it to distinguish itself from the world of things that surround it'
(Hurley, 42). The Ring's power to disintegrate the subject and transform it into something abject is most powerfully demonstrated in
Gollum but remains a constant threat to the identity of Frodo as
long as he remains the Ring-bearer. At the moment of crisis when he
must cast it into 'the very crack of Doom' he speaks with a voice
'clearer and more powerful than Sam had ever heard him use' and
claims the Ring for his own (*RK*, VI, iii, 265). Now in the sights of
the Eye of the Dark Lord, he is saved only by Gollum's bestiality in
biting off the finger that bears the Ring. Infected by the Ring,
Frodo's conscious will is not enough to complete the Quest.

There are vampiric resonances in *The Lord of the Rings*. The
insidious evil that the Ring represents infects the artefacts that serve
it and, by extension, those whose bodies who come into contact with
them. The knife that pierces Frodo in an early struggle takes from
him his strength in a way that is different from the trauma of a
normal wound. It also infects him with a nameless poison that
enhances the temptation of the Ring; like the bite of the vampire, it
infects him with desire. The Ringwraiths, possessors of nine of the
lesser rings, were once Mortal Men, but have long been reduced
to 'shadows under his great Shadow, his most terrible servants' (*FR*,
I, ii, 68). Éowyn's destruction of the Black Captain of the Ringwraiths on the Pelennor Fields is absolute: staked by her sword, he
becomes nothing, leaving an empty mantle and hauberk, his destruction evoking echoes of the end of Dracula as described by Mina
Harker: 'almost in the drawing of a breath, the whole body crumbled
into dust and passed from our sight' (Stoker, 377). One critic,

Gwenyth Hood, has offered a detailed comparison of Dracula and Sauron, using the image of the eye and vision as linking features between the two texts. Indeed, manifesting himself as a giant bestial eye, Sauron is an embodiment of another late Victorian Gothic preoccupation, the power of the eye. As Daniel Pick points out, long-standing theories about the forces projected from the seeing eye surfaced again in the late nineteenth century, to be subsumed into the speculations about mesmerism. The myth of the 'evil eye' is perhaps most dramatically represented in this period in the figure of Svengali but Pick also cites Conan Doyle's 'The Parasite', in which a 'rapacious and hypnotically dangerous' woman from the West Indies overpowers an eminent professor through the intensity of her gaze (Pick 2000: 169). Yet again it is possible to see the nineteenth-century anxiety about the integrity of the subject, as well as the twentieth-century fear of surveillance in the image of the eye of Sauron.

Tom Shippey identifies a contradiction between Boethian and Manichaean visions of evil as driving the plot of *The Lord of the Rings*. Hood's assertion that Sauron represents a twentieth-century vision of evil that is darker and more nihilistic than the evil of Dracula, 'which tempts with instinctual pleasure' (Hood 1987, 150), implies the Boethian vision of evil as absence, in the form of 'the Shadow'. Yet the Manichaean view of evil as a positive force, the 'Dark Power', seems to be demonstrated by the endowing of the Ring itself with evil powers. The Ring as symbol of evil may be seen as representing both of these apparently opposed visions: inscribed in Elvish letters but in the tongue of Mordor, it is, like Conrad's Kurtz, 'hollow at the core'. And what is at the core is the subject, human or humanoid.

Clearly, Tolkien was backward-looking in his choice of Gothic tropes from some 50 years earlier to represent deep fears of threats both external and internal. Yet in a twenty-first century that has already witnessed global politics increasingly framed in the Manichaean rhetoric of fundamentalism, the consolation of the happy ending or 'eucatastrophe' (to use Tolkien's own coinage [*Tree and Leaf*, 60]) of *The Lord of the Rings* seems to supply a deep-felt longing to some: perhaps to those who identify with the values of the Shire. Yet the destruction of Sauron cannot make Frodo what he once was – he is irreparably damaged – nor can it save the elves, who diminish further. For Ken Gelder, writing about Tolkien in the wake of 9/11, modern epic fantasy is a 'literary form of fundamentalism that troubles secular ideals', itself 'terroristic' in its attack on the modern world (Gelder 2003: 26). For those who find solace in Tolkien's fake mythology, there will be the hope of modest, reluctant heroes who offer themselves up to save their fellows from the worst that the modern world can do. So how should I have answered the bearded man with the folding bicycle who fixed me with an intense stare when I was rereading *The Lord of the Rings* on the train? Obviously believing he had spotted another devotee, he asked, 'So how many times have *you* read it?' The honest answer would have been, 'I read it every 35 years. I may not read it again.' In an uncanny, echoing coincidence we both left the train at Frodsham.

CHAPTER 4

THE ONE RING

Adam Roberts

WHY A RING?

To unpack the question a little: why might Tolkien light upon a finger-ring to embody the central force of his symbolic conception, making it the most powerful and most dangerous artefact in his imaginary world? More to the point, although each of the other magic rings (the three Elven, the seven Dwarvish and the nine Mannish) carries a precious stone, the one ruling Ring is a plain gold circle. Which is to say: it takes the form of a wedding band. Is there something strange in Tolkien, a devout Catholic with strong views on the sanctity and importance of marriage, himself happily married, taking a wedding ring as his supreme symbol of the corruptive power of evil in the world?

This question needs immediate qualification: of course the one Ring is not a wedding band in any literal sense; its resemblance is figurative and symbolic rather than literal. But to explore the way the Ring, and rings in general, signify in *The Lord of the Rings* is to open up some intriguing aspects of what I take to be Tolkien's fundamentally sacramental imagination, which in turn illuminate the way this book works, as a great Catholic as well as a great fantasy novel.

Immediate objections suggest themselves. Perhaps there is nothing especially remarkable about the use of a ring as the trigger or accelerant of Tolkien's large narrative. Some sort of item or treasure is frequently the focus (the 'mcguffin', as such narrative stratagems are sometimes dismissively called) of adventures in the Romance tradition; perhaps the object over which characters fall out, or after which characters quest. One of Tolkien's key strategies, as many critics have noted, is to invert the conventions of such tales. *The Lord of the Rings* is a sort of quest narrative, but with the difference that the quest is to destroy rather than discover an item of precious treasure. It is fair to ask whether there is any deeper significance to the Ring beyond its position as narrative facilitator. Perhaps there is nothing essential about the Ring apart from this functionality. It's possible that Tolkien could equally well have built his novel around a golden chalice, or a golden torc, or a golden coin, or – for all we know – a golden ankh, dolphin or miniature football boot. But to put it in those sorts of terms (they are ridiculous choices in this context, but why *should* they be ridiculous?) does at least highlight the *rightness* of Tolkien's actual choice. There is something intuitively appropriate about the Ring. Why might that be?

One way to start answering such a question is to look at the way the Ring functions within the logic of Tolkien's story, as well as to look at the symbolic and subtextual resonances of his creation, to have some sense of why he placed this particular artefact at the heart of his imaginative conception.

Actually, when one starts to look at *The Lord of the Rings* 'through the Ring', as it were, it starts to assume a certain ubiquity. The 'Fellowship of the Ring', the nine companions who take the Ring south, echo an Arthurian circle of knights (a round table). Mordor, the birth- and death-place of the Ring, itself externalizes a ring shape, surrounded on all sides by forbidding mountains. (Actually this is only partly true: according to the map the ring of mountains protecting the land of shadow falls away to the east; although there are no indications of this in the novel – no suggestion that Frodo and Sam should trek east to enter Mordor through eastern foothills, rather than clamber up the forbidding mountain ranges.) In *The Silmarillion* the council place of the Valar is called 'the Ring of Doom'; and the city of Doriath is protected by the 'ring of Melian', a type of magical fence protecting but also restricting the city. In an earlier draft of this material, collected after Tolkien's death in the volume *Morgoth's Ring*, the ring of the title is the whole of Middle-earth, through which (and especially through the gold ore threaded within it) Morgoth's malignancy circulates: only water is immune from his evil.

As an architectural or geographical feature rings are interestingly ambiguous. A surrounding wall might figure as protection against a hostile exterior world; or it might equally well figure as confinement, a prison wall preventing escape. Something of this semiological doubleness inflects the symbolic 'ring', focused on the One Ring, with an almost uncanny balance. And perhaps this also functions as a Tolkienian gloss upon the institution of marriage.

ANTECEDENTS

There are obvious points to make about Tolkien's choice of a 'ring' as key symbol. It is tempting, although rather fruitless, to list his possible sources, the many occurrences of magic rings in previous culture of which he was certainly aware. For some commentators the parallels with Wagner's cycle of opera *Der Ring des Nibelungen* are striking, although Tolkien repudiated them.[1] Of course, Tolkien's denial does not mean that Wagner can be dismissed entirely out of hand. John Louis DiGaetani has argued, in *Richard Wagner and the Modern British Novel* (1978), that Wagner's influence is pervasive in early twentieth-century British literature, citing in particular Conrad, Lawrence, E. M. Forster, Woolf and Joyce. But as DiGaetani points out:

> Wagner's *Der Ring des Nibelungen* is most basically about the relationship between love and power. The ring itself, which will give infinite wealth and power to the person who possesses it, can achieve its power only if its bearer renounces love forever.
> (DiGaetani 1978: 78)

This is not the dichotomy presented in *The Lord of the Rings*. Indeed, something of the reverse is true. The Ring achieves some of its sinister, uncanny effect in the novel precisely by creating a weirdly intense *parody* of the love relationship. Gollum loves his Ring as he might, under other circumstances, have loved a fellow being: he calls it his 'precious', talks to it and so on. Of course, this 'love' is not presented as a positive force; it is too claustrophobically exclusive, too much a version of unhealthy narcissism, and it overrides all other duties of care, love and honour.

More relevant to Tolkien's purposes (we might assume) are the many references to rings as precious objects and tokens of trust and fidelity in Old English literatures. From this perspective the Ring is interesting primarily because it represents, as *Great Expectations'* Wemmick might put it, 'portable property': valuable, displayable and easily transported, gold rings are a good way for a lord to reward his loyal followers. But there are problems here as well: a gold ring with an inset precious jewel would be a more valuable piece of portable property than a plain gold band; and yet, of course, in *The Lord of the Rings*, the reverse is the case – the plainer ring is the most powerful.

THE ONE RING

There are, as critics have noted, certain inconsistencies in the way the One Ring is portrayed in *The Lord of the Rings*. Sometimes it is inert; sometimes it seems to possess will and even agency ('the Ring,' Gandalf says, 'wants . . .'). It can be 'wielded' only by someone with a strong will; but some of the strongest wills (Boromir's for instance) are overwhelmed without even direct contact. There is also a, presumably deliberate, vagueness as to what the Ring might actually do in the wrong hands. Gollum possesses it for a very long time and does nothing more with it than use it as a means of becoming invisible. Yet the implication is that, on a properly skilled hand, it can wreak terrible damage (how? we wonder – does lightning lance forth from the beringed finger? Does it summon down atomic-bomb-like death on armies? Tolkien does not spell it out).[2]

Tom Shippey identifies some other difficulties. Gandalf's conversation with Frodo in the second chapter of the first book, says Shippey, contains assertions concerning the Ring which are 'at the heart of *The Lord of the Rings*' adding 'if they are not accepted, then the whole point of the story collapses'. He picks out three: firstly that 'the Ring is immensely powerful, in the right or the wrong hands'; secondly the Ring is 'deadly dangerous to all its possessors: it will take them over, "devour" them, "possess" them'; thirdly, 'the Ring cannot simply be left unused, put aside, thrown away: it has to be destroyed' (Shippey 1992: 126). And some characters (Gollum, Boromir) are indeed corrupted, devoured and destroyed by the Ring, consistently with these premises. But as Shippey notes there are many characters whom are untouched: including Sam (who hands the Ring back to Frodo without demur), Aragorn, Legolas, Gimli, Merry and Pippin, who all appear indifferent to it. At the beginning of the story Gandalf tells Frodo that he 'could not "make" you' relinquish the Ring 'except by force, which would break your mind'

(*FR*, I, ii, 80). Yet at the very end of the book Gollum wrenches the Ring from Frodo precisely by force, assaulting him and biting his finger off, and yet Frodo's mind remains unbroken. Shippey's solution to this is that 'all the doubts just mentioned can be cleared up by the use of one word, though it is a word never used in *The Lord of the Rings*. The Ring is "addictive"' (Shippey 1992: 126). Like a drug to a contemporary drug addict, the Ring can overwhelm the individual's power to 'just say no'.

There are problems, however, with the 'addictive' explanation. It seems, for instance, that Bilbo does not become 'addicted' to the Ring, even though he possesses it for decades, using it often. Boromir, on the other hand, becomes 'addicted' despite never possessing it. Moreover, addiction does not address the notion that the forceable removal of the Ring is described as something that will break Frodo's mind, and the later contradiction of this assertion. Rather, the imaginative logic of the novel suggests that a person with 'great will' might master the Ring and wield it (although his or her intents would be perverted to evil); whereas a 'little' person would be unable to master it, and would instead become mastered *by* it (like Gollum). It is hard to reconcile this with the idea of an 'addictive' Ring; on the contrary, it tends to play up the idea of the Ring as an agent itself, with its own will which must be wrestled with.

The Ring is clearly 'to do' with power; but more important than this rather nebulous fact is the point that the Ring is a *binding* agent, tying together all the other Rings of Power: a locus of connection ('One Ring to bring them all and in the darkness bind them'). 'Bind' is an interesting word. It means several things. It means to tie together or tie up, literally or metaphorically. It can also refer to marriage. It is etymologically connected with 'band' (a 'wedding band' is so called precisely because it *binds*). The Ring binds itself to its bearer. It binds together (by magic charm, as a form of marriage) all the other rings. In other words the resemblance between this 'binding' Ring and the ordinary marriage band is more than mere superficial appearance. There is a form of marriage – binding, exclusive, life-devouring – at the heart of Tolkien's conception of the Ring.

Nor is marriage an arbitrarily chosen trope. It is, after all, not merely a contract between two people, but a sacramental bond – sacramental in the strong, Catholic sense of the word. In other words, the key thing about marriage is that it is a sacrament. I am suggesting, in other words, that one answer to the question posed in the opening paragraph is that Tolkien chooses a Ring that resembles a marriage band precisely because, for a Catholic, the marriage ring is a sacramental icon. This is a crucial point, I think: because Tolkien conceives of his subcreated world in sacramental terms.[3]

SACRAMENTS

The Latin 'sacramenta' is the translation used of the New Testament Greek μυστήριον (musterion, 'mystery'); and in Christian theology a sacrament is 'a visible sign of an invisible grace'. Catholics recognize seven sacraments: baptism, confirmation, penance, the Eucharist, priestly ordination, marriage and extreme unction (or 'the anointing of the sick' as the latter has, since Tolkien's time, been renamed). These rituals are symbolic of divine grace entering into the material realm, but in a crucial sense they are *more* than symbolic. According to Aquinas 'the Christian sacraments are ways in which God lives in us and in which we, in this life, live in God' (Davies 2002: 210). The mystery of the sacraments is bound in with the mystery of the Incarnation: God, says Aquinas, was not obliged to incarnate himself in material form in order to confer his grace on humanity; but by choosing to do this he connected the spiritual world with the material world (in which we live). St Augustine saw sacraments as a physical 'signum', or sign, of non-physical (which is to say, spiritual) truth – so, for instance, that the water of baptism symbolizes the non-material spirit of God. Aquinas agreed that the sacraments were symbolic rites, but insisted that they were at the same time *more* than just symbolic.

> Aquinas firmly believes that God brings us to himself as creatures of flesh and blood. He thinks that, in the end, we are drawn into the life of God by someone like ourselves, by someone living a human life in our material world. And he believes this is where sacraments enter into the picture ... the sacraments of the Church are physical signs and genuine causes of grace. They are symbols which make real what they symbolize.
> (Davies 2002: 215–18)

This, I think, helps gloss Tolkien's repeated insistence of animadversion against allegory (we do, I think, need to take seriously Tolkien's statement of 'cordial dislike [for] allegory' and acknowledge that *The Lord of the Rings* is poorly served by that sort of reductive reading). A better way to think of *The Lord of the Rings* is not as allegory but as a sub-creative materialization – an incarnation, in a manner of speaking – of (what Tolkien took to be) certain spiritual realities.[4]

That *The Lord of the Rings* is a great work of Catholic literature, as well as a great work in the fantasy tradition, has been argued by several critics.[5] As Tolkien himself wrote to Father Robert Murray, a Jesuit friend, in 1953:

> *The Lord of the Rings* is of course a fundamentally religious and Catholic work; unconsciously so at first but consciously in the revision. That is why I have not put in, or have cut out practically all references to anything like 'religion', to cults and practices, in the imaginary world. For the religious element is absorbed into the story and the symbolism. However, that is very clumsily put, and sounds more self-important than I feel.
>
> (*Letters* 172)

This is not to suggest that the novel can be decoded as a religious allegory. But of course elements from Christian myth have shaped the imaginary world of Middle-earth – particularly a fascination with the Fall that introduces mortality to the world, and with ethical choice (writing to Milton Waldman in 1951 Tolkien said that 'all this stuff is mainly concerned with Fall, Mortality and the Machine' [*Letters* 145]). It tells the story of self-sacrifice, and a saviour who travels the paths of the dead only to return in triumph; of the tremendous significance of the moral choices people are presented with, particularly of ordinary people caught up in extraordinary times.

Bernard Bergonzi, in his article 'The Decline and Fall of the Catholic Novel' argues that 'the English Catholic novel . . . did not dramatize Catholic theology *tout court*, for there is no such single entity, but a particular and extreme theological emphasis, where religious beliefs were caught up with literary attitudes and conventions' (1986: 172–87). Assuming we wish to bracket *The Lord of the Rings* with the writers about which Bergonzi is here talking (Graham Greene and Evelyn Waugh predominantly) we might wish to go on and explore how 'particular and extreme' the theological emphasis of Tolkien's fantasy is. The particular element that articulates itself through the work is, I am suggesting, precisely this sacramental element.

One such element is the matter of free will, something profoundly important to Tolkien as a Catholic, and something with the largest resonance in the construction of this novel. As Colin Manlove points out, one malign effect of the Ring is to compromise Frodo's free will.

> Frodo has been 'chosen' for his task; by itself this is reasonable enough, for it would still leave him room to decide whether to take it up. But there are additional determining factors. Bilbo could voluntarily leave the Ring to Frodo because the Ring wanted to go to Frodo: as Gandalf says 'he would never have just forsaken it, or cast it aside. It was . . . the Ring itself that decided things. The Ring left *him*.' And since the Ring wants to be with Frodo, it is impossible for him to get rid of it as it was not for Bilbo: Gandalf tells him that he could not 'make' Frodo give it up 'except by force, which would break your mind'. Therefore, Frodo has to keep the Ring.
> (Manlove 1975: 176)

Later in the novel, Manlove suggests, 'this core of necessity is hopefully overlain with an apparent act of will'. Frodo, reflecting on his 'evil fate' recalls that 'he had taken it on himself in his own sitting room in the far-off spring of another year'. According to Manlove, however: 'this is not true to the facts'.

Certain difficulties do indeed present themselves. For example, how is it that Bilbo was able effectively to separate himself from the Ring? Manlove's answer (that the Ring wanted to leave) addresses the question on the terms of the localized rationalization provided by the text rather than according to its symbolic logic. But does this mean that Bilbo somehow has more free will than Frodo? That cannot be: Catholicism does not say that free will is distributed amongst human beings like height or wealth, some with more and some less. We all have the freedom to choose good or evil; and it's a choice equally important to all of us.

I think one way of answering this question would be to say that Bilbo can divorce himself from the Ring where Frodo cannot, because Bilbo's story (primarily *The Hobbit*) takes place within the ethical framework of Old Germanic culture; where Frodo's story in *The Lord of the Rings* – though set in the same fictive world – actually takes place in the different conceptual and ideological-theological climate of Tolkien's Catholic beliefs.

Free will in Christian theology means that we all have – at all times, whenever we make a choice – the freedom to choose to do good or evil. The fact that God (omnipotent, and knowing the future as He does) already knows all the choices we are ever going to make in our life does not diminish this freedom *as it presents itself to us*, in time, continuously. But marriage is something of a special case that divides Protestant and Catholic theologies. For a Protestant it is possible to choose divorce (which is to say Protestants have the freedom, under certain circumstances, to choose to end their marriage). Catholics do not. Of course (a Catholic might say) everybody who enters into a marriage does so, or *should* do so, of their own free will; which is to say, the proscription against divorce can be thought of as a way of saying merely that once a choice has been freely made it is then necessary to live with the consequences of that choice – which, if anything, places a higher value upon the notion of free will. Of course Catholics are perfectly capable of freely willing for themselves the evils of adultery, bigamy and so on. Marriage is no more a *practically* binding relationship for them than it is for a non-Catholic. But in Catholic belief it is a *spiritually* binding one: Catholics who go through a form of divorce and begin relationships with others are, their priest might say, only fooling themselves. In the eyes of God they are still married.

Frodo's ambiguous position with respect to the Ring mirrors this problematic. Once he accepts the Ring (although at that point he knows no better: we wonder – if Frodo had known all the trouble bound up with the Ring, would he have accepted it from Bilbo?), once he *has* accepted it, he is bound to it. He cannot divorce himself from it. Only death (the death of the Ring itself, which occurs at the moment of the death of Gollum) can break the bond.

This may seem like a rather bleak and incarceratory vision of marriage, but it is not out of keeping with Tolkien's thoughts on the subject. In a letter to his son from 1941 Tolkien wrote:

[Women] are instinctively, when uncorrupt, monogamous. *Men are not* – no good pretending. Men just ain't, not by their animal nature . . . It is a fallen world, and there is no consonance between

our bodies, minds and souls. However, the essence of a *fallen* world is that the *best* cannot be attained by free enjoyment . . . but by denial, by suffering. Faithfulness in Christian marriage entails that: great mortification. For a Christian man there is *no escape*. Marriage may help to sanctify and direct to its proper object his sexual desires; its grace may help him in the struggle; but the struggle remains. It will not satisfy him.
(*Letters* 51; emphasis in original)

This seems an extreme way to construe marriage ('for a Christian man there is *no escape* . . .'), especially when Tolkien ends this same letter by commending his son to 'the one great thing to love on Earth: the Blessed Sacrament' (*Letters* 53). There is, we might feel, something alarming in any free agent being so remorselessly bound to anything.

At that time when he was still friendly with C. S. Lewis, Tolkien wrote to offer an opinion upon Lewis's book *Christian Behaviour* (1943), in which the argument is advanced that there ought to be two forms of marriage: one a Christian commitment, lifelong and binding; the other a purely secular State-sanctioned contract which could be dissolved. Tolkien disapproved of this idea, insisting that

Christian Marriage – monogamous, permanent [lifelong], rigidly 'faithful' – is in fact the truth about sexual behaviour for all humanity: this is the only road of total health [total human health] (including [with] sex in its proper place) for all [*all*] men and women.
(*Letters* 60; emphasis in original; words in square brackets mark Tolkien's revisions to the original draft of this letter)

There is an interesting diremption between 'permanent' and 'lifelong' here. One of the pieces of prose not included in *The Silmarillion* is a fairly lengthy discussion entitled 'Of the Laws and Customs among the Eldar pertaining to Marriage and Other Matters Related Thereunto' (it is included in volume x of Christopher Tolkien's *History of Middle Earth, Morgoth's Ring*, 1994). Here we learn that the Elves lived according to strict notions of married chastity:

The Eldar wedded once only in life, and for love or at the least by free will upon either part. Even when in after days, as the histories reveal, many of the Eldar in Middle-earth became corrupted, and

their hearts darkened by the shadow that lies upon Arda, seldom is any tale told of deeds of lust among them.
(Tolkien 1994: 210)

But in a detail that strikes a note of almost Lewisian compromise, Tolkien adds a period of betrothal ('the betrothed gave silver rings one to another') that 'was bound to stand for one year at least, and it often stood for longer. During this time it could be revoked by a public return of the rings, the rings then being molten and not again used for a betrothal. Such was the law.' Should the betrothal lead to marriage the betrothed 'received back one from the other their silver rings (and treasured them); but they gave in exchange slender rings of gold, which were worn upon the index of the right hand' (Tolkein, 1994: 211).[6]

All this talk of the interchange of rings is very interesting. We might, in the light of it, want to read the One Ring as embodying a sort of malign anti-marriage, the photographic negative, as it were, of a blessed sacrament. The only major character in *The Lord of the Rings* whom Tolkien dramatizes as a functioning member of a happy marriage is also the only character in the book wholly immune to the power of the Ring, Tom Bombadil, who alone of the major characters in the book has a wife. He asks Frodo for the Ring, and Frodo 'handed it at once to Tom':

> It seemed for a moment to grow larger as it lay far a moment on his big brown-skinned hand. Then suddenly he put it to his eye and laughed. For a second the Hobbits had a vision, both comical and alarming, of his bright blue eye gleaming through a circle of gold. Then Tom put the Ring around the end of his little finger and held it up to the candlelight. For a moment the Hobbits noticed nothing strange about this. Then they gasped. There was no sign of Tom disappearing!
> (*FR*, I, vii, 175).

The point of this episode is to dramatize that the Ring has no effect upon Tom (when Frodo later slips the Ring on he becomes invisible to everybody except Bombadil). It is 'alarming' to see Tom's blue eye through the Ring presumably because it recalls and inverts the red eye of Sauron. But my suggestion here is that the episode depends as much upon Tom's status as happily married man as to his slightly inchoate status as 'spirit of the land'. Tom and Goldberry are the only functioning (i.e., loving, sacramental) marriage in the whole of *The Lord of the Rings* (until the Ring is destroyed and marriage again becomes possible) – *hence* Tom is immune to the malign power of the One Ring. Indeed, the Hobbits' sojourn in Tom and Goldberry's house is figured as the symbolic equivalent of travelling through a wedding band: 'the Hobbits stood upon the threshold, and a golden light was all about them . . . The four Hobbits stepped over the wide stone threshold' (*FR*, I, vii, 162).[7]

I am still, I hope, steering clear of the suggestion that we read *The Lord of the Rings* as an allegory of marriage; or even that it represents some sort of satire upon marriage as an oppressive power-trap. Rather Tolkien has taken 'marriage', in the broadest sense and with an understanding of marriage as a synechdocal sacrament for the connection between the material and the spiritual, as a structuring principle for his fantasy. What is wedded in *The Lord of the Rings* is not so much 'a man and a woman' (let us say, Sam and Rosie; or Aragorn and Arwen); it is the possibility of the connection of a materially embodied reality to a form of divinity. But what saves this aesthetic conception from a banal piety is precisely the double-edged valences of the Ring. It is both attractive and alarming: the ring around us protects, but also hems us in. Marriage is a connection founded in love, but also a restriction on the polygamous nature of man ('Faithfulness in Christian marriage entails . . . great mortification'). It draws us and it makes us suffer, but it also connects us with the grace of a bountiful and exacting God. This is the appeal, and the cost, of the central project of *The Lord of the Rings*.

PART II

SPACE, PLACE AND COMMUNITY

CHAPTER 5

INVISIBILITY

Robert Eaglestone

The Lord of the Rings is a book about evil. The title refers first to Sauron, the embodiment of evil: as Gandalf says angrily to Pippin, the 'Lord of the Rings is not Frodo, but the master of the Dark Tower of Mordor' (*FR*, II, I, 269). It is also about a ring of invisibility. This chapter shows how these two, evil and invisibility, are intimately connected and how this connection also shows that the evil on which the book focuses is inalienably characteristic of the twentieth century, precisely because it takes its most radical form in modernity. Moreover, I will argue that, because this form of evil exists in and characterizes modernity, a fantasy novel such as *The Lord of the Rings* is an excellent (and perhaps the only) form which can reflect on it. Finally, by examining the unheroic destruction of the Ring and the *failure* of the quest, I will argue that Tolkien shows that, in modernity, this evil cannot be avoided and can only be the subject of constant negotiation.

Shippey offers a well-known and convincing analysis of evil in *The Lord of the Rings*. He finds the novel to be suspended between two different conceptions of evil: one conception he locates in Boethius and argues that evil is simply the absence of good. This is an inheritance of one strand of a Platonic and neo-Platonic conception of evil: that wrongdoing comes from, for example, selfishness and that an evil deed is good for, or at least to the benefit of, the person that does it. In contrast, he suggests, is the Manichaean view that evil is an actually existing force in the world, struggling with good. One doesn't have to follow this dualistic view totally to believe in a Kantian idea of a 'radical innate evil in human nature' (Kant 1998: 56), a defect which 'negates the good or moral law' (Caygill 1995: 182). For Shippey, this 'crux' is central to the book (and, more, makes up the 'absolute heart of the Christian religion itself' [Shippey

2000: 141]). While it is clear that Shippey himself and, he believes, Tolkien, tend to the Manichaean, he rightly refuses to conclude on this matter, and suggests that Tolkien refuses a conclusion too, turning instead to the Lord's Prayer (Shippey 2000: 141; Shippey 2003: 145) concluding that the origin of evil is an aporia in Tolkien's work. For others, simpler explanations exist: for Caldecott, for example, it is 'the dark magic of the corrupted will, the assertion of self in disobedience to God' (Caldecott 2003: 60). However, I want to offer a contrasting view of evil that takes its origin from the prime feature of the Ring: its capacity to make the wearer invisible. The significance of this is often overlooked. At first, as Tolkien wrote, he thought it no more than a ring of invisibility, as often exists in fairy tales. But invisibility is at the core of what the Ring is: rings of invisibility, power and seeing have a profound ethical meaning.

Invisibility, ironically, is a highly visible form of evil. In *The Republic*, Glaucon tells the story of the ring of Gyges. A shepherd explores a chasm opened by an earthquake, and there, inside a bronze horse he finds the corpse of a giant with a ring. He takes the ring and finds that it makes him invisible. This leads him to seduce the king's wife, kill the king and seize the throne. (Herodotus tells a slightly different but cognate story: both Plato and he agree that the story of Gyges is about the moral implications of seeing but not being seen. See Herodotus 2003: 6–8.) Why does invisibility lead to this? For Glaucon, who wants to argue that 'morality is never freely chosen' (Plato 1993: 48) and is not real but socially enforced, the answer is simple:

> Suppose there were two such rings . . . one worn by our moral person, the other by the immoral person. There is no one, on this view, who is iron-willed enough to maintain his morality and find the strength of purpose to keep his hands off what doesn't belong to him, when he is able to take whatever he wants from the market stall without fear of being discovered, to enter houses and sleep with whomever he chooses, and generally to act like a god among men. His [the moral person] behaviour will be identical to that of the other person [the immoral].
> (Plato 1993: 47–8)

Invisibility, for Gaucon, is a way of avoiding the need to 'seem moral' – reputation – which in turn, even for the 'iron willed', allows immorality to flourish. Glaucon's description certainly does fit Gollum, and to some extent Bilbo (the burglar, and prone to show off with the Ring, as at his leaving party) and even Frodo (seen as 'a travelling magician of unknown powers' [*FR*, I, ix, 212] after disappearing in the Prancing Pony). And, of course, it fits the nearly immortal and extraordinarily powerful Sauron (as 'a god among men'). Of course, it is against this view that morality is about the simple benefits of reputation and for the innateness of morality that Socrates argues. However, this link between evil and invisibility dates at least to *The Republic* and Tolkien would certainly have been familiar with this, from Plato, or from a more contemporary telling of this myth, H. G. Wells' *The Invisible Man* (see Holt 1992). The story is about the power and consequences of seeing and not being seen: it is not by chance that Gyges is the first person whose power is described as a 'tyranny'.

The twentieth-century ethical philosopher Emmanuel Levinas draws more out from this story and finds in Gyges, in the gesture of seeing without being seen, both the phenomena of evil and one of the defining and unavoidable features of modernity. Levinas's starting point is that 'ethics is first philosophy': by this he means that our thought and daily lives are first in a relationship to the others that populate the world. Everything else is built on this fundamental relationship to the other, which 'happens' to us before we choose it. We can choose different ways to behave towards the other: we can help the other, or refuse to help, for example, but both of these already presuppose a primordial and unavoidable relationship with the other. For Levinas, to participate in this relationship means to act positively on this. When we participate with the others, we share the world of others: and to share (as anyone supervising small children knows) involves giving up one's rights and acknowledging both the rights of the other and one's own responsibility to them over and above yourself. For Levinas, 'participation is a way of referring to the other: it is to have and unfold one's own being without at any point losing contact with the other' (Levinas 1991: 61).

However, Levinas sees something at odds with this in modernity. He argues that Descartes, as a the quintessential modern figure, began his search for truth by doubting everything and withdrawing more and more from the world, doubting even his own senses, in order to more clearly apprehend what is certain and unquestionable. However, this 'withdrawing', this becoming invisible to the world, has another effect: separation, the opposite of participation. Descartes's search for truth gives the illusion of severing or covering up exactly the 'enrootedness' and 'primordial preconnection' (Levinas 1991: 60) which is participation in the world of others. (Another way to see this would be to say that 'reputation' – about which Galucon is concerned – has a deeper significance as, more simply, participation in a community: the state of one's reputation *already* presupposes an involvement with others. Once invisible, this no longer matters.) Thus, this apparent separation, which is summed up by the idea of invisibility, creates the illusion that one's subjectivity is, like Gyges, not derived from one's relation with others but rather existing independently without society or recognition from others. Levinas continues and argues that the 'myth of Gyges is the very myth of the I' (Levinas 1991: 61) which stands alone. 'Seeing without being seen' is at the same time an illusion of radical separation and uprootedness from others, and the grounds of the possibility of 'inner life'. This 'spontaneous freedom of the I [or read, here, "Eye"?] unconcerned with its justification . . . a being *no longer participating* and hence drawing from itself its own existence, coming forth from a dimension of interiority' – a being like Gyges, in short – invokes the 'impunity of a being alone in the world . . . for whom the world is a spectacle'. This is, for Levinas, 'the very condition for solitary, and hence uncontested and unpunished, freedom, and for certitude' (Levinas 1991: 90; italics in original). Invisibility seems to turn the world into a world of spectacle, in which the observer is disengaged and free from bounds or restraint (able to steal food from a stall, or enslave a continent). This radical freedom, this lack of participation, this spectatorhood is enacted by Descartes in his philosophy and by the ringbearers in invisibility: is it any surprise that Sauron becomes only seeing, an Eye, and is, indeed, only visible when he is consciously looking at the characters? It is also enacted by each of us in our common or garden assumptions about inner life.

This separation, which is unavoidable and characteristic of modernity, can – indeed does – as Levinas argues, become an isolating egoism. It is only 'I'/'Eye' that matters. Invisible in our towers of interiority, cut away from but looking out over the world, we forget 'the transcendence of the other', we banish 'with impunity all hospitality (that is, all language)' (Levinas 1991: 173). We think we become separate from our 'rootedness' in each other. This separation is 'not only dialectally correlative with transcendence' (that is, does not only happen inevitably) but is also 'accomplished as a positive event', chosen and enacted: as it were, we aggravate and exaggerate with another separation the separation that is inevitable. Levinas writes that

> Gyges' ring symbolizes separation. Gyges plays a double game, a presence to others and an absence, speaking to 'others' and evading speech; Gyges is the very condition of man, the possibility of injustice and radical egoism, the possibility of accepting the rules of the game, but cheating.
> (Levinas 1991: 173)

It is this invisibility that is the source of injustice: this is the illusion of separation that those who bear or are marked by the Ring exemplify.

It looks as if the contrast, then, in the novel is between separation and participation, that these make up the two poles of the novel. However, this is too simple precisely because it forgets that the separation is an illusion with which we deceive ourselves. Invisibility would not mean anything if it did not already presuppose visibility and so participation. The Ring is precisely this *illusion* of separation and a symbol to which this illusion of separation leads. Even evil is in community: the Orcs have a society, with rank, stories and moral choice ('She'd forgotten him, maybe, but we didn't touch him' [*TT*, IV, x, 437] says Shagrat: even wrong moral choices are moral choices). The Nazgûl are a fellowship of nine and work together; the Ring is to 'bind' the other rings together. Even Sauron, only an eye, is in the most minimal way in 'community', in that he can wrestle with Gandalf and Aragorn, and shape Saruman and Denethor to his will. A society built on the illusion of separation (a Hobbesian society, in fact) is one that bears a profound internal contradiction, as we are – really – inextricable from our enrootedness in each other. A key example of this inextricability occurs at the pool of Henneth Annûn. Frodo and Faramir see the strange shape of a 'small dark thing', an 'it' (*TT*, IV, vi, 363), not a bird or squirrel, fishing all alone: it's Gollum, of course, both exiled and self-exiled from society. Yet here he is already interpellated into a community, one of which he knows nothing, but which knows him, and which may bring death onto him as a judgement for a law he has unknowingly broken.

Frodo immediately serves to bring him into the community, first by stressing how he was lured there not by the evil of the Ring but by hunger, a need all in this community share, and then by going down to him and literally bringing him in.

The novel, then, is not about those outside society and those inside, but rather about contrasting views of society: about whether it should tend – as modernity leads us to believe – to the illusion of separateness in which we deny our 'enrootedness' in each other or whether it should tend towards a shared world that negotiates and respects otherness. But the novel is clear that theses two forces are in tension. There could be no one definite final position for each of us and life is a play between these centripetal and centrifugal forces. It is precisely this tension between the move for the illusion of separation, affirming self-will and so self, and the move towards the communal, which abnegates the self for the other, that is, I suggest, why Tolkien believed it to be 'fundamentally' a Catholic work. As Shippey correctly asks 'what did he mean by "fundamentally"?' (Shippey 2000: 175). The answer is that the Catholic church, in common with most other religious organizations, is principally and fundamentally about the construction and development of community, about coming together as 'the people of God'. But Catholicism and other religious and political doctrines, are also aware, as *The Lord of the Rings* is, that this 'coming together', which is a realization of our 'enrootedness', is always a process marred by our own selves and altered by the experience of the illusion of separation in modernity (not that modernity is opposed to this development of community, but that it offers specific and complex challenges that need to be taken into account). *The Lord of the Rings* charts this but does not offer any solutions, and is thus a modernist work. This incompleteness is illustrated by the recurrence of terms in Catholic rhetoric of journeying ('pilgrimage', 'pilgrim church') which stress the process of becoming, not the 'end result'. And, as I have suggested, this tension occurs throughout *The Lord of the Rings*: on every page, in fact.

The narrative form of the novel is a clear example of this. The narrative of books one and two (*The Fellowship of the Ring*) is unified: nearly all the events happen to the groups of characters together, and are told as a 'group narrative'. However, as the separation of the Fellowship, engendered by the Ring, takes place, so the narrative breaks into separate and isolated shards. From here to nearly the end of the novel, the narrative is full of strands of story and plot coming together (e.g., finding Merry and Pippin, meeting Gollum) and coming apart (Gandalf taking Pippin to Minas Tirith, Aragorn taking the paths of the Dead, even the separation and reunification of Frodo and Sam). However, once the Ring has been destroyed, the novel regains its unified narrative focus, for Aragorn's coronation, wedding and triumph. Then – reflecting the constant play of the forces of separation and participation – the narrative breaks apart again in the final chapters, and the characters go their different ways.

But this tension between participation and the illusion of separation is also clear in a range of other ways. For Levinas, the use of language is both a crucial symptom and illustration of our 'enrootedness' in others. And the use of language, as well as specific languages, are central to *The Lord of the Rings*. Indeed, the very paradox of an 'invented language' illustrates this (a paradox because an invented private language, while recognizable as a language, is uncommutative and so separate: yet language itself is about communication with others). Much in *The Lord of the Rings* depends on speech, and on how languages are put to use. Sauron, of course, never speaks, self-exiled from language. Orc-speech is brutal and circumscribed, while, in contrast, the Elves have a range of languages, all beautiful. When Frodo claims the Ring, he moves from proper speech to something else: silence and declamation ('clearer and more powerful than Sam had ever heard him use . . . it rose about the throb and turmoil of Mount Doom' [*RK*, VI, iii, 265]). This declaration contrasts, of course, with communication and reasoned debate speech at the Council of Elrond, which serves as a model of communal action. Gollum – but not Sméagol – is named, indeed, for his inability to speak and lives separately, a filthy 'gangrel' creature (*TT*, IV, vi, 363) unable to exist save a victim or aggressor. When Frodo and Sam talk to Gollum, and make him swear an oath, they draw him back, through language, into a participatory community.

Indeed, the special sort of language use that is an oath is crucial to this tension between separation and participation, and illustrates the continual 'in process' nature of the novel. Oaths are central to the novel: it is why the Rohirrim ride to Minas Tirith; it motivates the oath breakers at Dunharrow. An oath is a declaration, to the point of a law, of community: it appears to bind. However, the point of an oath lies not so much in its making, but in the decision to fulfil it when called ('Fealty kept he/Oaths he had taken, all fulfilled them' [*RK*, V, iii, 79]). Participation is not once declared and then set for good. It is a constant and daily, even momentary, decision and this is clear in what makes an oath an oath: its fulfilment or the failure to fulfil it.

Another form of language use that is central to the constitution or denial of a participatory community is 'the story'. Much has been made of the stories and narratives in poems that are scattered throughout the novel, mainly suggesting that this hinterland creates the depth of the novel and of Tolkien's world. However, stories themselves have a profounder significance and purpose, here and elsewhere. They are what binds and creates a community. As Alasdair MacIntyre argues,

> I can only answer the question 'What am I to do?' if I can answer the prior question 'Of what story or stories do I find myself a part?'. We enter human society, that is, with one or more imputed characters – roles into which we have been drafted – and we learn what they are in order to be able to understand how others respond to us and how our responses to them are partly to be constructed. It is through hearing stories about wicked step-mothers, lost children, good but misguided kings, wolves that suckle twin boys, youngest sons who receive no inheritance but must make their own way in the world and eldest sons who waste their inheritance on riotous living and go into exile to live with the swine, that children learn or mislearn what a child is and what a parent is, what the cast of characters may be in the drama into which they have been born and the ways of the world are. Deprive children of stories and you leave them unscripted, anxious stutterers in their actions as in their words. Hence, there is no way to give us an understanding of any society, including our own, except through the stock of stories which constitute its initial dramatic resources.
> (MacIntyre 1985: 216)

Stories shape ourselves and our communities, and the stories within *The Lord of the Rings* are no exception. They are not just 'narrative background' but part of the vital creation of community. The stories told to and by the characters – either directly relevant ones, such as told at the Council of Elrond, or seemingly irrelevant ones such as the song of Nimrodel (*FR*, II, vi, 445) (though it reappears [*RK*, V, iv, 106] as a foreshadowing of Aragorn and Arwen) – all serve to tie the characters into the shared participatory community: indeed, to help them inhabit it authentically. Thus, when Pippin asks to know the 'names of all the stars, and of living things, and the whole history of Middle-earth and Over-heaven and of the Sundering Seas' (*TT*, III, xi, 249–50) he is asking for more than information, he is asking to participate and be bound into the now much larger community in which he finds himself. This is a point recognized by Gandalf before meeting Denethor when he realizes that Pippin, through unavoidable ignorance and carelessness, does not know the context into which he walks ('See, Master Pippin, there is not time to instruct you now in the history of Gondor' [*RK*, V, i, 14] he says, and adds, unfairly, that Pippin might have learnt about it in the Shire: but the Shire knows nothing of Gondor). Pippin, however, is able to bind himself to the community through taking an oath and, more importantly, telling a story to Denethor. In contrast, those communities characterized by the illusion of separation have no stories, or have deficient ones. The name of the 'Mouth of Sauron' 'is remembered in no tale; for he himself had forgotten it' (*RK*, V, x, 191); Sauron's own story is not revealed in the novel. The Orcs do not share stories ('"You fool" snarled Shagrat. "You've been talking very clever, but there's a lot you don't know"' [*TT*, IV, x, 436]) or offer conflicting versions (rhetorically, '"Is Saruman the master or the Great Eye?"' [*TT*, IV, iii, 49]). The victory of Sauron, of course, will kill stories: Sam wonders if 'any song will ever mention it: How Samwise fell in the High Pass . . . No, no song. Of course not, for the Ring will be found and there'll be no more songs' (*TT*, IV, x, 430). And again Gollum is an odd exception: his story is told about him, not by him: he is bound into it with no choice, as it were.

The point about stories is that they represent a communal sharing and so a respect for the other telling the story: stories reflect both shape and are shaped by the community, and embody the deeper 'enrootedness' in community. However, in contrast, dominated by the illusion of separation, the world becomes a spectacle, and others are turned from people into objects. Indeed, this is summed up in the similarity between Denethor and Sauron: 'He uses others as his weapons. So do all great lords if they are wise' (*RK*, V, iv, 99). But objects are either to be dominated and used, or feared. Thus,

Sauron's desire for power is a direct correlative of the illusion of separation inherent in the power of invisibility of the Ring. In contrast, Gollum's long hiding below the mountains is a form of avoiding other objects. Sauron becomes – aims to become – a god, Gollum a beast.

As I have suggested, these two inclinations – towards separation, towards community – are constantly in play and cannot wholly and completely be identified with any one side. In fact, they often occur at the same time as each other and 'cross-fertilize': on the one hand, for example, Gimli and Legolas play a bloodthirsty game counting the Orcs they kill at Helm's Deep where the Orcs are reduced to merely numbers (contrast this with Gandalf: 'I pity even his slaves' [*RK*, V, iv, 92]). On the other, the Uruk-Hai display fine martial virtues and a communal feeling that heroic warriors might admire. Later, too, Legolas is amazed that the 'designs of Mordor' are overthrown by 'wraiths of fear and darkness' (*RK*, V, ix, 175) and Eomer's temporary madness 'Death, death, death!' (*RK*, V, vi, 133) and war chant are more appropriate to the servants of Sauron.

Yet it is at the climax of the novel at the Crack of Doom that the inextricable interweaving of these two trends come together very clearly. Frodo's quest to destroy the Ring – if that's what the task really was for Frodo – fails: ' "I have come . . . But I do not choose to do what I came to do. I will not do this deed. The Ring is mine!" ' (*RK*, VI, iii, 265). It is this taking ownership of the Ring that makes the Dark Tower tremble and leaves Sauron's creatures 'steerless, bereft of will' (*RK*, VI, iii, 266). This moment marks the failure of the quest, not because the Ring is not destroyed, but because a quest is not simply an attempt to achieve something: a quest is both an internal and external journey ending in an achievement that will set the world aright. Not only does this not happen, but it is frequently made clear that even destroying the Ring will not accomplish this: the world of Middle-earth will always be damaged, reduced and broken. Many critics ignore this failure, or brush it off. Jane Chance, for example, is conflicted when she suggests both that 'Frodo betrays himself enough to keep the Ring' (Chance 2001: 180) and that he 'succumbs to the power of the Ring, as he always knew he would' (121). (If he always knew he would, in what sense is this a betrayal? See also Shippey 2003: 144 ff and Shippey 2000: 140ff for accounts of this.) Gandalf, though, at Cormallen declares that the 'Ring-Bearer has fulfilled his Quest' (*RK*, VI, iv, 270) (note the capitals) and never uses the term again after he has (presumably) heard the story. This failure is also foreshadowed by Elrond, already weary at the 'many fruitless victories' (*FR*, II, ii, 318) he has seen: unlike Frodo (*RK*, VI, i, 220), he describes the mission of the Fellowship not as a quest but a 'task' (*FR*, II, ii, 355). Frodo foreshadows his encompassing of the Ring and all it means when he says at Elrond's council '"I will *take* the Ring"' (*FR*, II, ii, 355) (not a more neutral 'carry the Ring' or the more passive and suffering term that others use of him, 'bear the Ring', for example). And this phrase of Frodo's – along with his endless circumlocutions about his plans (two from many, '"It's my doom, I think, to go to that Shadow yonder"' [*TT*, IV, i, 256], '"I purpose to enter Mordor"' [*TT*, IV, iii, 301], not 'I have to destroy the Ring') – raise the spectre that despite the urgings of the wise, Frodo never meant to destroy the Ring. His offer to give it to Galadriel, for example, is – as she acutely recognizes – motivated by revenge and an enactment of his power as Ringbearer over her, leaving her 'shrunken' (*FR*, II, vii, 480). But as I have suggested, what the Ring really symbolizes – the movement towards the illusion of separation – cannot be destroyed, as it is inherent in modernity. At this moment in the novel, the tension between the drive to separation and the drive to community are juxtaposed, but not resolved. Gollum is only able to 'separate', to take the Ring, because of the community the Hobbits have given him (through oaths, through saving his life, through tentative friendship, though he has betrayed this) and it is this that restores Frodo to the community as 'the dear master of the sweet days in the Shire' (*RK*, VI, iii, 267). Likewise, Frodo is only able to declare himself the Lord of the Rings because of the community offered him by Sam. These two forces play each other out and come, as it were, to a draw: the Ring is destroyed, but so, really is Frodo. The events are profoundly unheroic, in that no heroic conclusion is reached, but instead we are left with a continuing struggle.

Finally, one might ask why the panoply of Middle-earth itself is invoked to explore to this most serious issue? Or, to put this another way, what does the setting bring to the understanding of this question? The answer is not simply biographical: that, for example, Tolkien preferred inventing languages, whereas another (Catholic) writer, say Graham Greene, preferred travel. Rather, it is the case that the world Tolkien created allows the ideas to be investigated in a specific, intense and important way, and it is this that, in no small part, makes the book so significant. It is precisely the 'fantasy' setting that is able to side step both the contemporary and the unavoidable anachronism of the historical novel and is then able to contrast so clearly this evil inherent in modernity with other forms of social organization. Moreover, the fantasy element means that the book can have no call on nostalgia: there is, in fact, no idealized past to which it refers. Instead, we have, so clearly drawn, this contrast between the illusion of separation (invisibility), from which (*pace* Levinas) injustice springs and participation, which more authentically embodies our fundamental ontology. What constitutes Tolkien's modernism (with Eliot, for example) and his achievement is that he is able to draw up this opposition: his limits are perhaps that in his art he is not able to move beyond it, nor to see that there are things in modernity, and in the illusion of separation, that are beneficial, nor that the ideal of being 'enrooted' can also lead to injustice.

CHAPTER 6

HOME

Simon Malpas

> Content the boatsman turns to the river's calm
>   From distant isles, his harvest all gathered in;
>   I too would gladly now turn homeward,
>   Only, what harvest but pain have I reaped?
> (Hölderlin 1998: 13)

There is a key difference between the protagonists' journeys in *The Hobbit* and *The Lord of the Rings*, which echoes the distinction between boatsman and narrator in Hölderlin's poem. Bilbo Baggins' adventure to the Lonely Mountain is, as the book's subtitle announces, a progress 'there and back again' that ends with the reassertion of domesticity and the harvest of wealth and experience. In contrast, Frodo's quest is not to acquire a treasure but to destroy one, his pains remain as bodily marks (the scar from the Morgul knife, Shelob's sting and, of course, the missing ring finger) that can never fully be healed, and the Shire that he has saved which can never again be home. His final speech in the novel captures this perfectly: 'I tried to save the Shire, and it has been saved, but not for me' (*RK*, VI, ix, 376). This difference is not simply accidental; rather, it is a product of the transformation of Middle-earth itself which takes place in *The Lord of the Rings* and goes to the heart of the presentations of identity and community in the two texts. Both protagonists' journeys are regularly punctuated by invocations or memories of home, but the ways in which this trope is produced and developed by the narrative of the later book generates a world in which homelessness appears to be the norm. If Bilbo's adventures lead him through a series of comparatively stable homelands, from Elrond's 'last homely house', via Beorn's homestead, the Elvenking's palace in Mirkwood, Laketown, the eventually re-inhabited Dale and Lonely

Mountain, and back again to the Shire, the journey undertaken by Frodo and his companions is through a world whose peoples exist in states of continual conflict, threat, migration and vagrancy, which even the destruction of the Ring only problematically renders secure. By opening out the frame of reference, both geographically and historically, *The Lord of the Rings* transforms the meaning of being in Middle-earth fundamentally. Home, in this text, remains the wished-for destination of a resolved narrative, but comes to be achieved only on the basis of a profound redefinition of its foundational status.

An exploration of this difference between the two texts opens up the possibility of reading *The Lord of the Rings* as a novel that raises important questions about the politics of environment, technology and community in our own contemporary world. On the basis of such a reading, I want to discuss Tolkien's text in terms of some of the arguments about art, technology and homelessness deployed in Martin Heidegger's discussions of poetry, especially in his readings of Friedrich Hölderlin (Heidegger 1996). Besides the historical congruity between these two (the composition of the novel between 1936 and 1949 is roughly parallel to the vast majority of Heidegger's exegeses) each, I think, struggles to make sense of the possibility of community during a period where industrialization, war and rapid transformations of technology threaten to destabilize traditional notions of being in common. In each case the central question is what, in the midst of a violently changing world, might constitute 'being at home'?

MODERNITY, TECHNOLOGY AND THE WORLD

For both Tolkien and Heidegger, home is a category under threat by technological innovation, and it is the acknowledgement of this that produces the attitudes towards the modern that their writings display. More generally, the resonance of the term 'home' has not remained stable in the face of the restless processes of modernization and conflict that the last few centuries have witnessed. What has come to be called modernity is, in its most simple formulation, the period that takes transformation and development as its central categories of self-identification.[1] Change is not something that happens accidentally or occasionally to a preceding stability, but is, rather, the essence of experience. Marshall Berman describes this experience of modernity in the following terms:

> To be modern is to find ourselves in an environment that promises us adventure, power, joy, growth, transformation of ourselves and the world – and at the same time threatens to destroy everything we have, everything we know, everything we are ... It pours us into a maelstrom of perpetual disintegration and renewal, of struggle and contradiction, of ambiguity and anguish. To be modern is to be part of a universe in which, as Marx said, 'all that is solid melts into air.'
> (1983: 15)

This characterization of modern experience as rapid and radical transformation in which the certainties and stabilities of the pre-modern agrarian community (itself perhaps no more than an idealized back-formation of the modern) are annihilated in a 'maelstrom of perpetual disintegration and renewal' is, according to Berman, driven by technological development and capitalist economics. Together, capitalism and technology provide the core of modern existence, the driving forces of destruction and creation that break open each moment of perceived stability and relentlessly propel us into a future that promises to be radically different from all that has gone before. These processes are, simultaneously, hopeful (in that the future advances in technology will allow us to ameliorate the suffering of contemporary life) and threatening (community, tradition and even our environment is constantly under threat of annihilation), but, most of all perhaps, they appear inevitable and irreversible. In threatening 'everything we have, everything we know, everything we are', they challenge all that might come to count as home with the radically migratory homelessness of modern development.

This thoroughly modern conflict between technologically-driven expansion and the threatened home of an organic community lies at the heart of *The Lord of the Rings*. Treebeard's description of Saruman as having 'a mind of metal and wheels' and not caring for 'growing things, except as far as they serve him for the moment' (*TT*, III, iii, 84) encapsulates a key struggle in the novel, and has frequently been taken as the basis of Tolkien's presentation of the conflict between the oppressive power of technological development driven forward by Sauron and his minions and the rural freedoms and communities of the 'natural' world of the so-called 'free peoples'. Tolkien himself states in a letter that 'all this stuff is concerned with Fall, Mortality and the Machine'.[2] On the basis of this, one might even go so far as to claim that the purpose of Frodo's quest is to rid the world of the technological imperative produced by the very existence of the Ring. Patrick Curry argues that 'the Ring epitomizes the strongest economic and political power in Middle-earth, which already threatens to dominate all others in one vast autocratic realm' (Curry 2000: 284), and in this manner comes to stand in as a literary instantiation of modernity's power to dissolve which must be opposed at all costs. While this approach to the novel can be persuasive, I want to argue that its depictions of the conflict between technology and nature can only problematically be reduced to a simple opposition that can straightforwardly be overcome by the destruction of the Ring and the defeat of the forces of darkness. Instead, the novel produces a much more ambivalent conclusion, one which gives rise to a complex set of compromises between agrarian stability and technological development. Victory for the allies does not put an end to history, safeguard their communities from change or restore a 'natural balance' that Sauron and Saruman's imposition of industrialization had come to disrupt. In fact, Tolkien is quite explicit throughout the novel that nothing can simply resist or ignore change: the Elves must continue their exodus, the Entwives remain lost, the lives of Men continue to dwindle as the strain of Numenor diffuses, and even the seclusion of the Shire will be lost as its borders are opened to the world.[3] To read the text as a straightforward depiction of victory over development is to produce an account of Tolkien's novel as an escape from the modern world into a Middle-earth in which the transformative power of the modern can be still be overcome. It is, in other words, to trivialize both the pressures faced by today's society and the text's presentation of these conflicts. Rather, I want to follow a suggestion that Slavoj Žižek makes about the representation of religion in *The Lord of the Rings*, that only 'a devout Christian could have imagined such a magnificent pagan universe, thereby confirming that paganism is the ultimate Christian dream' (2002: 580), to argue that only in the face of the modern technological reproduction does a fantasy world such as Middle-earth make sense, and that, as such, the world of Tolkien's novel is meaningful precisely because it evokes and interrogates the rural fantasies from which technological development draws its power without simply evacuating the latter of all meaning and force. If the conclusion of the novel does reassert the possibility of home, I want to argue that it does so only problematically and not as the result of a return 'back again' to a secure and unchanging community.[4]

It is with regard to this impossibility of simply returning home that Tolkien's work might be read in the light of Heidegger's philosophical engagement with modernity. A sense of the modern as a process of unceasing technological transformation and development provides the impetus for his thought from the 1930s onwards. Like Tolkien, Heidegger refuses to present modernity and community as a straightforward binary opposition, and sees no hope in the sentimental idea of a return to a pre-technological past. Although there are moments in his writings that might strike the reader as overly romantic or (given his well-known political affiliations in the 1930s) ultra-rightwing invocations of an agrarian homeland under threat from industrial development, his analyses of philosophy's history of thinking of the world in terms of its capacity to be 'put to work' for human ends remains irreducible to a simple nostalgia for a lost mode of life. Rather, he argues that technology forms an inescapable horizon for contemporary existence that is at once 'the supreme danger' (Heidegger 1977a: 26) and, yet, also the site at which the 'coming to presence of truth' (1977a: 33) might remain possible.

According to Heidegger, the most fundamental challenge facing modern philosophy is produced not just by the new technologies themselves but by the processes of what he calls technological thinking. This essence of technology is, he argues, 'by no means anything technological' (1977a: 4), and so long as 'we represent technology as an instrument, we remain held fast in the will to master it' (1977a: 32), which will to mastery lies at the heart of the technological thought that treats the world entirely in terms of means and ends. According to Heidegger, existence and experience have become essentially technological, our day-to-day being in the world has come to be 'Enframed' (*Gestellen*) by technology, and this 'coming to presence of Enframing is the danger' (1977b: 41). What he means by 'Enframing' is 'the way in which the real reveals itself as standing-reserve' (1977a: 23); or, in other words, the attitude towards the world that encounters the object as material to be used as a means for an end, as an energy or resource whose value lies in its potential to be employed. The world of objects comes to be experienced as a stockpile of resources that humankind exploits in order to shape its destiny. For Heidegger, this approach to the world generates a contradiction, which, he argues, gives rise to the 'supreme danger':

> As soon as what is unconcealed [the world] no longer concerns man even as object, but does so, rather, exclusively as standing-reserve, and man in the midst of objectlessness is nothing but the orderer of the standing-reserve, then he comes to the very brink of a precipitous fall; that is, he comes to the point where he himself will have to be taken as standing-reserve. Meanwhile man, precisely as the one so threatened, exalts himself to the posture of lord of the earth. In this way the impression comes to prevail that everything man encounters exists only insofar as it is his own construct.
> (1977a: 26–7)

In thinking the world as a standing-reserve for technological innovation and presenting itself as the master of this process, humankind precipitates itself towards a situation in which it too is in danger of becoming nothing more than the material to be put to work in the name of progress. It is this 'precipitous fall', analogous to the 'Fall, Mortality and the Machine' with which Tolkien claims his novel is concerned, that the technological imperative of the Ring presents to the peoples of Middle-earth.

The 'supreme danger' that Heidegger identifies cannot be avoided by simply thinking otherwise or even by any straightforward strategy of environmental or technological regulation. Only by working through the history of how technology has come to dominate existence as an essential component of human understanding and experience can its dangers and potentials be grasped. He argues that technology, as the Enframing horizon of modern existence, produces the means by which the world is revealed to us, and that through a questioning of what is at stake in this process thought can begin to clear the path for an alternative way of experiencing our being-in-the-world. In fact it is precisely through such questioning of and reflection on its essence that a space might be opened up within the technological imperative that provides such an alternative. In order to demonstrate this, Heidegger argues that technology is 'no mere means . . . It is the realm of revealing, i.e., of truth' (1977a: 12).[5] In other words, although it is the 'supreme danger' it is also the realm in which this danger might be averted. Tracing the meaning of *technē* back to its Greek origins where it signifies 'the bringing-forth of the true into the beautiful' (1977a: 34), he relates it to the *poiēsis* of art, and claims that the problematic relation between the two provides the conditions of possibility for the fundamental questioning of modern technology:

> Because the essence of technology is nothing technological, essential reflection upon technology and decisive confrontation with it must happen in a realm that is, on the one hand, akin to the essence of technology and, on the other, fundamentally different from it. Such a realm is art. But certainly only if reflection on art, for its part, does not shut its eyes to the constellation of truth after which we are *questioning*.
> (1977a: 35)

Because of the relation between their fundamental differences and shared structures of revealing, technology and art are capable, Heidegger argues, of being thought in terms of a 'constellation' that opens the possibility of grasping the relation between *poiēsis*, *technē* and being-in-the-world, and thereby of exposing the 'supreme danger' that modern technology threatens, but only on the basis of a thinking that draws out the concealed interrelationships of their productive, revealing powers.

The question to which I should now like to move is how might this constellation be thought with regard to *The Lord of the Rings*?

LOCATING MIDDLE EARTH: TOLKIEN'S *POIĒSIS*

This riddling tale, to what does it belong?
Is't history? vision? or an idle song?
Or rather say at once, within what space
Of time this wild disastrous change took place?
(Coleridge 1993: 485–6)

The 'Friend' in Coleridge's poem asks the 'Author' how his tale is to be received, and in this gesture evokes a problem with which both

Tolkien and Heidegger wrestle: how, in the constellation of *poiēsis* and *technē*, is literary meaning to be grasped critically? Within 'what space/Of time' can the events of Tolkien's text be read? Is *The Lord of the Rings* 'history? vision? or an idle song?' How, in other words, might we approach the central conflict between Sauron and the free peoples of Middle-earth in a manner that allows us to think through the apparently analogous tensions which we face today?

The question concerning technology in *The Lord of the Rings* has been raised before by critics of Tolkien, and his work has come to play an important part in contemporary critical discussions of eco-theory and green studies. Explaining the inclusion of a chapter on *The Lord of the Rings* in *The Green Studies Reader*, Laurence Coupe, the book's editor, claims that Tolkien's text 'foresees the need to foster human pluralism and natural diversity', because 'far from encouraging . . . readers to evade environmental disaster by indulging in dreams of another world, "Middle-earth" is presented as a site of struggle, much like our own' (2000: 255). This is an important observation, and worth pursuing as it challenges the trite but still too common-place description of fantasy as little more than a form of escapism from day-to-day reality, and opens the text up to a range of critical analyses that allow us to explore its capacity to generate political questions about the environmental pressures with which contemporary culture is faced. What Coupe's assertion leaves unexamined, however, is the question of what might be meant by the phrase 'much like our own'. What correspondences are traceable between Tolkien's fantasy land and the contemporary world? In what terms might the posited similarity be formulated? How, in other words, might the novel help us to gain a sense of the 'need to foster human pluralism and natural diversity'?

One does not need to be familiar with Tolkien's well-known assertion in his foreword to the novel that *The Lord of the Rings* is not to be read as allegorical to see the absurdity of simply and mechanically equating the tree-felling in Fangorn with the destruction of the Brazilian rainforests or the eruption of Mount Doom with any recent volcanic disturbance. A one-to-one mapping of textual episode and real-world event is, with regard to all criticism, trivial. Equally, however, it is misguided to read the book as having a universal 'message' – another term that Tolkien refuses in his foreword – about ecology, technology or home that can straightforwardly be spelled out as the 'intention' of its author and thus the 'moral' of the text. Instead, what is required is a reading based on what Tolkien calls in that same foreword 'history, true or feigned, with its varied applicability' (xvii). This notion of 'applicability' puts the onus on each particular reading of the novel to reveal its own correspondences, or, to use the terms of the previous section of this essay, to open its eyes to the 'constellations of truth' that the text discloses. Reading does not happen in isolation, and the applications that become available are not simply the product of arbitrary decisions on the part of readers. Rather, they emerge from within the horizon of a culture, which, in Heidegger's terms, is always already 'Enframed'.

If this notion of 'Enframing' is taken seriously, the production of meaning by a text requires investigation as a complex formation or constellation that remains irreducible to allegory or moral as such meanings would remain within the framing of the technological imperative. Instead, Heidegger characterizes art as 'the becoming and happening of truth', which

> . . . is never gathered from objects that are present and ordinary. Rather, the opening up of the Open, and the clearing of what is, happens only as openness is projected, sketched out, that makes its advent thrownness.
> (Heidegger 1975: 71)

What he means by this is that what is revealed in the work of art is not simply a new definition or meaning that remains within the frame of reference of a culture's beliefs or modes of thought (that are themselves given by the Enframing of the technological imperative), but the opening of those beliefs and modes to other possibilities or projections. This does not posit art as producing a wholly new world-view, but rather finds in the work a recognition that existing world-views are already Enframed in a way that limits, closes and subsumes thought and object within the 'already known'. In Heidegger's philosophy, art is not valued for its power to represent a familiar world, its task is to open or disclose what in the Enframing of that world has been concealed. For the purpose of this chapter, what I want to argue is disclosed in *The Lord of the Rings* is the problematization of home in the Enframing of modern technology. In other words, what is important is not that Tolkien presents Middle-earth as an alternative world, like or unlike 'our own', in which the question of home is resolved as a symbol or allegory that we can take away as the text's 'message', but rather that the novel might be read as a 'feigned' history of the processes of modern Enframing that discloses the possibility that these processes are not final or absolute, and that sites remain from which a resistance to technological rationality might be launched.

HOME AND HOMELESSNESS

If simply stepping outside of the Enframing nature of technology is impossible, a reading of that process of Enframing might be opened by returning to the notion with which this chapter began: the figure of 'home'. As I have attempted to show, modern transformation and change continually threatens to foreclose the possibility of home. Heidegger describes, in a lecture he delivered in Meßkirch (his home town) in 1961, how modern humanity is precipitating itself towards homelessness by way of its fascination with technological innovation and development:

> Spellbound and pulled onward by all this, humanity is, as it were, in a process of emigration. It is emigrating from what is homely [*Heimisch*] to what is unhomely [*Unheimisch*]. There is a danger that what was once called home [*Heimat*] will dissolve and disappear. The power of the unhomely seems to have so overpowered humanity that it can no longer pit itself against it. How can we defend ourselves against the pressure of the unhomely? Only by this: that we continually enable the bestowing and healing and preserving strength of what is homely to flow, to create proper channels in which they can flow and so exert their influence.[6]

From the foregoing discussion of technology, it should be clear that Heidegger's remedy for modern homelessness, enabling the 'bestowing and healing and preserving strength of what is homely to flow', is not as simple as it at might appear. What is at stake here is a re-description of home: no longer a secure ground, a point of origin that resists the transformative flux of the modern to hold open the possibility of an undisturbed identity, home must be preserved in the midst of the dissolving forces of the unhomely so as to retain its sustaining and nourishing powers in the face of the loss of its foundational status.

In the summer of 1942 Heidegger gave a series of lectures on Hölderlin's poem 'The Ister' that explore the questions of homeliness and the foreign in detail. In a key passage from these lectures, he makes the following claim:

> [C]*oming to be* at home in one's own in itself entails that human beings are initially, and for a long time, and sometimes forever, not at home. And this in turn entails that human beings fail to recognize, that they deny, and perhaps even have to deny and flee what belongs to the home. Coming to be at home is thus a passage through the foreign. And if the becoming homely of a particular humankind sustains the historicality of its history, then the law of the encounter [*Auseinandersetzung*] between the foreign and one's own is the fundamental truth of history, a truth from which the essence of history must unveil itself.
> (1996: 49)

Home is presented here not as an origin to which modern humanity can straightforwardly return, but rather as something to be realized through the essential historical encounter between the foreign and 'one's own'. It is, in other words, not a ground located outside of historical transformation as a foundational point from which history can be experienced as an objective process. Rather, it is only through a recognition of humanity's thrownness into the flux of history (which Berman characterizes as its modern predicament) that it becomes possible to secure a sense of home in the midst of the fundamental homelessness of our 'passage through the foreign'.

The depiction of home in *The Lord of the Rings*, I want to argue, follows a similar trajectory, disclosing in its narrative development precisely the transformation of the term's meaning that Heidegger's reading of Hölderlin produces, and yet retaining in its resolution the sense of a redemptive 'becoming homely in being unhomely' (Heidegger 1996: 21). What the novel presents is a double movement: the gradual dissolution of the pre-modern, agrarian image of the Shire as an isolated and secure idyll, which occurs when the Hobbits are swept up in the radically modernizing narrative of the War of the Ring, is accompanied by the production of a modern sense of the power of 'home' as an, albeit entirely altered, site of resistance to the unhomeliness of being. In other words, *The Lord of the Rings* stages the transformation of the notion of home that Heidegger's argument posits, discloses for us what might be at stake in a modern experience of home, and thereby exposes the relation of home to the meaning of being in the contemporary world.[7]

When the Ring is first identified, Frodo's decision to undertake his quest is justified precisely through reference to the Shire as home: 'I feel that as long as the Shire lies behind, safe and comfortable, I shall find wandering more bearable: I shall know that somewhere there is a firm foothold, even if my feet cannot stand there again' (*FR*, I, ii, 82). The Shire is presented here as a foundational space, an ontological ground for the Hobbit's identity, that lies securely outside of the conflict he is about to enter: Frodo's journey will be bearable given that there is always the possibility of imaginative recourse to the stability of a home that retains its life-sustaining virtues irrespective of the threats and difficulties of the protagonist's unhomeliness.

As the narrative develops, however, this vision of home as a stable space whose redemptive efficacy is inexhaustible is dissipated by encounters with the foreign that radically transform its resonance. Before he has even left the Shire, Frodo is told by the Elf Gildor that 'it is not your own Shire . . . Others dwelt here before Hobbits were; and others will dwell here again when Hobbits are no more' (*FR*, I, ii, 111). Gildor's comment opens the Shire to history, making contingent that which had appeared foundational and transforming its status by bringing it into the historical space of conflict and migration that shapes Middle-earth. And this is no isolated incident: Tolkien is relentless in repeating, varying and amplifying this sense of the Shire, and by extension of Hobbits themselves, as caught up in history and struggle. To cite just a few of the most intense examples of this, Frodo's realization that the mithril coat he wears is more valuable than the entire land he had thought of as home introduces a vertiginous sense of economic insignificance; Sam's vision of the destruction of Hobbiton in the mirror of Galadriel foresees the integration of the Shire into the war; the entry of Hobbits into Treebeard's list of the races undoes their isolation from the world and history; the dawning recognition that Gollum, perhaps the most resolutely homeless character in the text, is himself a Hobbit shatters not just the sense of the Shire's history but the entire ontological consistency of Frodo's self-identity; and even the planting of the

Mallorn-tree during the rebuilding of the Shire symbolically opens its borders to the wider world. Cumulatively, these events, and the numerous others that occur both for the Hobbits and the other races presented in the novel, dissolve the ontological consistency of the separate communities that are introduced, transforming identities through their interactions and conflicts so as to redefine what is at stake in social being.

As a counter to this movement of dissolution, the narrative's depiction of the interconnectedness of the different groups and races of 'free peoples' stages a sense of being in common that is irreducible to a foundational 'racial' identity and emerges on the basis of an ethical imperative of self-sacrifice in the interests of communal survival. This counter-movement continues the dissolution of the stable, extra-historical sense of home, but redefines it in relation to unhomeliness in a manner that holds out the possibility of redemption. What is required to win the War of the Ring is the forging or renewing of alliances, the willingness of peoples to go to war far from home, to integrate themselves into foreign cultures and to redefine their identities in order to defend the existence of their homes and communities from the threat of Sauron's power. Continually at risk in these alliances is the sense of the stability of home: to cite only the most obvious examples in the novel, Sam's loyalty to Frodo prevents his return to the Shire when he sees the vision of its destruction; the Ents' attack on Isenguard marks the end of their isolation and their re-entry into history; Rohan's decision to answer Gondor's summons risks leaving their homes unprotected if they are defeated; and the Wild Men imperil the security of their homeland in Druadan Forest by allowing the riders to pass through it on their journey to Minas Tirith. In each case, the characters are forced to put their homes at stake in order to make victory possible, and (with the exception, perhaps, of the resolutely pre-modern Wild Men whose borders are reasserted by the victorious King) lose the isolated security they had previously enjoyed. What Tolkien's novel insists upon again and again, then, is the encounter with the foreign, and the risk of self-sacrifice it entails, that transforms each character's sense of homeliness as a foundation of identity into the notion of home as something to be produced anew through the engagement, struggle and conflict that modern existence requires.

The result of this double movement is that, by the end of *The Lord of the Rings*, the term 'home' has come to signify something

fundamentally different. To return to Heidegger's reading of Hölderlin once more, one might argue that a 'counterplay is played out
between being unhomely in the sense of being driven about amid
beings without any way out' (1996: 118), which is what is threatened
by the Ring's technological force, and 'being unhomely as becoming
homely from out of a belonging to being' (1996: 118), which is the
goal of the free peoples' struggle:

> Being is not some thing that is actual, but that which determines
> what is actual in its potential for being, and determines especially
> the potential for human beings to be; that potentiality for being
> in which the being of humans is fulfilled: being unhomely in
> becoming homely. Such is our belonging to being itself.
> (1996: 120)

The Lord of the Rings stages this counterplay between the homely
and unhomely that produces the potential of a redefined home in
which being might come to be freed from the threat of annihilation,
presents the risk of absolute loss that technology imposes on the
'standing reserve', and explores the necessity of self-sacrifice that
resistance to the technological must be prepared to make. The final
line of the novel, Sam's 'Well, I'm back' (*RK*, VI, ix, 378), testifies to
this risk, to the concomitant change in the meaning of home, and
discloses that the home to which he has come back is anything but
familiar or trite.

PART III

GENDER, SEXUALITY AND CLASS

CHAPTER 7

WOMEN

Jennifer Neville

It is a commonplace that the women in Tolkien's fiction are disappointing. Some damn his fiction for its old-fashioned, misogynist depiction of women (e.g. Partridge 1983, Wood 2000, Frederick et al. 2001). Some defend it as a product of its time (e.g. Crowe 1992: 272). Some defend it as a product of a more distant time, the medieval period that occupied Tolkien not only in his professional life but also in the creation of his fiction (e.g. Ringel 2000: 165–6, Donovan 2003: 106, Crowe 1992: 272). That is, it can be argued that Tolkien's fiction merely reflects the position of women in the types of society that he depicted. In the case of the Riders of Rohan, for example, Tolkien presents a society very like the Anglo-Saxon world most famously depicted in *Beowulf*, a society in which women have traditionally been seen as decorative but ultimately powerless, as pawns in a man's world (Hill 1990: 239).

In this chapter I shall argue that this latter view, at least, is not valid. Tolkien underestimated the women depicted in texts like *Beowulf*, and so women in Rohan are, I believe, more marginal than those in *Beowulf*. Yet Tolkien should not be singled out for blame for the limits he placed on women. The best nineteenth- and early twentieth-century scholarship left no room for active women in Old English poetry, and late twentieth- and early twenty-first-century feminist criticism of Old English literature continues to create an image of the powerless, voiceless, and hopeless woman who can do no more than weep. In what follows, I shall briefly outline the links between Tolkien's Rohirrim and the Anglo-Saxons and then argue in detail against a traditional reading of Wealhtheow, the queen of the Danes in *Beowulf*. I shall then examine how Tolkien drew upon this reading and reread it for his own purposes in *The Lord of the Rings*.

Tolkien denied a direct equivalence between the Riders of Rohan and the Anglo-Saxons (Shippey 2003: 123). Nevertheless, the Riders of Rohan are clearly modelled on the heroic society described in Old English poetry – a literature that Tolkien knew better than most – and the modern reader can derive a fairly good sense of the spirit of that literature from reading *The Lord of the Rings*. For example, while the importance placed on horses in Rohan does not figure in our records of Anglo-Saxon England, the close, personal relationship between King Théoden and his men and the emphasis on earning glory in battle before death coincide neatly with, for example, the relationship between Byrhtnoth and his men and the priority placed on glory rather than survival in *The Battle of Maldon* (e.g. *TT*, III, vi, 151 and vi, 156; *RK*, V, v, 120 and vii, 137). The relationship persists in more particular details, too. For example, the Rohirrim speak and name themselves using the Mercian dialect of Old English (Shippey 2003: 123). They privilege a relationship between maternal uncle and nephew – the 'sister's son' – that is marked in Old English texts: Beowulf, like Éomer, is the son of his king's sister.[1] They appear to share a common poetic tradition, for Aragorn quotes part of *The Wanderer* to illustrate Rohirrim poetry (*TT*, III, vi, 130–1). Finally, Beowulf's *meduseld* 'mead-hall'[2] corresponds in name, importance, ceremonial function, and many other particulars to Théoden's 'Meduseld' (e.g. *TT*, III, vi, 129).

The parallels are many and have been noted many times before, as have the parallels between the role of women in these male-oriented societies. For example, Éomer states that women will mourn for Théoden (*RK*, V, vi, 132), as Hildeburh does for her male relatives in *Beowulf*, and Éowyn passes the cup around the mead-hall, as Wealhtheow does in *Beowulf* (*Beowulf* 620–41, 1162b–96). Éowyn's role is explicitly *meant* to be the classic feminine role of helpless, passive waiting for the active male to achieve glory in battle (*RK*, V, ii, 55ff; *RK*, V, viii, 162ff). Yet Éowyn famously rejects this role, despite her king's orders, for a limited but significant time. It could thus be argued that, far from being old-fashioned in his portrayal of women, Tolkien has been radically modern in depicting a woman who dares to do what would have been unthinkable in the culture upon which he based the Rohirrim.

The problem with this argument is that female helplessness and passivity are easier to find in scholarship about Old English poetry than in Old English poetry itself. The traditional passive female of Old English poetry is not as old as we might think. She is Victorian, not Anglo-Saxon. Where did she come from? Although assuredly not the only source, a major contributor to our understanding of women in *Beowulf* is Frederick Klaeber. Like all readers of the poem, Klaeber read *Beowulf* according to his own view of the world; unlike most, however, his reading of the poem, first published in 1922, has shaped almost every other reader's view ever since and continues to define the shape and meaning of *Beowulf* today (Bloomfield 1999: 130).[3] His version of the poem remains the standard scholarly edition for literary scholars and translators and thus remains the indirect source for archaeologists, historians, and art historians, as well as the general public (Bloomfield 1999: 129–30). Tolkien knew Klaeber's work well and valued it (Drout 2002: 103).

Klaeber was a great scholar, and it is helpful to have one's view of a difficult text shaped by such a reader, but some of his views reflect his own time more than the time depicted in *Beowulf*. For example, Josephine Bloomfield analyses five words associated with Wealhtheow; these possess a range of meanings including 'generous', 'fitting', 'glorious', 'persuasive', and 'friendly invitation', but all are glossed by Klaeber as 'kind' or 'kindness'. As a result of this insistence on kindness, 'we see Wealhtheow's motivations regulated and her role transformed from peace weaver and power-broker to tender maternal care-giver' (Bloomfield 1994: 184). Bloomfield contends that Klaeber's 'likely world view' included women who were 'biologically, intellectually and emotionally capable of serving only as wives and mothers'; as a result, he was, 'perhaps unconsciously, forced to "rewrite" her, to create her as a person guided by sentiment rather than by the realities of tribal politics, in order to make her intelligible to him as a "good" mother' (Bloomfield 1994: 202). The Wealhtheow that most modern readers experience consequently reflects not only Anglo-Saxon ideas of women but also nineteenth-century German ideas of women.

Tolkien read *Beowulf* along with Klaeber's interpretation of it, and the Anglo-Saxon culture that he reflects in his Rohirrim can be seen to reflect Klaeber's nineteenth-century German values as well as his own twentieth-century English values: like all readers, Tolkien saw patterns of behaviour consistent with his own values. I, of course, do the same. Assuming that neither Klaeber, Tolkien, nor I do violence to the text, however, it is useful to see how different a picture we can derive from the same text. In the next few paragraphs, I shall describe the roles traditionally assigned to women in Old

English poetry. Our assumptions about these roles may tell us more about our own expectations than they do about women in Anglo-Saxon England, for Old English poetry allows women more power than critics even now allow – or, more accurately, ascribes powerlessness more equally to both men and women. This is not to say that women are equal to men, but that no clear-cut dichotomy of power and powerlessness exists between them. Although it requires a fairly long excursion into Old English poetry, it is necessary to explore this point thoroughly, for this state of affairs did not suit Tolkien's purposes.

The traditional roles attributed to women in Old English poetry include those of hostess, peace-weaver, and ritual mourner.[4] We see all of these in *Beowulf*: Wealhtheow acts as a hostess, welcoming Beowulf and his men into the hall; Freawaru, her daughter, will soon be a peace-weaver, since she has been promised in marriage to a neighbouring kingdom as part of a peace-treaty; and Hildeburh mourns the death of her brother and son in battle. It seems natural, from a modern perspective, to assume that these roles are marginal – that a hostess is a servant, that a peace-weaver is an objectified token of male exchange (Rubin 1975, Fee 1996), and that a mourner is a passive victim (Chance 1990: 251). It is possible to explode each of those assumptions, but given the limited space available I shall focus my attention on the role of the hostess, which is the most prominent of the three in *The Lord of the Rings*.

A twenty-first-century audience expects little of a hostess, and the view of Wealhtheow is consonant with such expectations. Many readers see her as merely decorative and excluded from the central conflicts engaged upon by men. This conception of the hostess is, however, incomplete. To understand it fully, it is necessary to recall the early part of the poem. Hrothgar was in a desperate situation, for the monster Grendel had been eating his men for 12 years, thus damaging his reputation as a defender of his people.[5] His people's reputation as strong warriors had also been undercut; Beowulf's comment that Grendel found no need to fear the *Sige-Scyldinga* 'victorious Danes' (*Beowulf* 597b) hints at their loss of reputation. Beowulf's promise to do all that Hrothgar and the Danes could not thus puts Hrothgar in an uncomfortable position. Beowulf apparently realizes the problem, for he enters Hrothgar's realm respectfully and positions himself as a suppliant: he begs for permission to fight Grendel (*Beowulf* 426b–32). In private, Hrothgar is eager to welcome him (*Beowulf* 372–90a), but in public he carefully revises Beowulf's reasons for travelling to Heorot: Beowulf says that he has heard about the plight of the Danes and come to rescue them (*Beowulf* 409b–14), but Hrothgar says that Beowulf has come to repay the favour that he did for his father and to honour the oaths that he swore (*Beowulf* 457–72).

Hrothgar thus attempts to subordinate Beowulf to his authority by reminding him of past obligation. The poem never indicates that Beowulf accepts this obligation; indeed, Beowulf's next comments suggest that his intention is rather to demonstrate his own people's superiority (*Beowulf* 601b–3a). This statement is the immediate context and perhaps the provocation for Wealhtheow's first appearance in her role as welcoming hostess: she approaches Beowulf, offers him a cup of mead, and publicly announces that her wish has come true (*Beowulf* 612b–28a). Modern readers can underestimate the significance of this act, for such drinking is not merely entertainment or slaking of thirst, especially since, in this case, at least, drink has already been served (*Beowulf* 494b–6a): drinking from the king's cup is tantamount to making a pledge to him (Robinson 1985: 75–9, Damico 1984: 54–6). In addition, Wealhtheow's statement of faith in the hero not only flatters but demands that he live up to her expectations. That is, like Hrothgar, Wealhtheow attempts to inscribe Beowulf into a place in the Danish court and make him subordinate to its order. Her actions are part of the Danish hierarchy's efforts to assert their control over a powerful newcomer. Hrothgar's attempt may or may not have been successful, but Beowulf accepts Wealhtheow's imposition of obligation and formally pledges to fulfil her wishes or die in the attempt (*Beowulf* 632–8; cf. Damico 1984: 67–8, 93–4). Wealhtheow is thus not simply a waitress or greeter; she is a political force in her own right, influencing loyalty, status, and honour within the Danish court in a way that complements her husband's own power.

Later, however, Wealhtheow becomes a political force that opposes her husband's power. During the celebrations following the death of Grendel, Wealhtheow publicly addresses first her husband, who seems to have planned to adopt Beowulf as his heir instead of their sons; second, indirectly, Hrothulf, her nephew; and third Beowulf himself (*Beowulf* 1168–1231). Her complex speech can be simplified as follows. To Hrothgar she says: 'Celebrate and be generous to the Geats, but do not forget what you yourself have received.

I have heard that you want to adopt Beowulf. Enjoy what you have and then leave the kingdom to your children when you die.' To Hrothulf she says: 'You will do what is right and support my sons, because of what we have done for you in the past.' To Beowulf she brings another cup, rich gifts, and another speech: 'Here is another gift. If you treat my sons well, I will reward you well. Such good deeds have made you famous. There is no weakness in this place. Men follow my commands.' The unstated threat between Wealhtheow's compliment to Beowulf and her statement of men's obedience to her ('You may be famous but I have the power to oppose you') is particularly notable. We see here Wealhtheow not only commanding her own men in the hall but also determining the succession. Importantly, she does this not only in accordance with her husband's agenda, but also in opposition to it.

Many readers have felt uneasy about this speech, and it is interesting to observe that Wealhtheow has been accused of undermining Hrothgar's authority, destroying opportunities for peace, or, more commonly, being pathetic or ineffective (Damico 1984: 127, Irving 1989: 74, Horner 2001: 77–81, Renoir 1975: 229–30; cf. also Overing 1990: 90–101). That is, modern readers of the poem reject Wealhtheow's political power as either destructive or absent, even though the poem does not comment negatively upon Wealhtheow's actions and Beowulf is not, after all, adopted. Even if one rejects Wealhtheow as a failure, however, she is not alone.[6] Hrothgar notably fails to defend his people from Grendel, and Beowulf predicts that Hrothgar's attempts to secure peace with the Heathobards will also fail. Beowulf fails to prevent his kings' deaths (first Hygelac, then Heardred); he also fails to end the ongoing hostilities with the Swedes. It is a commonplace to see women in *Beowulf* as helpless to change the world around them, but the poem demonstrates that even the greatest kings and heroes share in this helplessness.

Wealhtheow is also not alone in her physical passivity. Although it is easy to stress the binary oppositions between male and female characters in the poem, doing so risks missing that there are other ways of grouping characters in the poem. For example, in comparison with Beowulf, Wealhtheow and the other women in the poem are passive. However, in comparison with Beowulf, every character in the poem is passive. No one else wrestles with Grendel; no one else dives into the mere; no one else volunteers to fight the dragon alone. By Beowulf's standard, for example, Hrothgar is indistinguishable from Wealhtheow. Like her, he is physically passive, incapable of the physical action that is seen to be the particular domain of men as opposed to women.[7] Yet he is acclaimed as a good king (*Beowulf* 863b), and he achieves great deeds through his words: the building of the hall, the creation of political alliances, the distribution of treasure, and the ordering of a peaceful society. Wealhtheow, too, achieves deeds through her words.

That is, even in Old English heroic literature, focused as it is on men and martial deeds, there are many ways to be 'active'. Excellent sword-work and great physical strength, although highly prized, are not the only routes to success, and in some cases physical heroism would be neither appropriate nor successful. This point is central to *The Lord of the Rings*, both in the main story of the destruction of the Ring and in the episodes that echo it.

Tolkien inherited a view of women in *Beowulf* rather different from the one for which I have argued here, a view which, as mentioned earlier, derived from a traditional, patriarchal understanding of the roles of women. In what follows, I shall argue that Tolkien was complicit with this view of women in Old English society. In doing so, however, I do not reject his fictional work as misogynist. Rather, I see the contrasts between Tolkien's character, Éowyn, and the Old English queen upon which she was at least in part modelled as evidence of a view that ultimately seeks the transcendence – or even the deconstruction – of such dichotomies as strength/weakness, activity/passivity, and effectiveness/helplessness.

The power exercized by Wealhtheow in Heorot does not appear in Edoras. Tolkien does not include even Klaeber's Wealhtheow, a sentimental queen focused exclusively on her children. This absence is significant. Jane Chance has argued that the end of *The Lord of the Rings* shows the 'return of female difference to balance harmoniously with the masculine' (Chance 2001: 61), and it is striking that male characters without female counterparts often fare poorly in Tolkien's work (Gollum, Saruman, Sauron, Boromir, Denethor, the Ents, arguably Frodo himself), while heterosexual couples embody the positive forces of Middle-earth (Tom Bombadil and Goldberry, Galadriel and Celeborn, Aragorn and Arwen, and Sam and Rosie). Théoden lacks this balancing, feminine principle, but, for the purposes of this chapter, it is more significant that he lacks someone to play the roles that Wealhtheow fulfils in *Beowulf*. He lacks someone who might goad, counsel, or compete with him for political control. If he had, the story of Wormtongue would necessarily have been quite different, for the danger posed by Wormtongue is dependent upon the alienation of the king. Yet even Klaeber's Wealhtheow was not quite marginal or powerless enough for his story, and so Tolkien does not include one.

Éowyn is *not* Wealhtheow; she is, if any character in *Beowulf*, Freawaru: the daughter (or sister's daughter) who could have been married to the visiting hero but is not in the cases of both Beowulf and Aragorn, although for different reasons.[8] Freawaru may be a cup-bearer like her mother (2020–1) but she is not yet a queen and does not possess a political voice. Similarly, in contrast with Wealhtheow's speeches to Beowulf, Éowyn's interactions with Aragorn are personal, not political (*TT*, III, vi, 150); in fact, she bitterly resents her political duty (*RK*, V, ii, 55). If Éowyn had done what she was told, she, like Freawaru, would have been truly marginal as her society faced threats of destruction from both internal and external threats – from Wormtongue's insidious advice and military attacks by Saruman and Sauron. A Wealhtheow in Théoden's court might have been able to oppose the imprisonment of Éomer, for example, but Éowyn can only watch and wait in sorrow and fear.

Although Éowyn soon demonstrates that she can do much more, she shares the essential identity of the traditional marginal female. It is important to Tolkien's overall theme that she should do so. One of the very modern ideas in his plot is that it is not the impossibly heroic and superhuman Beowulf-figure, Aragorn, who has the power to defeat Sauron; rather it is Frodo, a Hobbit, someone even smaller and weaker than the average man, who must do the deed. The deed and the character are heroic, but not in a traditional way, and ultimately Frodo triumphs not because of great strength or skill but because he receives aid from his equally sub-heroic helpers, Sam and Gollum (cf. Chance 2001: 72). Such a figure is unthinkable in and absent from *Beowulf*, but in *The Lord of the Rings* he becomes the centre. Great heroes merely serve as a diversion.

This well-known central plot is prefigured in the battle of Éowyn against the Lord of the Nazgûl. While great male heroes like Gandalf, Théoden, and Éomer struggle with increasing despair against the besieging army from Mordor, the key opponent, the Witch-king of Angmar, is immune to the greatest heroic action. He can be killed only by someone who is *not* a man, *not* a hero. Again, like Frodo,

Éowyn does not achieve this crucial deed because of great strength or skill: she possesses these, but ultimately she triumphs because of the help she receives from another sub-heroic Hobbit. Her great heroic deed does not make Éowyn the same as or equal to male heroes, even if 'her deeds have set her among the *queens* of great renown' (*RK*, V, viii, 163, emphasis added): her marginal position is essential – and not simply because of the demands of the prophecy within the plot of the text. If she were not marginalized and assumed to be powerless, her action would not resonate with the central story of Frodo and Sam.

It is intriguing to note that there is another Old English poem in which this reversal of central male action and marginal female action occurs: in *Judith*, the widow of the apocryphal Bible story who seduces a general is transformed by the Old English poet into a chaste maiden endowed not only with the traditional attributes of women in Old English poetry (brightness, jewellery, etc.) but also the traditional attributes of heroes: she displays courage and skill as she beheads the enemy of her people. More significant than the parallels between the descriptions of Judith and Éowyn, however, is the function of her action in the plot. Judith's beheading of Holofernes, the Assyrian general, takes place in secret, outside the arena of war, but it determines the outcome of the war between the Hebrews and Assyrians. In the same way, Éowyn's 'beheading' of the Witch-king takes place outside the knowledge of male leaders of armies and outside the 'main' battle, but it is arguably the most significant factor in the victory on the Pelannor Fields.

Comparing Wealhtheow to Éowyn reveals that Tolkien's portrayal of women in Rohan, at least, is not simply derived from early, unenlightened, male-oriented literature. Tolkien saw in Old English poetry what he wanted to see, and he probably believed – like Klaeber and many feminist critics of Old English poetry – that passivity and helplessness characterizes women in *Beowulf*. He did not destroy, invert, or even question the patriarchal system that relegated women to a marginal position in his fiction, as modern feminist readers may have wished. Thus Éowyn renounces the role of warrior of which she had demonstrated herself capable and embraces traditional female roles (wife, healer), to the disappointment of many readers.

At the same time, however, Tolkien's fiction proclaims that male power is not the only way to achieve victory, and, in fact, is incapable of winning the most important contests (cf. Drout 1996). In making this point the expectation of female helplessness proved as useful to Tolkien as it was essential to the fictional heroine of the Old English *Judith*. For Judith, these expectations provide a disguise that allows her to penetrate the enemy camp and carry out an assassination (Koppinen 2003). For Tolkien, these expectations provided a framework within which to pursue a different idea of strength and effectiveness. Tolkien assigned value to the marginal and apparently ineffectual, and he gave her (and him) a role at the centre of his story. In her own, small way – indeed, *because* her way was small – even a woman could win a war, while an even smaller person could save the world. As we live our modern lives, we may choose to feel patronized by Tolkien's women, but, unless we can claim to be a Beowulf or Aragorn (a route not open to normal men, either), Tolkien's message may not be so disempowering as has been thought.

CHAPTER 8

MASCULINITY

Holly A. Crocker

In one sense, to speak of masculinity in J. R. R. Tolkien's *The Lord of the Rings* is ridiculous, since Men are just one group among an assortment of *kind*, including Hobbits, Elves and Dwarves.[1] This loose taxonomy of the inhabitants of Westernesse, moreover, is but one part of a larger topography of difference that might more fairly be said to distinguish groups along lines that are overtly racialized.[2] The Easterlings *look* different than those peoples of the South, just as the Dúnedain of the North, as protectors of Hobbits, friends of Elves, and descendents of Isildur, gain at least part of their rugged mystique from keeping the forward borderlands. Mordor's description as a place that yields nothing but evil shapes is the ultimate expression of this spatialized differentiation between the many kinds who populate Middle-earth. Yet this localization also relentlessly insists that the range of somatic and dermal variations that distinguish amongst and between regional sorts is social in its origin, moral at its base.[3]

The Orcs and their lands are twisted into degenerate forms by wastrel habits; bred from Elves, they are similar to the Black Númenóreans, whose captain is so distorted by his evil practice that he retains affiliation with his former kind only through the overt declaration that he is not a Ringwraith but 'a living man' (*RK*, V, x, 191); like those decayed worthies who were corrupted by their desire for power, such ruined figures highlight the trilogy's recurring concern with the failures responsible for the distinctions that divide groups. But it is not just social or moral deficiency that produces differences in kind; promise, whether bound up with habit or principle, also fashions various peoples. So it is with Hobbits, whose general temperament and outlook is wholly calibrated to a pristine life in the unspoiled Shire, which is characterized by 'peace . . . quiet and good tilled earth' (*FR*, Prologue 1). Similarly, those other groups that unite to fight the forces of Sauron's oppression – Elves, Dwarves, even Ents – clearly reflect the parts of the West that they make their own. Kind, then, is a social and moral category that takes corporeal and geographical root through the time-worn practices of peoples.[4]

And it is in the narrative's concern with the racializing effects of time that masculinity assumes presence in Tolkien's epic. As the most unsure participants in the Fellowship – ever on the cusp between failure and promise – men have a vexed relation to time that threatens to dislodge their claims to place and even to kind.[5] After Isildur fails to destroy the Ring of Power, men have an increasingly tenuous hold on their realm, until Gondor itself becomes a kingdom governed under stewardship awaiting the return of its rightful heir. Those descendants of Isildur too, whose very classification as 'Rangers' bespeaks their mobile anonymity, are unable to inhabit a stable model of identity. Faramir's classification of the three types of Men – the High, the Middle, and the Wild – faults the 'evils and follies . . . idleness and ease' of the Númenóreans for Gondor's demise and their increasing likeness to the middling Rohirrim (*TT*, IV, v, 354, 355). Despite the foibles of particular groups of Men, however, masculinity emerges as an idealized identity that is able to exceed other nodes of difference by the trilogy's end.

Even in his moment of failure Boromir identifies traits that define masculinity as the foundation of promise in this quest: 'True-hearted', incorruptible, 'staunch' and not desiring 'the power of wizard-lords' but only 'strength to defend ourselves' (*FR*, II, x, 523). Fortitude, faithfulness and lack of aggression: in his ploy to take the Ring Boromir identifies the promise of masculinity that actual Men have never been able to realize since Isildur's failure. Gimli's evaluation of Men's craftsmanship provides a larger commentary on their fallibility: 'And doubtless the good stone-work is the older and was wrought in the first building . . . it is ever so with the things that Men begin: there is a frost in Spring, or a blight in Summer, and they fail of their promise' (*RK*, V, ix, 170). But Legolas's reply offers canny insight into masculinity's dependence on kind for its ultimate claim to authority: 'Yet seldom do [Men] fail of their seed . . . And that will lie in the dust and rot to spring up again in times and places unlooked-for. The deeds of Men will outlast us, Gimli' (*RK*, V, ix, 170).

As I shall suggest in what follows, Tolkien's *The Lord of the Rings* produces kind as a differentiating system in order to invest masculinity with the timeless privileges of invisibility. As an authority that is ever mobile, masculinity may remain a loose set of traits that retains a claim to purity for its lack of embodiment.[6] This invisibility is neither transparent nor opaque, though as a 'peculiar, visible invisibility', this kind of masculinity stakes claims to both (Bhabha 1995: 57–65). Functioning as an unlocated mode of becoming that subsumes all those who subscribe to its principles, this masculinity compels others to see it as invisible. Even in its abstraction, however, this rendering is not simply a redeployment of a heroic or classical model of *virtus*.[7] Although the promise of masculinity is progressively associated with Aragorn, the trilogy is nevertheless careful to retain distinctions of kind, as Pippin's objection to Gandalf's introduction of him in Minas Tirith as a 'valiant Man' attests (*RK*, V, i, 8). In arguing that masculinity is a mode that subsumes all kinds, then, I also suggest that the narrative's preservation of differences among groups is ultimately a way to install hierarchy in an empire where one *kind* of Men – the High Men of the West – gives order to those others who inhabit their realm.[8]

PROMISE OF KIND

In its exposition of kinship between Hobbits and Men, Tolkien's Prologue outlines the nebulous affiliations that give masculinity privilege as a unifying mode across groups. The suggestion that Hobbits 'liked and disliked much the same things as Men did' (*FR*, Prologue 2), creates an affinity of temperament designed to make many features of Hobbits recognizable as components of a universal masculinity empowered by its unbounded scope.[9] Indeed, as the quest to unmake the Ring of Power coalesces, it becomes clear that Hobbits realize one aspect of the kind of masculinity that Aragorn promises to fulfill. The nature of Hobbits, the narrative demonstrates, is richer than the initial qualities of congeniality and simplicity would suggest. Indeed, as even the different Hobbit-members of the Fellowship discover, these 'little people' possess courage, resolve and strength. While these traits might be said to define a heroic character more generally, each articulation of these traits is particular to Hobbits in a different respect.

Hobbits' indifference to suffering, which becomes manifest in the exchange between Merry and Pippin during their Orc-captivity, is doubtless related to Hobbits' affability:

No listener would have guessed from their words that they had suffered cruelly, and been in dire peril, going without hope and towards torment and death; or that even now, as they knew well, they had little chance of ever finding friend or safety again.
(*TT*, III, iii, 65)

Yet this propensity, as Gandalf puts it, 'to sit on the edge of ruin and discuss the pleasures of the table, or the small doings of their fathers . . .' (*TT*, III, viii, 196), is significant because it affirms Hobbits' sense of their own unimportance in the larger affairs of the world.

This conscientious smallness is elsewhere characterized as 'plain Hobbit-sense', and is a crucial part of Sam's ability to aid Frodo in carrying the Ring towards its ultimate destruction (*RK*, VI, i, 206). When Sam frets about his worthiness to assume the burden of the Ring after Frodo's fall to Shelob's sting, he struggles against an awareness of his own insignificance in this grand scheme: 'What? Me, alone, go to the Crack of Doom and all?' (*TT*, VI, x, 425). His reluctance is not lack of courage, but a feeling that 'it's not for me to go taking the Ring, putting myself forward' (*TT*, VI, x, 425). As the Ring begins to exert its evil pull on Sam, working on his psyche with images of his glorification, it is only his awareness of his smallness that gives Sam the strength to resist its ruses of power. Even as he dreams of 'Samwise the Strong, Hero of the Age' he checks himself with continual reminders of his own insignificance: 'he knew in the core of his heart that he was not large enough to bear such a burden' (*RK*, VI, i, 206). Sam trudges onward, vowing to carry Frodo up Mount Doom if necessary, mainly because he sees himself as a small player in this massive errand.

Hobbits are not the kind to make bold interventions, as Merry's almost accidental stabbing of the Nazgûl makes clear. While Merry rides with the Rohirrim more out of a desire for company than honour, it is only when the Ringwraith fells Éowyn, herself an unlikely and surprising warrior, that the 'slow-kindled' courage of Hobbits is stirred (*RK*, V, vi, 129). Moments earlier Merry fights to maintain the commitment he has sworn to Théoden with his nearly incantational repetition ' "King's man! King's man!" ' (*RK*, V, vi,

128). Only when Éowyn answers the black chieftain's menacing threat by revealing she is 'no living man' but a woman (*RK*, V, vi, 129), does Merry find the strength that derives from the seeming insignificance that comes with being a Hobbit.

Merry's success against the Nazgûl is true to his kind, insofar as it confirms Théoden's earlier characterization of Hobbits as a group who 'do little, and avoid the sight of men, being able to vanish in a twinking' (*TT*, III, viii, 195–6). When the Ringwraith dispatches Éowyn he considers his victory complete, failing to understand the dangerous potential that the small Hobbit standing before him represents. Because the black captain overlooks Merry, the Hobbit is able to wound him, though even this deed does not bring Merry or Hobbits more generally into visibility amongst the gathering of warriors who fight the forces of Mordor. After this tide-changing feat, Merry must pick his way back to safety, only receiving relief for his injured arm when Pippin finds him. With his doleful comment, 'one poor hobbit coming in from the battle is easily overlooked' (*RK*, V, viii, 152), Pippin acknowledges that the most salient characteristic of Hobbits is their insignificance.

But Merry affirms this aspect of Hobbit-identity as the strength of their kind, replying 'It's not always a misfortune being overlooked' (*RK*, V, viii, 152). Certainly it is the cultivated smallness of Hobbits that makes Frodo a good candidate for the office of Ring-bearer, for even with his surveying gaze Sauron is unsure where to look to find such seemingly unimportant creatures. Early on, when Frodo tries to press Galdalf to take the Ring, the Wizard's refusal suggests that it is the Hobbit's very lack of manifest strength that makes him appropriate to carry the Ring: 'With that power I should have power too great and terrible. And over me the Ring would gain a power still greater and more deadly' (*FR*, I, ii, 81). Frodo's resolve to carry the Ring into the heart of Mordor, moreover, is furthered by his sense of personal insignificance in this larger struggle. Unlike Bilbo, who shows his weakness by his proprietary regard for the Ring, Frodo disavows its possession for as long as he can manage. As he explains to Faramir, 'It does not belong to me. It does not belong to any mortal, great or small' (*TT*, IV, v, 335).

The Ring's corrupting power manifests itself in Frodo's growing consideration of the errand as his alone. When he accuses Sam of trying to take charge of his burden, Frodo presages his final failure to destroy the Ring. Like Bilbo, who defines his identity through his adventures with the Ring, Frodo increasingly identifies his destiny with that of the Ring, suggesting an investment in large worldly affairs that is otherwise un-Hobbit-like. When Sam realizes that they will probably not survive their quest, his resolve is nevertheless bolstered by the fantasy that has hitherto sustained him: the return to the Shire. Sam's wish 'to see Bywater again, and Rosie Cotton and her brothers, and the Gaffer and Marigold and all' (*RK*, VI, iii, 249) illustrates the local investment that he maintains in the matter of the Ring's destruction. His first motivation is his unwavering love for Frodo, but even that devotion is borne of his desire to preserve the form of life they enjoyed in the Shire. Sam nearly panics when Galadriel earlier shows him a vision of the Shire's degradation, and when he returns home from his adventures, his main task is restoring the Shire to its former state.

His lack of obsessive interest in a single locale differentiates Frodo from other Hobbits, but it also suggests the dividing line between Hobbits and the kind of Men that Aragorn will consolidate through his accession.[10] The conscientious insignificance that characterizes Hobbits is recognizable in Boromir's articulation of masculinity, particularly in his (ironic) insistence that true-hearted Men disavow ambitious power. This disavowal, so uncharacteristic of any of the Men who have come before Aragorn, promises to produce a new kind of Men, a sort who can be ever mindful of the corruption that their desire for power may breed. Rather than being confined to a bounded region, however, Men like Aragorn are legitimated in their expansive claim to rule over others by the cultivated smallness that they share with Hobbits. The masculinity that Aragorn comes to embody, then, subsumes kind insofar as it gathers strength from those groups it rules. It preserves difference, however, in its ability to assert for itself a broader range of characteristics than any other kind can approximate alone.

THE INVISIBLE MAN

Although my discussion has focused on the affinities between Hobbits and the type of masculinity that will renovate the High Men of the West, it is equally true that the kind of manhood Aragorn promises is also inflected by Elves, Dwarves, and even a spare Wizard. Aragorn's personal affiliations with Elves are most pronounced in the trilogy; yet through his associations with all these groups, who 'shall fade or depart' with the coming 'Dominion of Men', a new model of masculinity emerges that consolidates power through its claim to invisibility. As you might expect, this kind of masculinity is not a category that is easily inhabited. Aragorn cannot readily assume the mantle of masculinity that his lineage provides because its claim to power is staked on the personal visibility of rule. Even if, as Frodo acknowledges to Faramir, Aragorn is the only mortal who may claim the Ring, were he to do so he would set himself up as the definitive marker of the failures of Men, finally destroying that which he sought to preserve through his assumption of power. When Aragorn disavows his right to the Ring, he proves what Legolas calls his noble will: 'In that hour I looked on Aragorn and thought how great and terrible a Lord he might have become in the strength of his will . . . But nobler is his spirit than the understanding of Sauron' (*RK*, V, ix, 175).

Instead, Aragorn must refashion the masculinity of his kind to avoid their missteps, ultimately by taking a role in the Fellowship that reveals his leadership through gestures of service that avoid visibility. His support of Frodo's errand, therefore, is simply the culmination of a long formation of masculinity that is fostered by contact with groups who protect Middle-earth using quiet modes of dominion. Elves can make themselves as invisible as Hobbits, as Galadriel's forces demonstrate in the forest of Lòrien. But this sense of invisibility is not simply literal; Gandalf's homey congeniality prevents those with whom he commonly comes into contact from perceiving the might of his power. It is only after he survives his ordeal in Moria that he is revealed in all his Wizardly strength as Galdalf the White; moreover, that emergence is marked as serving the pointed purpose of defeating the forces of Sauron before his final exit from Middle-earth. While the Hobbits and Men of Bree may view Rangers like Strider with suspicion, those who know their purpose appreciate their invisibility as an important component of their protection. Before he becomes king, then, the new masculinity that Aragorn realizes is enabled by its ability to pass unseen amongst those it protects.

Yet it is also clear that this masculinity's time has come, that the power of this mode of governance must be revealed, and must be identified with one figure in order to exert shaping effect over all regions of the new empire. The trilogy thus figures Aragorn's final emergence as the sort of 'true man' that Boromir characterizes, but it does so in an incremental fashion that seeks to negotiate the problems that potentially attend the increasing visibility of this position. As Frodo's avowal of the Ring at the edge of Mount Doom demonstrates, concern for one's own place in larger affairs threatens to erode the Hobbit-like smallness that will divide this mode of masculinity from others of the past. This masculinity must emerge into the visible field as *invisible*, which means that its revelation must appear to present that which was already perceived though never acknowledged by anyone. For, as the lessons that Dwarves, Elves, and even a spare Wizard indicate, the power that emerges from this covert mode of identity must finally be affirmed, but in a manner that preserves its cultivated unimportance in a larger scheme.

Of all the wisdom that Aragorn draws from Elves, one of their most important contributions to the masculinity he incorporates is negative. Although Tolkien's narrative presents the withdrawal of Elves from Middle-earth as a product of time and kind – their age has passed – their departure also signals their indifference to the challenges of Men, a loss of faith that cannot be recovered by the promise that Aragorn represents. That said, Elrond's mentorship and Galadriel's support, not to mention the marriage of Aragorn and Arwen, suggest that the relationship between Men and Elves is renewed through this brand of masculinity. But the estrangement of Men and Elves bespeaks an isolationist attitude that this new masculinity must avoid. While local investment may be appropriate for Hobbits, there is a danger if such provincialism becomes an alienating preoccupation. Taken together with the Elves' disaffection, the ruins of Moria serve as a foreboding warning concerning the dangers that attend the absolute invisibility of isolation.

As Gandalf points out, the decayed path to Moria is a remnant of happier times, when different races – Dwarves and Elves especially – were more friendly. The door to Moria was not designed only to admit Dwarves; rather, it connected these great inhabitants of the inner caverns to others on the outside, as even the Elvish password 'friend' indicates. The fear and suspicion that surrounds this place when the Fellowship approaches, however, suggests that Moria's demise was a product of estrangement, a breaking of bonds that isolated these Dwarves from their neighboring kinds. What was a magnificent kingdom becomes a ruinous tomb without external contact. Aragorn's hestitation is particularly telling, especially since it is he who later forges an alliance with those oath-breakers who are stranded upon the Paths of the Dead. He does not wish to enter Moria again, and the memory of his first visit is 'very evil' (*FR*, II, iv, 390). The dread of Moria, it seems, is the destruction of Fellowship that isolation threatens.

Although the party of the Ring survives this passage due to Gandalf's seeming self-sacrifice, the company is fractured by the experience, as Sam's later lament suggests: 'Things went all wrong when [Gandalf] went down in Moria' (*RK*, VI, iii, 249). Indeed, with the loss of Gandalf, Boromir is killed after he tries to take the Ring, Frodo and Sam leave the group to set out on their own, and Pippin and Merry become captives of the fast-moving Uruk-kai. The party that Aragorn leads is reduced to three, and forms a most unlikely alliance, as he acknowledges: 'We will make such a chase as shall be accounted a marvel among the Three Kindreds: Elves, Dwarves and Men. Forth the Three Hunters!' (*TT*, III, i, 14). The breaking of the Fellowship initially signals a personal failure to Aragorn, whose momentary indecision shows that he is not yet ready to assume his role as leader: 'This is a bitter end. Now the Company is all in ruin. It is I that have failed. Vain was Gandalf's trust in me. What shall I do now?' (*TT*, III, i, 6).

But when Aragorn takes a moment to reflect upon the best course for all involved in the group: 'Let me think . . . And now may I make a right choice' (*TT*, III, I, 13), he realizes that he does not control the Ring's destruction: 'the fate of the Bearer is in my hands no longer' (*TT*, III, i, 13). This awareness is important, because it allows Aragorn to comprehend the true meaning of Fellowship, which must define his masculinity for his rule to gain authority beyond a single community. As he understands, others also play an important part in this larger design, and those players direct their own paths as events unfold. Unlike Sauron, who uses agents he controls to execute his sinister plans from a position of unseen power, Aragorn must allow for the autonomy of others. His ability to let Frodo go his own way actually expands Aragorn's potential, because in viewing himself as one player among many who seek to bring about Sauron's overthrow, Aragorn may chart a different course, which is also crucial in fighting the power of the lidless eye. His ability to forge a brotherhood with Gimli and Legolas ultimately allows them to save Pippin and Merry, recover an alliance with the Rohirrim, destroy the forces of Sauron, and bring reinforcements to Minis Tirith in its hour of greatest need.

These feats are not as important as Frodo's task, but in diverting Sauron's attention from his search for the Ring, they provide Frodo and Sam with the needed opportunity to carry Gollum's 'precious' to its unmaking. Just as important, perhaps, these deeds forge connections that establish Aragorn's credit in the larger community. As Éomer makes clear, Aragorn will be an effective ruler because he has built ties of affection between himself and various peoples: 'Since the day when you rose before me out of the green grass of the downs I have loved you, and that love shall not fail' (*RK*, VI, v, 298). Through a Fellowship that allows for the autonomy of difference, Aragorn incorporates a model of manhood that others revere. Even when the Hobbits attempt to explain Aragorn's ascension to the plain folk of the North, Butterbur's response reveals that it is the familiarity that different individuals feel with Aragorn that will allow him to unite widely diverse peoples: ' "Strider!" he exclaimed when he got back his breath. "Him with a crown and all and a golden cup! Well, what are we coming to?" ' (*RK*, VI, vii, 331). The elevated figure that Aragorn has become is immediately familiarized through the notion that he might have tasted and approved the beer at 'The Prancing Pony'.

MANAGING KIND

Though Butterbur's affection is markedly different than Éomer's, both suggest that it is their personal intimacy with Aragorn – which he achieves by refusing to distance himself from those whom he will rule – that gives his identity power. Aragorn's invisibility, then, is of a completely different sort than that of Sauron. The manner in which Aragorn allows for differences amongst groups, it must be added, is nothing like the ways in which this dark master manipulates his various subjects. In his effort to set up a realm that encompasses all, the dark Lord uses invisibility to further a panoptic technology of surveillance that subjects all to a singular emanating gaze. This Foucauldian exercise of power is akin to other partitioning disciplines insofar as 'it imposes on those whom it subjects a principle of compulsory visibility'; yet in his domination of Orcs, Easterlings and Southrons, Sauron does not respect the autonomy of difference amongst these groups (Foucault 1995).[11] Instead, as the quarrelling Orcs demonstrate, Sauron's authority extends to each individual subject, and every particular servant is a disposable entity readily sacrificed for his larger plans.

Snaga's defiance of Shagrat's commands suggests that each Orc is left to shift for himself because there is no cohesion amongst them. The only grouping that is respected in Mordor, it becomes clear, is produced by common oppression: the narrator discusses the huge slave fields in the south of Mordor, and the roads which bring food and fresh slaves to Sauron's realm. Because each servant of Sauron is subjected to his withering gaze, there is no way for any of these conscripted forces to resist their domination. The dark Lord thus asserts an impersonal strategy of disciplinary seeing: known only by a totemic name and a disembodied eye, his authority produces each subject as a faceless yet individual member of a larger regime of power.

Aragorn, by contrast, does not strip away the particularities of identity to consolidate his rule, but rather preserves distinctions of kind to recruit the loyalties of different groups. Aragorn's emergence as ruler depends on the perpetuation of kind, because all groups must see him as rightful king of their own accord. Each group affirms him in the way that befits their people, as Éomer's and Butterbur's differing responses suggest. Because assent is not compulsory, the consolidation of power in Aragorn makes his visibility a seemingly transparent marker of a just community united through a boundless respect for difference. Yet the broad support that Aragorn's emergence galvanizes, it must be added, depends upon the putative invisibility of his masculinity. As I have argued, the masculinity Aragorn promises is defined by dis-avowal, a refusal to assume authority over others through visible gestures.

Even the manner in which his rightful rule is discovered, through a folk adage that identifies the king as a servant of the people, suggests that Aragorn's authority is founded upon protection that defies visibility: 'For it is said in old lore: *The hands of the king are the hands of a healer.* And so the rightful king could ever be known' (*RK*, V, viii, 154). As the old wife Ioreth's chatty revelation demon-strates, this power does not announce itself through bold gestures of control. Even as the Ring's destruction clears the way to make his power known, it is his brand of masculinity, defined as service and protection, that others come to see as the (in)visible markers of Aragorn's authority:

Tall as the sea-kings of old, he stood above all that were near; ancient of days he seemed and yet in the flower of manhood; and wisdom sat upon his brow, and strength and healing were in his hands, and a light was about him.
(*RK*, VI, v, 296)

The central place in the field of sight that Aragorn finally assumes, I suggest, asserts masculinity's invisibility by defining it as the standard of identity that will consolidate all kinds in this new reign.

Masculinity, then, subsumes kind because it becomes a mode of identity that is not simply identified with Men, or with Aragorn for that matter. And it is in this respect, finally, that Aragorn's production of a universal mode of identity to mobilize affinities of kind for his singular authority is most similar to strategies of racist domination that are all too familiar from our own cultures of 'Westernesse'. Tracing the privilege of white identity in American society, Robert Bernasconi argues that 'Whites have secured their own disappearance as white . . . [they] do not thematize their identity but disappear into the norm' (Bernasconi 2000). Because kind is presented as a system of difference that is more permanent due to its embodied status and its geographic distribution, masculinity can float free as a prosthetic identity that may be assumed by all those who subscribe to its principles. Éowyn's challenge to the Nazgûl suggests as much when she dons the strength of a fierce warrior even as she retains her womanly identity.[12] By refusing to identify with a particular kind, the masculinity that Aragorn consolidates secures Men at the apex of a hierarchically ordered domain.

In a prescient critique of masculinity's authorizing strategies, Abigail Solomon-Godeau argues 'that what has been rendered peripheral and marginal in the social and cultural realm, or actively devalued, is effectively incorporated within the compass of masculinity' (1995: 68–76). Here she identifies femininity as that other which masculinity mobilizes for its own influence, falling too easily into a binarization of power that overlooks the transversal benefit that structures of race yield to men, particularly white men. If masculinity seeks to establish itself as a universal, *The Lord of the Rings* suggests, it cannot do so by fitting itself into a binary. Rather, in crossing the very divides of difference that it maintains for others, masculinity may assert its boundless universality. By positing kind as a racializing geography that exceeds the human, Tolkien's trilogy calls attention to the status of masculinity as 'the apparatus of cultural difference', as Homi K. Bhabha puts it (1995: 58). In a final sense, then, to speak of masculinity in J. R. R. Tolkien's *The Lord of the Rings* is *not* ridiculous, since this trilogy reveals that masculinity's privileged invisibility is staked on the production of difference as a strategy of rule.

CHAPTER 9

HOMOEROTICISM

Esther Saxey

Two moments made me aware of the ambiguous appeal of the Peter Jackson adaptation of *The Lord of the Rings* for a male audience. First: in a CD/DVD store in London, I notice a circle of motionless, open-mouthed men has formed around me. I look up and see Viggo Mortensen lying on top of Sean Bean on the huge screens above me. I have no idea how the men around me sexually self-identify, but every one of them is frozen, apparently waiting to see Aragorn kiss Boromir on the forehead.

Second: British comedian Will Smith, performing in a club in Reading, states that straight men (like himself) can all think of one man with whom they would consider having sex. He mentions his own choice, and then several choices, then a long list. A male member of the audience heckles: 'No! You're wrong!' Smith assumes this is a prequel to homophobic abuse, but when challenged, the indignant man responds: 'You left out Sean Bean. And Viggo Mortensen. And Orlando Bloom.' He lists, to a surprised comic and crowd, most of the male cast of *The Lord of the Rings*.[1] Moments such as this imply that the recent film adaptations of *The Lord of the Rings* bridge the homosocial and the homoerotic. Is this a plausible extension of the homosocial world of the novels, or a modern misinterpretation specific to the films? How homoerotic is Tolkien?

I am not the first reader or critic to interrogate the treatment of sex and gender in *The Lord of the Rings*. Tolkien's gender politics, in fiction and in life, have often been found wanting, usually when held up to an ideal of heterosexual maturity. Edwin Muir remarked that all the male characters are 'boys' – the Hobbits 'boys irrevocably, and will never come to puberty' (1955: 11). Catherine Stimpson also calls Tolkien's views on sex 'childish' (1969: 20). Biographical information on the male friendships between the Inklings can be used to demonstrate that Tolkien was interested in intellectual life as a 'boy's club' – intensely homosocial and perpetually juvenile. Critics have also emphasized the limited roles for female characters, and the 'nasty' and 'evasive' attitude to sex (Stimpson 1969: 20). The spider Shelob is seen as an embodiment of Tolkien's fear of women's sexuality (by Stimpson 1969, Partridge 1983 and Craig 2001, alike). Thus either retarded emotional development, or a fear of sexual women, prevents Tolkien and his characters from a fully mature, equal heterosexuality. These criticisms may be valid, but linking heterosexuality to maturity and respect for women allows little space to discuss a mature, non-misogynist homoeroticism. Brenda Partridge and David M. Craig do suggest homoerotic aspects to the text, particularly within the relationship of Frodo and Sam. Partridge notes how Norse Mythology attracted Lewis and Tolkien because 'war provides a context in which men can be acceptably intimate because they are at the same time being seen to live up to the socially desirable stereotype image of the aggressive male' (1983: 184). Craig (2001), in contrast, gives a more historically specific account, showing how British interwar culture rejected pre-war aggression and militarism in favour of more feminized national values. Closer friendships in wartime were made acceptable, Craig argues, by an absence of women, rather than because of the presence of stereotypical male violence.

These assertions of infantilism, misogyny and subconscious homoeroticism are matched by similarly fierce arguments for the maturity and heterosexuality of both text and author. Daniel Timmons (2001) is a fine example: in 'Hobbit Sex and Sensuality' he advocates taking Tolkien at his word on these matters, and denies that the author projects, displaces or communicates symbolically his anxieties around sex and gender. For example, where Partridge (1983) asserts Tolkien's 'submerged homoeroticism' (in fiction and life), Timmons (2001) splendidly responds that to know Tolkien's real feelings about sex, Stimpson (1969) need only have taken the collected letters and 'looked at the index entry for "women" and "marriage"' (72). Timmons soothes the reader: 'We need not wonder how Hobbits 'reproduce' or whether they have sex or not, anymore than we wonder how our own communities experience these matters' (74–5). For theorists of sex and gender who investigate how 'our own communities experience these matters', this confident assurance seems misplaced. His final line is a rousing call to arms: 'it may be hard to see in a modern or post-modern society that matters of honour, decency, abstinence and fidelity can still resonate powerfully with readers, while real sexual deviance blights life and literature . . . one thing appears all too clear: the path of "free love" or heedless lust leads to degradation and despair. Is that what Tolkien's detractors would have us choose?' (79). Timmons might be surprised at the number of Tolkien *fans* who wish us to choose the path of free love, heedless lust and post-modern 'real sexual deviance'. Speaking as one such, I think it timely to build on previous critics of Tolkien's sex and gender structures, and approach the novels and films with a backpack of critical tools developed in the last decade by gay, lesbian, bisexual and queer theorists.

THEY ARE LOVERS – FRODO AND SAM AS POSTERHOBBITS

To begin, I use as my guide an article on *Xena: Warrior Princess* by Elyce Rae Helford (2000). Helford moves with agility between a 'queer' reading that recognizes many different viewer investments and responses, and a 'lesbian' reading that supports lesbian identity politics. She discusses how ambiguous connotations of lesbianism have been a useful tool of heterocentrism – keeping queer readers happy while reassuring heterocentric audiences. She notes the homophobia of many Xena fans. Because of these twin concerns 'one (political) statement this chapter needs to make regarding Xena and Gabrielle is: THEY ARE LOVERS' (144).

The Lord of the Rings and *Xena* certainly share similarities; they are examples of the fantasy genre, have reached cult levels of fandom. Both have, at their heart, a loving same-sex partnership travelling across an inhospitable land: Gabrielle and Xena, Sam and Frodo. Queer readings by fans of both texts have been numerous. Xena can boast themed cruises and club nights; *The Lord of the Rings* has many online communities of homoerotic fanfiction writers and artists (depicting relationships between Legolas and Aragorn, Aragorn and Boromir, any or all of the Hobbits). But in both cases, the text is redeemable for a heterosexual reading; the homoeroticism can be safely designated as a 'subtext'.

With these compelling comparisons, is it important for me (politically) to make a similar statement? Should I pick a pair of characters and say: SAM AND FRODO ARE LOVERS? To answer this, I should take into account all that Helford considers: not only the textual 'evidence', but also the viewer reactions and thus the political expedience of such an assertion.

Textually, one can accumulate moments that seem to connote that Sam and Frodo are in a sexual relationship, but these can (should the reader wish) be re-heterosexualized by using other features of the texts. The novel tells us that Hobbits usually marry and generate large families, but the protagonists are pairs and groups of single male Hobbits; Frodo and Bilbo's non-reproductive family unit gives way to Frodo's 'special friends' Pippin and Merry, and then to Sam and Frodo. The textual justification for this is that these characters are in their 'tweens' and could be expected to be single. Bilbo never marries, but for this Timmons blames the 'non-productive love' of the Ring (75).

The first chapter uses the word 'queer' often: of Bilbo's relatives ('no wonder they're queer' [FR, I, i, 29]) and Bilbo and Frodo ('Bag End's a queer place and its folk are queerer' [FR, I, I, 31]) – this repeated usage recalls *The Well of Loneliness*). The riches and youth of Bilbo 'will have to be paid for' – 'it ain't natural'. But the Hobbit view espoused in these commentaries is deliberately provincial, and the range of expression in Hobbit pub conversation limited – if Bilbo and the Brandybucks are 'queer' so are the 'queer folk crossing the Shire' (FR, I, ii, 59). After Bilbo's departure, Frodo remains different (FR, I, ii, 56) – he lives alone and wanders all over the Shire, sometimes at night, shaping up well to be a melancholy queer t(w)een. But by this time, he has inherited the isolating, 'non-productive' Ring.

So potential 'queer' difference jumps out of the text but is retracted again by the novel's canonical explanations. Any queer reading must abandon Timmon's acceptance of face-value explanations, and note that Tolkien has written get-out clauses into the novel, so that his characters need not, or cannot, marry, and must form close male friendships.

At the centre of any argument for Sam and Frodo as a sexual or romantic couple is the faithful love between the two. Sam's extended meditation on Frodo as he sleeps is exemplary:

[H]e saw his master's face very clearly . . . Sam had noticed that at times a light seemed to be shining faintly within; but now the light was even clearer and stronger . . . it looked old, old and

beautiful . . . He shook his head, as if finding words useless, and murmured: 'I love him. He's like that, and sometimes it shines through, somehow. But I love him, whether or no.'
(*TT*, IV, iv, 321)

The quest narrative facilitates physical contact: Sam carries Frodo, and shelters the sleeping Frodo with his body. Sam's most intimate interactions with Frodo centre on the pressing and stroking of Frodo's hands, most suggestively when Frodo recovers in part from his sword injury at Rivendell:

> He ran to Frodo and took his left hand, awkwardly and shyly. He stroked it gently and then he blushed and turned hastily away.
> [. . .]
> 'It's warm!' said Sam. 'Meaning your hand, Mr. Frodo. It has felt so cold through the long nights.'
> (*FR*, II, i, 295)

Why, when he has already stroked the hand, does Sam feel compelled to add 'meaning your hand'? Does Sam's blush indicate his awareness that physical contact is inappropriate, now the dangers of armed conflict and illness are (briefly) over?

The appendices heterosexualize many of the characters, giving wives and children to Merry and Pippin, and heirs to Aragorn. But they also reunite Sam and Frodo: '[T]radition is handed down' that after Rose Cotton's death, Sam calls at his daughter's to say goodbye, then goes to join Frodo in the Western Isles (*RK*, appendix B 470). Similarly, Gimli is also rumoured to have sailed there; possibly for heterosexual devotion to Galadriel, possibly for his 'great friendship' with Legolas: 'More cannot be said on the matter' (*RK*, appendix A 447). The use of the traditional romance narrative to contain Sam's queer potential breaks down even within the text itself.

Laying out instances of textual 'evidence' such as these exposes the confusion inherent in the search: what can be considered evidence? And evidence of what: sexual contact, romantic devotion, non-heterosexual identity? This brings into question the sociology of this fantasy world. Tolkien's 'subcreation' of Middle-earth doesn't make obvious mention of same-sex desire or sexual identity. Some fans have taken this as the final word, suggesting that as Tolkien didn't put male-male sex into his world, it cannot be plausibly 'seen' there. Other fans argue that homosocial closeness is a feature of Hobbit society, and is never sexual. Anti-homophobic fans can reach similar heterosexualizing conclusions: 'American men cannot deal with two literary characters supporting and loving each other in a time of dire need, so it becomes a gay issue when it never really was' (Clifford Broadway, Quickbeam on www.TheOneRing.net, quoted in Behrens (2002) – many Internet film discussion boards chart similar debates).

These attempts to use the sociology of Middle-earth to avoid homosexuality ignore the strong similarities between that world and our own. Heterosexuality in Middle-earth seems to be organized around an idealized Catholic version of 'our' (Western, middle-class) heterosexuality. Without our understanding of heterosexual romance and family norms, the text would lose half its resonance. It should, then, be logical to interpret same-sex relationships the same way, through parallels with our own world. Anything else is an avoidance tactic.

As viewers we could certainly look for normative, non-gender-specific features of romantic love: commitment, exclusivity, permanence, cohabitation, sexual activity. Or in a deeper parallel between worlds, the reader can draw on histories of homoeroticism or homosexual identity. For example, Sam and Frodo strongly recall a British history of cross-class gay relationships; E. M. Forster's eponymous Maurice and his lover Scudder are also a middle-class homosexual man and a working-class bisexual (Sam is a gardener, Scudder a gamekeeper). The physical class characteristics are certainly suggestive of erotic readings:

> In his lap lay Frodo's head, drowned deep in sleep; upon his white forehead lay one of Sam's brown hands, and the other lay softly upon his master's breast.
> (*TT*, IV, viii, 403)

Sam is work-hardened, sun-beaten, and being used as Master Frodo's cushion. A less homosexually aware viewer may simply notice the erotics of one man calling another 'master'. This historical comparison helps locate the 'queerness' of *The Lord of the Rings* within intense hierarchical homosocial relations, as discussed shortly, rather than (for example) effeminacy, or a sense of difference.

The textual 'evidence' for Hobbit same-sex desire, then, is partial, riddled with interpretative problems and dodging de-sexualizing explanations within the text. However, the evidence for Hobbit *heterosexuality* is just as flimsy, if not more so. Shawna Walls, a Tolkien historian who runs the gay-friendly site www.BagEnd Inn.com, argues: 'The thing is, Tolkien didn't talk about sex at all, so using sex as a litmus test to decide whether or not Sam and Frodo are a gay couple doesn't really apply' (Behrens 2002). Charles Nelson (1994) charts the uneven development of the novel's heterosexual romances, in part to answer his title question, 'But who is Rose Cotton?' While the film attempts to bring the romances more centrally into the plot (as described later), and shows Rose at Bilbo's birthday party, Sam's interactions with her are still peripheral. The Hobbits' meeting with Lady Goldberry is used by Timmons to suggest their maturing into heterosexuality (2001: 76), but although their responses are powerful they are only ambiguously sexual.

With these problems of the legitimacy of textual 'evidence', it is helpful to move from asking 'Are Sam and Frodo lovers?' and ask 'What would it *mean* or *achieve* to assert that they are lovers?' Helford (2000) asserts Xena and Gabrielle's relationship as lovers to support a beleaguered fanbase, pressurize homophobic fans and emphasize the show's potential as a site of resistance in mainstream TV. The political/pragmatic point is not identical for *The Lord of the Rings*. Xena has a huge lesbian fanbase, but gay fans have not responded as fervently to Tolkien's work. The only equivalent fanbase I can find with a vested interest in homoeroticism is, as I mentioned, that of slash fanfiction writers and artists. The slash fanfiction community, while often anti-homophobic, have different needs to the lesbian fans of Xena in their requirements, for pleasure, identification and politics. For example, slash writers use a range of canonically heterosexual characters; lesbian viewers seeking lesbian characters, as Helford describes, have far less choice.

Also, the fact that the stars of Xena are female changes the meaning of dissident viewing. One of Helford's main criticisms is that connotations of female-female eroticism have been used to attract viewers who can then dismiss the reality of lesbian identity and solidarity. Popular culture has not to the same extent, and in mirrored ways, used male homoeroticism to lure in straight viewers. Women's pleasure at seeing attractive men in homoerotic situations, has (I would argue) been *under*estimated; Orlando Bloom's role as

Legolas, and his subsequent strong and ambiguous partnership with Johnny Depp in the film *Pirates of the Caribbean* (2003), have apparently appealed to his female fans.

However, there *is* strong fan resistance to the idea of Frodo and Sam as sexually involved. This resistance is a good reason, as it was for Helford with *Xena*, for me to insist on the sexual nature of their relationship. Online fans have expressed disgust at the idea of the Hobbits as lovers. Often this accompanies a double-layered homophobia that (while superficially tolerant of same-sex sex) feels unease at having to identify Sam and Frodo in particular as lovers. The infantilization of the Hobbits may be notable here; while juvenile heterosexuality can be innocent and cute, same-sex sex and child-like characters spark homophobic protest. The intense identification inspired by these novels, through childhood games or adolescent enthusiasm, may also contribute to the defensive tone of responses.

Considering textual 'evidence', political considerations and fan satisfaction, it becomes clear that these films are not the male *Xena*. However, homophobic resistance to such a reading encourages me to suggest the possibility of a sexual relationship.

Choosing two characters, though, and using their sexual relationship as the basis for a queer reading of the films would isolate the pair, and let the rest of the characters slip into heterosexuality. I wish rather to show the homoeroticism of practically every pairing in the films. This would include other key moments: Aragorn and Boromir with their death-scene kiss, but also Aragorn and Legolas' Elven exchanges, Legolas and Gimli's 'great friendship', Merry and Pippin's anguished wails on parting, and the joyful and playfully physical reunion of the Hobbits near the close of *The Return of the King*. So while I do not wish to say SAM AND FRODO ARE LOVERS, I certainly do not wish to say that Sam and Frodo are *not* lovers. I aim to emphasize what writers of slash fanfiction already know; that most of the characters and relationships are ambiguous, and could easily be sexual. I use the remainder of this chapter to explore one explanation for this.

MEN WITHOUT WOMEN; WOMEN WITHIN HOMOEROTICISM

The dominant model of interpersonal relationships has shifted in the transition from novels to films. In the novels, hierarchical male relationships predominate. In the films, this is extended to include heterosexual romance. This is not a complete shift of emphasis; it would be insane to propose that the quest narrative, the relationships of rivalry, mistrust and leadership have been subordinated to a romance narrative. But the text, as suggested above and further argued below, was already poised on difficult, intensely homosocial ground. Decisions made in the film adaptation have destabilized that precarious homosociality.

The novels provide an amazing range of male-male relationships that are often hierarchical, articulated in the text around the war-time leadership of a captain, and the peace-time ruling of a king. This also includes less formal examples of leadership and authority, including Gandalf's guidance of the Fellowship, and Sam's fealty to Frodo. An example can demonstrate how different relationships in the text share similar resonant images of fealty, extending outside the purely feudal or martial: one of the high-points of the Hobbits Merry and Pippin's 'coming of age' is their swearing of allegiance to King Théoden and Lord Denethor. Merry's allegiance is expressed by the Hobbit kissing the ruler's hand. This formal gesture gives a context for Sam's continual holding, kissing and stroking of Frodo's hand.[2]

Passionate allegiance is often named 'love'; Faramir is referred to in relation to Beregond as the captain whom he loved. To show that this is not an isolated 'love', Pippin chimes in a page later acknowledging that many men would follow Faramir.

The titles involved in these exchanges are worth noting. A text involving many men can confuse because of pronoun use, often leading to unintentional erotics (as when the ownership of body parts is ambiguous – 'He stroked his cheek'). In this text, the con-fusion is partially solved by the use of titles (also, the use of races – 'the Dwarf', 'the Elf'). But these titles do not only serve to indicate who is touching or loving whom; they also serve to mark clearly the variety of gesture, the kind of love involved. When Beregond loves his captain, it is in the manner of a soldier loving his leader. Although, as noted, insanely homoerotic, Sam's continually referring to Frodo as 'Master' also provides a *less necessarily* sexual context for his devotion.

I say 'less necessarily' because any comparison with our own world shows us that these frameworks do not exclude sex as effec-tively as Tolkien might have wished – servants and masters, captains and soldiers, kings and subjects have all had sexual relationships. Sexuality is not prohibited by such relationships. But these models do mean that sex is not central to the narrative; a sexual reading is made optional.

How do these formal relationships thus translate to the film version? The language of admiration precisely and formally delineated through titles can perhaps only clumsily be expressed through lingering shots of the lead characters which leave the viewer to their own personal form of appreciation. In the text, a servant views his master or a soldier views his captain: onscreen, when two characters face each other (especially if excerpted from the narrative flow in a publicity still) they are simply two men. The gaze or gesture between them can be contextualized by costume or props or scenery, but these have a hard time approximating the formal designations that support the novel's hierarchies. Boromir's onscreen dying words use the titles to the full: Aragorn is designated 'My brother, my captain, my king . . .'; the acknowledgement of Aragorn's emotional importance to Boromir is framed by fraternal explanations, then capped by first a martial, then a monarchical, context as well, as though the eroticism is so potent it needs a triple containment. But the kiss is still a kiss.

And something more than the accidental eroticism of fealty is at work in the films. Romance and sex, previously optional and supplementary to the action, are drawn in to supplement (or conflict with) the hierarchical model of relationship. I conclude this chapter with an exploration of this shift, through the two characters most affected: Arwen and Éowyn.

The relationships of the male characters are altered because the roles of female characters, and of romance, are enhanced. This enhanced female/romantic presence raises the possibility that sexual relationships exist alongside the hierarchical and military homosocial relationships. This destabilizes any confidently asexual (or less-sexual) reading of the relationships between men. Rather than romance narratives being subordinated to, and expressed through, the language and gestures of all-male hierarchies, romance is now vying for equal dominance as the ideal form of relationship.

The part of Arwen is the most substantially enhanced. To participate in this action film, she becomes an action heroine; she lays her sword against Aragorn's neck, leads the company to Rivendell, rescues Frodo on her horse, and defies the ringwraiths: 'If you want him, come and claim him!' She replaces Elrond and Gandalf in calling the flood that saves the company.

Aragorn becomes less self-sufficient, so that Arwen can help him explore his duty and carry it out. At Rivendell, a conversation between them conveys necessary plot information to the viewer, but also demonstrates that Arwen is an assured confidante and advisor for the future king: 'Why do you fear the past? You are Isildur's heir, not Isildur himself. You are not bound to his fate.' The film narrative is altered so that Arwen becomes the instigator for Isildur's sword Narsil being reforged from its fragments and passed to Aragorn. She supports Aragorn in a nocturnal vision; he states in Elvish 'My path is hidden from me', and she responds, 'It is already laid before your feet. You cannot falter now.' She also seems to rescue him when he falls from a cliff into a river (kissing him with the words 'May the grace of the Valar protect you'); whether her appearances are concussed/insomniac hallucinations or mystical communications, he couldn't have done it without her.

And their romantic relationship becomes dramatic, rather than static, because Arwen's 'choice' (to either remain with Aragorn, or leave Middle-earth with her father Elrond) is played out in far more detail. In the novels, her 'choice' is foreshadowed from when they first meet. Her father lays down preconditions ('She shall not be the bride of any man less than the King of both Gondor and Arnor') and states his objections, but does not otherwise intervene. In the film, a devious and full-blown tug of love takes place; Elrond lies to Arwen about her future, and pressures Aragorn to leave her. The audience is encouraged to invest emotionally in each of Arwen's decisions and reversals: she tells Aragorn she will stay, is told by him to leave, rides for the Grey Havens but (after a vision and a confrontation with Elrond) stays after all.

Finally, Arwen is interwoven with the quest narrative in a way that is frankly clumsy. In an implausible intervention, Elrond advises Aragorn that 'Arwen's life is now tied to the fate of the Ring.' Does this hastily conveyed information significantly shift the narrative focus? Probably not, but it attempts such a shift. Romance may be intended in part to compensate for the loss of Tolkien's intricate histories; the casual viewer cannot be expected to grasp the implication of one of the race of Numenor taking the throne of Gondor – but everyone recognizes romance.

So in action, in supporting Aragorn and in romance plot, Arwen has been enhanced. Peter Jackson spoke of the changes in an early interview (with *Ain't It Cool News* in 1998):

> For example, the Aragorn/Arwen romance is a lovely part of the story . . . but if it was filmed exactly as Tolkien wrote it, they would have maybe ten minutes screentime together over six hours of film. So we have to find a way to include Arwen in more of the story, to have a chance at creating a meaningful screen romance. However, we won't do anything radical . . . It's a fine line that we walk.

The 'fine line', I would argue, has been crossed; a romantic relationship has achieved prominence in the film, where in the novel same-sex hierarchical relationships ruled supreme. In the novel, sex is not central to the plot; it is optional, and one can imagine as much or as little as one likes. In the film adaptation, the viewer is encouraged to emotionally invest in romance, and seek it out and speculate about it, with contradictory effects; the viewer may notice how flimsy the heterosexual relationships are in contrast with the male-male bonds, how much more the men admire and owe one another.

Éowyn's relationship with Aragorn perfectly demonstrates the martial being supplanted by the romantic. In the novels, their unrequited romance is powerfully rooted within the context of fealty. Éowyn admits her love by using a comparison with the soldiers that follow Aragorn: 'They go only because they would not be parted from thee – because they love thee' (*RK*, V, ii, 55). Later, when Faramir describes Éowyn's love for Aragorn, it is again in an explicitly hierarchical and martial frame:

> You desired to have the love of the Lord Aragorn. Because he was high and puissant, and you wished to have renown and glory and to be lifted far above the mean things that crawl on the earth. And as a great captain may to a young soldier he seemed to you admirable. For so he is, a lord among men . . .
> (*RK*, VI, v, 291)

Éowyn's future fiancé agreeing that Aragorn is lovable is not calculated to surprise the reader. Éowyn loves Aragorn as his men do, for the same reasons his men do, *as does Faramir*. Even Éowyn's first sight of Aragorn is through the frame of his regal inheritance: 'tall heir of kings, wise with many winters.' Éowyn's martial love for Aragorn is communicated through understated glances and exchanges in the novel; the film transforms this into far more of a traditional cinematic romance. The film allows them more inter-action, and their relationship is more informal and relaxed; they share a joke about female Dwarves' beards. It is Éowyn's question about the jewel Aragorn wears that provokes thoughts of Arwen; Aragorn is positioned briefly as the romantic hero, torn between two lovers.

Rather than the elegant and hierarchical explanation for Éowyn's love given by Faramir, we are treated to this from Aragorn: 'It is but a shadow and a thought that you love. I can not give you what you seek.' This is phrased in a fantasy lingo, but its theme is familiar from standard cinematic romance: *you don't really love me, you don't know me, I'm not who you want me to be*. It's a far cry from Faramir's martial model. So rather than romance being framed by hierarchical allegiances, as was Éowyn's case before, the quest is now partially framed by the romance narrative.

When women weren't part of the picture, the male relationships could be more easily de-sexed. Men were kings and kings-in-waiting, captains, masters and servants, batmen, soldiers and subjects. We should note also Galadriel's role as a queen, and Arwen's as a princess: dynastic and hierarchical. With the introduction of romance, these relationships become confused. For example, the use of Elven language as a token of love between Aragorn and Arwen adds a suggestive note to his exchanges with Legolas, at Helm's Deep and elsewhere. The physical gestures that expressed male homosocial relations – grasping shoulders, pressing and kissing hands and fore-heads – is now also available for heterosexual encounters, and this recontextualizes the fervour of the homosocial. When the physical now includes Aragorn kissing Arwen, what is meant by his kiss for Boromir?

It may seem perverse to argue that improved roles for female characters in the film open the possibility of homoeroticism. The reverse is often the case; Mark Doty notes that 'using a woman to mediate and diffuse male-male erotics' is a conventional device in film (1993: 11). But in the novels of *The Lord of the Rings*, without female characters, the viewers can believe that sex has been effaced from every set of relationships. Women *are* the possibility of sex;

they *are* the romance plot. Craig (2001) shows how the absence of female characters can make male bonds look 'queer' as men are forced to behave like women (perform domestic tasks, express 'soft' emotions and form close bonds [15]). But at least with no women present, sex can be nominally ignored. If female characters are then returned to the text, and sex made central to the plot *with the male bonds and roles still intact*, the 'queerness' is doubled.

I do not mean to reinforce this state of affairs by highlighting it. It seems to me obvious that sex is present in a council with seven men, just as it is present on a bridge with a man and a female Elf. But I can't deny that the conversion of the dominant frame of the text from primarily homosocial relationships, to containing some female-male sexual/romantic relationships, has had an effect.

Observing this, I must note the potentially reactionary side of queer readings of the films. My own queer reading depends on women being the bearers of 'sex', and many viewers who saw the Hobbits as gay did so out of a homophobic fear of male intimacy (as noted by Broadway in Behrens 2002), which is not noticeably more challenging then reading them as resolutely heterosexual. I also have a sense of the limited political advantages of 'appropriating' mainstream films, or even asserting an obvious subtext; will a positive homoerotic reading ever 'stick' to this multi-million pound franchise? Even when Boromir's forehead is tenderly kissed, he dies shortly after – Saint Sebastian-style – stuck full of arrows. But I assert my reading: they are potentially *all* lovers.

CHAPTER 10

SERVICE

Scott Kleinman

In *The Lord of the Rings* there is a sustained meditation on the nature of social relationships in which one person is bound to serve the will of another. Service relationships entail a diminution of the freedom and autonomy of the servant, whose subordination raises troubling questions about the nature of the bonds that secure the service and the social inequalities they produce. In the discussion below, I attempt a modest outline of some of the ways Tolkien addresses these questions in his depiction of the peoples of Rohan, Gondor and the Shire. Drawing on literary and historical models of service from the past – particularly the medieval and Victorian periods – Tolkien reflects upon the history of service and its continued viability as a form of social cooperation.[1] In this admittedly incomplete survey of service relationships in *The Lord of the Rings*, I hope to demonstrate that Tolkien systematically explores the strengths and weakness of service cultures of the past in order to imagine an ideal form for today.[2]

LOYALTY AND AUTONOMY

Tolkien's view of service was profoundly influenced by the Germanic model depicted in Anglo-Saxon poetry. Shortly before the publication of the first volume of *The Lord of the Rings*, he discussed his view of this model in an essay accompanying 'The Homecoming of Beorhtnoth Beorhthelm's Son', his 'sequel' to the Old English poem 'The Battle of Maldon'. In this essay, Tolkien contrasts the nobleman Byrhtnoth's 'chivalrous' (by which he means excessive) pursuit of honour with the heroism demonstrated by his subordinates, whom he leads to their deaths in the poem. 'The Battle of Maldon',

Tolkien argues, draws into relief the separate responsibilities of lords and thegns. In the Germanic model of lordship, the lord's chief obligations were, as Jane Chance puts it, 'wise leadership, protection from enemies, and food, shelter and reward for valor in battle' (Chance 2002: 117). By contrast, Tolkien defines a subordinate as 'a man for whom the object of his will was decided by another, who had no responsibility downwards, only loyalty upwards. Personal pride was therefore in him at its lowest, and love and loyalty highest' (Tolkien 1953: 14). This intimate connection between love and loyalty characterizes the relationship between lord and thegn, making Byrhtnoth's irresponsibility condemnable, and the loyalty of his thegns all the more worthy of praise.

Tolkien draws on this Germanic model of service extensively in his depiction of the Rohirrim. Théoden states precisely the expectations of lord and servant when Merry asks him why he has accepted him as his 'swordthain':

> 'I received you for your safe-keeping,' answered Théoden; 'and also to do as I might bid.'
> (*RK*, V, iii, 80)

The obligation to do as one's lord bids is entered into voluntarily out of a feeling of camaraderie, which Théoden engenders in Merry by inviting him to eat, converse and ride with him (*RK*, V, ii, 70). Likewise, when Théoden rallies the Riders of the Mark, he does so by reminding them equally of their oaths to 'lord, land and league of friendship' (*RK*, V, v, 122). Service in Rohan does not imply social stratification; even when Merry performs the most servile of tasks, waiting on the king, he is nevertheless invited to sit beside him (*RK*, V, iii, 70).[3] The intense emotional bond between Théoden's subordinates and their king is frequently expressed using a paternal metaphor, such as when Éowyn (disguised as Dernhelm) stands over him after he has fallen: 'he had loved his lord as a father' (*RK*, V, vi, 128). Merry's anguish is experienced in the same terms: 'You must stay by him. As a father you shall be to me, you said' (*RK*, V, vi, 128). One result of this camaraderie is that the thegn's obedience to his lord is grounded in their personal relationship. Hence, when Théoden rides to Gondor, he cannot command Merry to serve: instead, he releases him from his service (if not his friendship) and asks him to serve Éowyn, if you will (*RK*, V, iii, 77).

But such an arrangement comes at a price; the servant's degree of autonomy, combined with his love for his master, can place him in awkward situations, in particular when he lacks his lord's guidance or doubts his wisdom. The extent to which a thegn is obligated to follow his lord's command, 'be it folly or wisdom', as Gandalf puts it (*TT*, III, vi, 134), is not laid out. Hence Háma, allowing Gandalf to enter Théoden's hall with his staff, argues that 'in doubt a man of worth will trust to his own wisdom' (*TT*, III, vi, 135). Yet, under the influence of Gríma Wormtongue, this latitude has been undermined in Rohan, and Théoden later tells Gandalf that he has imprisoned Éomer because 'he had rebelled against my commands, and threatened death to Gríma in my hall' (*TT*, III, vi, 141). Wormtongue's deception of the king is in fact made possible by his depiction of himself as a loving *and* obedient servant, conflating the cause and effect of the thegn's subordination. When Théoden declares his intention to go to war and bids him, 'Come with me and prove your faith', Wormtongue praises the king's courage but adds:

> But those who truly love him would spare his failing years. Yet I see I come too late. Others, whom the death of my lord would perhaps grieve less, have already persuaded him.
> (*TT*, III, vi, 146)

He goes on to suggest the appointment of a steward, himself, as 'one who knows your mind and honours your commands' (*TT*, III, vi, 146). But the 'cured' Théoden can now see the deceit here. A few pages earlier, he accuses Háma and Éomer of disobedience, but with a nod and a wink: ' "The guilty shall bring the guilty to judgement," said Théoden, and his voice was grim, yet he looked at Gandalf and smiled and as he did so many lines of care were smoothed away and did not return' (*TT*, III, vi, 141). Later, in an exchange of maxims with Gandalf, Théoden recognizes that faithful service may involve dissent: ' "I owe much to Éomer," said Théoden. "Faithful heart may have forward tongue" ' (*TT*, III, vi, 149). The problem for the Germanic model of service is that lord and servant have no certain criteria for love and good service other than loyalty in battle. Off the battlefield, the lord must discern whether his thegns behave in his interests, and his thegns must make the same judgements about their own autonomous actions, where they run counter to their lord's commands. The potential for ambiguity extends even to those whose fidelity is unquestioned. In the end, when Théoden is thrown from his horse, the Rohirrim cannot reconcile the beast's love for the king, with his part in his downfall; they place on his tomb the contradictory epithet: 'Faithful servant, yet master's bane, / Lightfoot's foal, swift Snowmane' (*RK*, V, vi, 134).

A MAN'S WORD IS HIS BOND

Although Tolkien finds evidence for the survival of the Germanic model of lordship and service as late as the fourteenth-century *Sir Gawain and the Green Knight*, he nevertheless recognizes that 'The Battle of Maldon' takes place at a transitional moment, when the English aristocratic consciousness was beginning to shift towards 'a whole code of sentiment and conduct, in which heroic courage is only a part, with different loyalties to serve' (Tolkien 1953: 16). With the rise of feudal vassalage from the eleventh century onwards, the personal ties that bound lords and thegns were weakened by the growing importance of property exchange, particularly since a single vassal could hold multiple fiefs from different lords.[4] Other developments, such as the growth of royal power and of national consciousness, provided additional alternative locations for servile devotion (see Turville-Petre 1995). As the Middle Ages progressed, the makeup of lordly households moved increasingly towards the model of contractual affinity, a model that dominated the politics of the fourteenth century (Given-Wilson 1986). Although such attempts to formalize the relationship between lord and vassal can be seen as a response to the collapse of more personal loyalties between individuals, the process of so defining these relationships ironically forced lords and their subordinates into ever more rigid positions in exercising their responsibilities and duties. It is no wonder that there was great anxiety over the binding quality of formal oaths of fealty at this time. Hence in *Sir Gawain and the Green Knight*, the poet places Gawain in positions where he is bound to fulfil the terms of his oath, even at the cost of his life and honour (Thomas 2002).

In Gondor, service relationships are organized around such formal promises, creating dilemmas for the servants of Denethor that are similar to that faced by Gawain. Pippin's oath, which he repeats verbatim from Denethor's prompts, highlights later medieval conceptions of fealty-based service:

'Here do I swear fealty and service to Gondor, and to the Lord and Steward of the realm, to speak and to be silent, to do and to let be, to come and to go, in need or plenty, in peace or war, in living or dying, from this hour henceforth, until my lord release me, or death take me, or the world end. So say I, Peregrin son of Paladin of the Shire of the Halflings.'

'And this do I hear, Denethor son of Ecthelion, Lord of Gondor, Steward of the High King, and I will not forget it, nor fail to reward that which is given: fealty with love, valour with honour, oath-breaking with vengeance.'

(*RK*, V, i, 17–18)

The formal and formulaic language of reward in Denethor's answer to Pippin's oath highlights the contractual nature of the exchange of duties. This model of service renders the servant obliged to perform duties precisely as stipulated in the oath, without the leeway afforded to Háma in Rohan, as Tolkien demonstrates through the character of Beregond, who reluctantly violates his orders in order to save Faramir's life. Although Gandalf believes that Pippin's offer to serve Denethor touched his and pleased his humour, he also notes that Pippin is 'at his command' (*RK*, V, i, 22); and Denethor in fact relegates him to menial tasks, to 'wait on me, bear errands, and talk to me, if war and council leave me any leisure' (*RK*, V, iv, 83). Whilst Denethor speaks of rewarding fealty with love, Pippin's own motives for offering his service are feelings of pride and indebtedness, rather than affection for the recipient of his service. His oath in fact designates that his fealty belongs, not to Denethor specifically, but to the State, Gondor and to the Steward, transferring his allegiance from *pater* to *patria*. Whereas in Rohan the obedience of Théoden's servants is based on a filial affection, Denethor inverts this principle by requiring absolute obedience even from his own sons.[5] Thus he resents Gandalf's influence over Faramir and objects to his son's taking his own counsel (*RK*, V, iv, 91); by contrast, he insists that 'Boromir was loyal to me and no wizard's pupil' (*RK*, V, iv, 91). Loyalty is here conceived in the binary terms specified in Pippin's oath. That Faramir has been forced into this service paradigm becomes clear in his response to Denethor's refusal to send further troops to Cair Andros: 'I do not oppose your will, sire. Since you are robbed of Boromir, I will go and do what I can in his stead – if you command it' (*RK*, V, iv, 96).

Denethor, for his part, rejects those who act autonomously out of such devotion, as Pippin does in trying to comfort him. In part, this is because of the 'release' clause present in Pippin's oath, which Denethor later invokes, using language reminiscent of that used by Théoden in releasing Merry from his service. But Denethor's intent differs from Théoden's desire for Merry to serve Éowyn. Denethor simply has no further use for Pippin and therefore grants him autonomy to 'do as you will' (*RK*, V, iv, 108), just as earlier he tells the men of Minas Tirith to 'follow whom you will' (106). Instead, he calls for the servants whom he knows will obey him unquestioningly, even to the point of bringing about his death. Whilst the formal oath of affinity in Denethor's household may help to define his servants' duties and allay concerns about their loyalties, it also colours the expectations of both lord and servants in troubling ways by preventing the servants from acting autonomously and by undermining the respect they have from their lord. Although Denethor's actions may be a result of his madness and despair, he is not a failed Germanic lord, a monstrous parallel to Théoden. His behaviour is at least partly the result of problems inherent in the formal and contractual service culture of Gondor. These problems are likewise revealed in his servants, whose oaths force them to aid in his suicide. But Denethor never becomes truly monstrous because he does not ask his servants to do more than they have sworn to do; he does not go so far as to exploit them.[6]

CULTIVATION AND EXPLOITATION

Medieval aristocratic and courtly models of service were little concerned with the lower orders of society such as the large class of peasantry, most of whom were serfs, that is, people legally designated as 'servile'. Although serfdom had declined by the end of the Middle Ages, the colonization of the New World and the rise of the slave trade in the early modern era reconstituted this class of exploited agricultural workers. There are hints that Tolkien had in mind such colonial conditions when fashioning the Shire, the most 'modern' of the three societies discussed here.[7] The history of the Shire is indeed conceived as a colonial one. Its first settlers, Marcho and Blanco, are calqued on the leaders of the Anglo-Saxon settlers of Britain, Hengest and Horsa, whose arrival also had great resonance for the colonists of the New World, as can be seen from Thomas Jefferson's plan to place Hengest and Horsa on the Great Seal of the United States.[8] Such associations between the Shire and colonial societies are made more concrete in the apparently digressive section of the prologue entitled 'Concerning Pipe-weed', a plant of New World origin.[9] Although there is no slavery in the Shire, affinities with exploitative plantation cultures begin to take shape once Saruman gains power there. Saruman has already employed Orcs as slaves in Isengard, and his attraction to pipe-weed shows his continued predilection for such exploitation.[10] Hence, when Frodo and his companions return at the end of the book he has virtually reduced the Hobbits to slaves. This is not to say that we are meant to identify the Shire they return to with colonial America. Rather, they suggest the potential for exploitative forms of service, even in a nominally egalitarian society.

This is where the cultural resemblance of the Shire to Victorian England becomes particularly resonant. Victorian models of service differed significantly from those of the medieval past. Gone were the days when young gentlemen entered service as a part of their training. Service activities were increasingly restricted to the lower ranks of society in the early modern period, widening the social gap between master and servant. From the Tudor period onwards legislation was introduced which placed the servant entirely at the beck and call of the employer, strengthening the social divide between them. This placed the servant in a position of vulnerability and, although many were treated kindly by their masters, others endured terrible mistreatment and exploitation (Horn 1975: 3). Victorian culture maintained the social distance between master and servant through an elaborate etiquette for servant behaviour which emphasized deference towards the master in all ways (Horn 1975: 110–13). Despite increasingly egalitarian modes of thought and the decline of service amongst men in favour of other opportunities such as factory labour, the extreme social stratification of Victorian society did not begin to erode significantly until the twentieth century (Horn 1975: 71).

The Shire is characterized by some vestiges of this social hierarchy. The Thainship is hereditary in the Took family – whose naming conventions (e.g., Isengrim II) even recall those of European monarchs – and the Sackville-Bagginses likewise appear to represent a large (and suitably pretentious) moneyed interest. Bilbo and Frodo strongly resemble members of a squierarchy similar to the gentry that dominated the local populations of Victorian England, and, as Jane Chance has persuasively argued, the social tensions surrounding the breakdown of Victorian class divisions are played out in the early chapters of *The Lord of the Rings*, where the 'queerness' of Bilbo and Frodo derives in part from the fact that they cross the social divide through their relationships with Sam, Gaffer Gamgee, and other poorer Hobbits (Chance 1992: 22–34). The apparent absence of a servant class in the Shire may reflect the decline of such a class at the end of the Victorian period. The exception to this trend was in the employment of outdoor servants, especially gardeners, who were probably the most prominent form of male servant in Tolkien's youth.[11] It is perhaps no accident, then, that it is a gardener, Sam, who is the primary example of the servant in *The Lord of the Rings*. Sam's deferential behaviour towards Frodo – powerfully conveyed by his use of the titles 'Mr. Frodo' and 'master' – is the vehicle for Tolkien's evocation of Victorian social division, rather than any clearly defined class relations. At the same time, Bilbo's and Frodo's spirit of generosity towards their social inferiors – and even selected deference, as when Bilbo consults Gaffer Gamgee on the growing of vegetables – reflects the growing twentieth-century spirit of egalitarianism. Such gestures are arguably what prevent those at the top of the Shire's social hierarchy from exploiting those at the bottom. In fact, examples of involuntary service are decidedly missing from the Shire communities; none of the 'poorer Hobbits' seem to have entered service out of necessity. Nevertheless, Sam's deference to Frodo makes clear that Tolkien has not eliminated the social divisions of Victorian service culture from the Shire; rather, he constructs a scenario in which the reader is forced to confront the breakdown of social hierarchies by imagining a form of subordination without exploitation.

QUEER SERVICE: SUBORDINATION AND DESIRE

Egalitarian idealism in the twentieth century has led to an increased scepticism about many traditional kinds of service-based cultures – including the culture of social deference – because they have become associated with exploitative cultures of the past. Service relationships, whether entered into voluntarily or not, have been tarred with the same brush, even those based on personal and national loyalties. This can be discerned in the growing disillusionment with the institution of monarchy, the status of which became more precarious in 1936, the year before Tolkien began *The Lord of the Rings*, when Edward VIII abdicated the throne. The 1937 film *The Prisoner of Zenda* (based on Anthony Hope's 1894 novel), the plot of which revolves around an English gentleman who successfully impersonates a European king and in fact rules with considerably more virtue, reveals something of the anxiety at the time about the basis for service to a king.[12] Tolkien was a monarchist and wished to affirm a basis for this sort of service. He too was to create a sort of model English gentleman in the form of Aragorn, for whom one could genuinely be willing to accept the subordinate role of a subject. However, the film adaptations reveal the discomfort with such subordination felt by many people today. At Aragorn's coronation scene, the four Hobbits bow before the king. Aragorn then says, 'My friends. You bow to no one'. He then leads the crowd in kneeling before them.

For Tolkien, such deference was unproblematic.[13] He was much more concerned with the issues raised by making admiration the basis of subordination, particularly the possibility that admiration may turn to desire. Tolkien explores this possibility through the character of Éowyn, who falls in love with Aragorn. But, as Faramir tells her, her desire was a reflection of her desire for glory. Aragorn has inspired in Éowyn the devotion of a soldier, but this desire has caused Éowyn to eroticize that devotion. Faramir's assessment seems correct if we recall Éowyn's angry response when Aragorn reminds her that she must attend to her duties rather than follow him: 'All your words are but to say: you are a woman, and your part is in the house. But when the men have died in battle and honour, you have leave to be burned in the house, for the men will need it no more. But I am of the House of Eorl and not a servingwoman' (*RK*, V, ii, 55). It is Faramir's job to convince Éowyn that such service is noble; her marriage to the King's steward, his chief servant, ultimately subsumes her erotic devotion into a servile relationship.

A similar dynamic seems to play out in the more 'modern' characters of Frodo and Sam, whose relationship is frequently read, particularly in the popular imagination, in homoerotic terms.

Amongst the many passages in which we can locate such potential, one will have to suffice: the vignette we have of Frodo and Sam asleep on the stairs of Cirith Ungol:

> Sam sat propped against the stone, his head dropping sideways and his breathing heavy. In his lap lay Frodo's head, drowned deep in sleep; upon his white forehead lay one of Sam's brown hands, and the other lay softly upon his master's breast. Peace was in both their faces.
> (*TT*, IV, viii, 403)

Passages like these are so frequently read as homoerotic, that the film adapters appear to have taken the extraordinary counter-measure of making Sam precede Frodo's famous and repeated words at Sammath Naur – 'I am glad you are here with me' (*RK*, VI, v, 268 and *RK*, VI, iv, 272) – with a comment about Rose Cotton: 'If ever I was to marry someone, it would have been her'. Although today's readers may arguably eroticize the homosocial relationships more than Tolkien intended, their propensity to find Frodo and Sam's relationship 'queer' may derive from the same confusion of servile and erotic devotion demonstrated by Éowyn.

Today's reader may also see Frodo and Sam's relationship as 'queer' because Sam's love for Frodo is manifested almost entirely through his servility. Initially, he is introduced as a local gardener, albeit 'on very friendly terms' with his employers (*FR*, I, i, 28). Sam himself describes his relationship to Bilbo and Frodo in these terms, saying that he 'works for' Mr. Baggins, though he also points out that he has had many a talk with Bilbo when he was a lad (*FR*, I, ii, 59). Although Tolkien twice lists Frodo's closest friends and intimates (*FR*, I, ii, 56; *FR*, I, iii, 89), Sam is not amongst them. Hence his intense emotional devotion to Frodo at the end of *The Shadow of the Past* comes as something of a surprise. By all appearances, Merry and Pippin have drafted him as part of the 'conspiracy' because of his access to Bag End. After Sam is caught, he is delighted to accompany Frodo primarily because it will allow him to 'see Elves and all' (*FR*, I, ii, 85), as if he were being taken to see one of Bilbo's stories come true. Sam's devotion to the Bagginses is primarily a response to their kindness to him; just as in Victorian England, servants could discern bad masters and good masters by their kindness, with the latter inspiring greater devotion. Hence, as

Frodo rightly detects, Sam has come to 'care about' him (*FR*, I, ii, 84). What makes the relationship between the two so unsettling for today's reader is that they continue to behave in dominant and submissive roles as the plot progresses. Sam is never able to place himself on an equal footing with Frodo, even when he questions Frodo's treatment of Gollum:

> It had always been a notion of his that the kindness of dear Mr. Frodo was of such high degree that it must imply a fair measure of blindness. Of course, he also firmly held the incompatible belief that Mr. Frodo was the wisest person in the world (with the possible exception of Old Mr. Bilbo and of Gandalf).
> (*TT*, IV, iii, 305).

The incompatibility of Sam's beliefs mirrors the irrationality of his devotion to Frodo. The bond that ties Sam to Frodo is 'queer' in that, unlike the Germanic model in which service is inspired by love, Sam comes to love Frodo through his service to him. At the same time, Sam's subordination to Frodo is not based on any formal oath of fealty or homage; ultimately, he is Frodo's 'man' because he admires him and he admires him because he is his 'man'.

Readers today may find in this circularity an uncomfortably conservative response to the social changes that have taken place over the course of the twentieth century. Tolkien's model of service is, admittedly, an uneasy one, since by nature the servant's devotion pushes at the boundaries of the hierarchical relationship between master and servant. However, it is often remarked that Sam is the true hero of *The Lord of the Rings* – or at least of the final book – even as the trajectory of the novel moves towards the return of the king. Even as Tolkien builds his ideal lord, he also builds his ideal servant, and, in doing so, he valorizes service itself. In this respect, we can observe genuine movement towards the egalitarian ideals which problematize service cultures today. At the same time, Tolkien bridges the gap between the centuries. Like the poet of 'The Battle of Maldon', he makes heroism a virtue and a status which anyone may achieve.

PART IV

TOLKIEN'S FUTURES

CHAPTER 11

GAMES

Barry Atkins

When the initial screens full of corporate logos and company slogans finally clear at the start of the video game *The Battle For Middle Earth* (2004), and the player actually gains access to the game itself, he or she is greeted by a sight that will be comfortingly familiar to readers of the original books. The inked lines of what looks suspiciously like Tolkien's hand-drawn map of Middle-earth, that had itself acted as gatekeeper to successive editions of the books, briefly comes into focus before swiftly giving way to something more suited to the expectations of this new medium as the map moves from two to three dimensions. As the old technology of pen and paper gives way to the new technology of polygons and texture maps it is apparent that this digital Middle-earth has both depth and movement, populated as it is by the great eagles circling above the western mountains and wheeling Nazgûl over Mordor, while rivulets of lava stream down the side of an animated Mount Doom and the Eye of Sauron roams the landscape. In this move from the flat planes of the conventional map to the illusion of a third dimension in which there is already evidence of mobility, we can immediately see something of the kind of promise of a specific form of engagement that the video game holds out to its players. This differs in kind from the audience engagement with either Tolkien's literary text or Peter Jackson's trilogy of films. The animated map both locates the player in the recognizable world of Middle-earth that might be expected to have previously been encountered by many players in other media forms, and signals its specificity as a different kind of experience, representing an immediate invitation to think of Middle-earth in terms of a space to be penetrated and explored, and as a place where it might finally be possible to move off the beaten track and indulge any fantasies we might have of the inhabitation of Tolkien's fictional world. To use the language adopted by that growing group of scholars who are now subjecting the video game to serious critical analysis, what the game appears to offer is the possibility of 'immersion'.

The video game relies upon the player's desire to immerse themselves, at least metaphorically, in the virtual space opened up on screen. As Marie-Laure Ryan (2001) has observed in *Narrative as Virtual Reality* of the problematic reception of the concept of immersion, it is an idea that has not been given sufficiently sensitive treatment by critics to date:

> The self-explanatory character of the concept is easily interpreted as evidence that immersion promotes a passive attitude in the reader, similar to the entrapment of tourists in the self-enclosed virtual realities of theme parks or vacation resorts. This accusation is reinforced by the association of the experience with popular culture. 'Losing oneself in a fictional world,' writes [Jay] Bolter [in *Writing Spaces*, 1991], 'is the goal of the naive reader or one who reads as entertainment. It is particularly a feature of genre fiction, such as romance or science fiction.'
> (11)

Computer game criticism has often shown a rather simplistic acceptance of the idea that the immersive potential of some games, and particularly those games that present the illusion of three-dimensional space on their necessarily two-dimensional screen, marks a radical departure from that available in earlier forms of media.[1] It should not be forgotten, however, that there is something marketable about a perceived desire to believe that computer games and video games might allow their players a different relationship with a fictional world through something akin to a form of presence. To think that one might 'lose oneself' in a fictional elsewhere may be 'naive', but it evidently has appeal. In some forms of contemporary video game, and in all of *The Lord of the Rings* games produced following release of the film trilogy, there is a literal illusion constructed that we can potentially enter the space on the screen before us, and that we can negotiate what Henry Jenkins (2004) has called its 'narrative architecture'.[2] It is as well to be sceptical of claims for the uniqueness or novelty of this immersive promise, even if we do not go so far as Katie Salen and Eric Zimmerman (2003: 450–5) and label this gesture (as if it necessitates the loss of orientation with reference to real world co-ordinates and a suspension of any under-standing of what is real space and what is game space) the 'immersive fallacy', but even if we restrict ourselves to comparing the visual aesthetics of the video game to those of film it is important to note that the video game offers the possibility of both presence and action through its mobilization as played experience only through the manipulation of the player/game interface with reference to this representation of three-dimensional space in the process of play.[3] Having recognized that what is represented on screen is spatially organized, the player is then faced with an imperative to act within that space. This is not simply an experience of surfaces, as the very term 'film' declares itself to be, but an experience of material space as well as representational space that combines real movement in space (of the hand controlling the mouse and keyboard, or the game-pad controller of a console game) with movement of and within the screen image.

The video-game industry and its players have always had an affection for, and a recognition of the commercial potential of, the works of J. R. R. Tolkien, that dates back to the days when the only available interface that would allow movement in the game world of text adventures was by typing 'go north' at the command line.[4] While relatively few directly licensed games based on the books have been released due to the tight control kept for many years over the permissions granted for software development, the influence of *The Lord of the Rings* as a core reference text is everywhere apparent in the fantasy worlds that have been realized on personal computers and various video-game consoles since the 1980s. It might always be possible, and even advisable given the careful protection of copyright engaged in by the Tolkien estate, to sidestep direct reference to Tolkien when tracing the network of influences that underpins a game such as *Everquest* (1999) or *Baldur's Gate* (1998) and cite his own source texts or the more general genre of fantasy literature as the major influences on the content and structure of such games, but there is something lacking in generosity about any denial of Tolkien's place as a primary source of reference. As with *Dungeons and Dragons*, the non-computer role-playing game that sees its parties of adventurers battling in a cod-medieval fantasy world of Wizards, Orcs, Elves, Dwarves and Halflings where magic rings and enchanted swords are commonplace, the allusions to Tolkien may be indirect, but they are always present.

One of the key reasons for the interest in Tolkien's work for large numbers of games players rests not in the heroic story told over the course of *The Lord of the Rings*, but in the complexity of the evocation of place within the work. As with two other fictional spaces that have seen far more long term exploitation in video-game form, *Star Wars* and *Star Trek*, Tolkien's work has primarily been seen as a source text for games not in terms of plot, but in terms of providing a ready made geography of the imagination that comes complete with an already established audience who show every sign of having a desire to find a way of exploring its spaces. The tourist authorities in New Zealand certainly understand the desire of members of the film audience to somehow penetrate the screen, marketing the locations in which the film was shot in the terms of an opportunity to visit the 'real' Middle-earth.[5] Through his books Tolkien had constructed a Middle-earth with a geography, a history and a mythology that always appeared to gesture off to the possibility of further revelation of a consistent world if only we had access to texts as yet unread. In Jackson's films that world was then clothed in a consistent visual aesthetic, and given a representational style as distinctive as that of *Star Wars* or *Star Trek*. In providing both a consistency of visual design and a consistency of what in video-game development would be referred to as 'backstory' the intersection between original literary text and the subsequent films might therefore be expected to provide a particularly appropriate space in which a video game might insert itself.

Any tourists to New Zealand, of course, are likely to be disappointed (although perhaps not the passive victims of Ryan's 'entrapment') if they take the claims to be able to access a meaningfully 'real' Middle-earth too seriously – Jackson's films were self-consciously the product of a meeting between the conventional cinematic techniques of live action (the mechanical record of the material presence of an object on film) and the new possibilities opened up by the computer generated image (CGI). For anyone seeking to explore the space at which contemporary video game and cinema meet, examination of the relationship between *The Lord of the Rings* video games and films can be rewarding because it, too, appears to be a place of unresolved conflict and unsettled resolution. The Middle-earth of the films is already a virtual space, and already a virtual space in which the material image and CGI are not entirely comfortable in each other's company as they compete for screen presence. What is intriguing about the initial four video games for personal computer and major games consoles released between 2002 and 2004, is that they have not taken on board the radical potential of what their reliance on spatial representation means for the player who wishes to immerse themself, or their possibility of providing plural outcomes as a result of player interaction. Instead they seem to have joined the films in what appears to be a conservative wariness towards their own technology. Like the films, the video games owe their very existence to shared CGI technology, but where the films reach closure at a point where there will be no more need for CGI in Middle-earth – with the departure of the Elves and the destruction of Sauron we see not so much the coming of the 'Age of Men' as the departure of the 'Age of Special Effects' – they gesture back constantly to the films as if they are unable to confidently let go of firm reference to their point of origin. It is always dangerous to generalize too much from specific instances and examples, but it may even be possible to see *The Lord of the Rings* video games as representative of the wider current state of dialogue and negotiation between two media forms which have not yet worked out how to co-exist.

THE GAMES OF THE FILMS OF THE BOOKS

When the video-games developer and publisher Electronic Arts secured the licence to make and distribute games closely tied in to the Peter Jackson trilogy of films, they followed a tradition within the industry of seeking the security of a ready-made audience base on which to build a video-game franchise. For all the hyperbole that exists in video-game journalism and professional organizations whose role it is to promote the video-games industry, that would claim that its commercial worth now approximates or even surpasses that of Hollywood, this appeared to be another indication of the position of any 'game of the film' as little more than another example of branded merchandising, where its own aesthetic qualities or specific successes as a pleasurable playing experience are of little consequence compared to the clarity of the association with the film.[6] Unlike the process of transformation from literary to cinematic text that saw Jackson's films scrutinized by the many Tolkien readers who are almost obsessive in their demand for any treatment of Middle-earth to remain consistent and faithful to the original texts, very little seems to be at stake in what the New Media theorists Jay Bolter and Richard Grusin (1999) have termed the 'remediation' from one media form to another in the movement from the big screen of the cinema auditorium to the small screen of the television set or computer monitor in the home. The process of remediation from books to film might initially have generated concern amongst Tolkien's readers, but there was little comparable anxiety about a transfer to a game incarnation. There is an expectation, now, that the branding of a game is as much a commercial inevitability for an action film with a huge budget as a promotional link with a fast-food chain, or the release of an accompanying range of action dolls. Whether it is *The Lord of the Rings*, *Spiderman 2* or the latest production from Walt Disney and Pixar studios, the contemporary big budget cinema release will almost inevitably be accompanied with a video-game tie-in.

Caught among the fractured and dispersed recycling of image and logo for the film among a slew of other licensed products whose appropriateness for branding may often be questionable, the public relationship between the films and the games is, at first, one of clear hierarchical dominance by the films. Their fidelity to Jackson's vision (and not Tolkien's) is contractually policed, as the initial screens of any of the video games make clear through their copyright notices that mark out the limits of ownership for EA when compared to that of New Line Cinema. Much effort has obviously gone into capturing the look of the films, from the modelling of facial features and body shapes of the members of the Fellowship so that they are recognizable, if crude, approximations of the actors, to the replication of the action of the film closely enough for the promotional material to see direct cuts between game sequences and film sequences. The games also seem to recognize the superiority of the film's images over their own in the use of film stills on their packaging, with actual screen-shots from the games relegated to diminutive frames on the back of the CD case while the covers feature the images of the actors, rather than their digital models. Cut scenes, those segments of film shown in pauses between action in the game that act as non-interactive sequences between stages of differing game play to tell their snippets of story and reward and indicate successful play, do not even use the animations of the game, but are taken directly from the film. In the case of *The Battle for Middle Earth* (2004) film images are shown within a discrete window on one of the game screens, anchoring even the practice of one element of gameplay in the continuing context of the films. In part, this points up the technological disadvantage that games have if they are ever evaluated as a purely representational medium. To simply claim that films and games are inevitably converging because of their shared technology as dependent on the computer generated image is to be blind to the way in which what is achieved on screen in the films in terms of the sheer scale of the spectacle provided and the polish given to the computer generated imagery is far in excess of that of current, or foreseeable, games technology.[7]

Everything points to the video game as film's poorer cousin. As the printed material on the case notes for the video game of *The Lord of the Rings: The Return of the King* indicates, the initial promise made in the games is that the player 'Live the Movie. Be the Hero' and 'Live the Epic Adventure'. As such, the games do not gesture towards making a version of Middle-earth available as a space in which the player may engage in free play, but as a space in which the player is engaged in the re-enactment of the extant cinematic text. The video game, at least in the case of the specific example of the Electronic Arts *Lord of the Rings* games, do everything they can to reinforce the primacy of the films of the games.

A negative reading of such fidelity to Jackson's version of Middle-earth might recall Roland Barthes' essay 'Toys' in *Mythologies* (1972: 61), where he bemoans the 'literalness' of those toys that position the child 'as user, never creator; he does not invent the world, he uses it: there are, prepared for him, actions without adventure, without wonder, without joy'. Within the video-game versions of both *The Two Towers* (2002) and *The Return of the King* (2003) the player takes up the role of a member of the Fellowship who moves from action sequence to action sequence, freed for player control only when there are scores of enemies to dispatch. A role-playing video game exists, *The Lord of the Rings: The Third Age* (2004), but the party of adventurers available to the player are a form of fellowship-lite, and feature a Ranger, an Elf, a Dwarf, and other figures whose only major departure from their originals is a random reassignment of genders. Any illusion of complex agency (I can act within the game space according to its rules but in ways not immediately prescribed) in these games is tempered by the constraints of the available freedoms allowed in play. The possibility of the plural in terms of both action and outcome that is inherent to imaginative and creative (video game) play is disabled in a process which is less the enactment of free action in narrative space, and more the re-enactment of actions from the films. And if Barthes is looking back with nostalgia to the wooden toys of the craftsman that had pre-ceded the plastic mass-produced toys of the 1960s, then he could hardly be expected to have approved of this new form of play that moves even further away from the world of the material and the craftsman. Like Barthes' children, playing out roles assigned to them by the literal associations of their toys, it is possible to see an absence of any creative or imaginative possibility in the player as user. The player manipulates the interface to fight off the cave troll in Moria, or to repel the hordes of Orcs and Uruk Hai at the Deeping Wall at Helm's Deep, but any more meaningful choices are denied the player who is, in this limited sense, restricted in role to re-enact rather than even have the illusion of freedom of action. This is not to deny that the games are in themselves successful and pleasurable playing experiences. Indeed, their structure of basic linear movement between moments of button pressing and joystick manipulation as screens are cleared of their population of opposing figures place them firmly within a tradition of gameplay interaction that differs from the action of play in early video games such as *Space Invaders* only in the complexity of the interface and the complexity of the contemporary graphical representation of the action on screen.[8]

The corporate slogan of Electronic Arts might be 'challenge everything', but in their handling of *The Lord of the Rings* licence they certainly did not seek to exploit the potential for video games to challenge established media forms. This is less 'remediation' in Bolter and Grusin's terms, where something new is created at the moment of contact at which new media borrows and adapts and changes the vocabulary of existing media, and more a dressing up of existing video game conventions in the superficial clothing of a film licence. The relationship between film and game iterations of *The Lord of the Rings*, however, might still have something interesting to tell us about a collision between contemporary popular film and con-temporary video games that might see the ushering in of a new and different relationship. That relationship is certainly of a different order than that between the films and any other product that has associated itself with the marketable brand that is *The Lord of the*

Rings, as is evident in the way games and films are cross-marketed. Advertisements for the video game preceded the showing of the films in cinemas, and made much of the possibility of cutting directly from film to game and back again as if seamless transition from one to another were possible. As the DVD releases of the films include promotional material for the games among the 'extras' for which consumers would be expected to pay more, so the games promise 'exclusive movie content' as one of their own selling points. Here films and game both exploit the commercial potential of portraying themselves as sites of potential excess, rather than as closed and complete objects in and of themselves. We might have seen the credits roll at the end of any of the films, and particularly *The Return of the King*, but New Line and Electronic Arts both gesture towards a future in which we will have access to other products that will allow a revisiting of the primary experience of the watching of the films, an iterative return with difference in a re-encounter that will see us always offered another release, be it in the collector's edition on DVD, or in another game. It is here that the video game has the potential to exploit the immersive desire of its consumers to test the limits of consistency in this fictional world. As Tolkien discovered after the eventual success of *The Lord of the Rings*, he had generated interest in a place, and not just a plot, and readers were keen to revisit that space. Where Tolkien provided *The Silmarillion* and (posthumously) *Unfinished Tales*, Jackson and New Line had their special collector's editions with their additional footage and their other additional content, but such traditional media will inevitably be exhausted, and far quicker than the essentially plural video game. It is in this possibility for something other than simple repetition that the games represent something new and different that implies anything but a passive consumer mindlessly immersed in pre-scripted and prescriptive experience.

To some critics, including Bolter and Grusin (1999), the transformative power of the new media forms, including video games, that technology has given birth to is something to be cherished. What is most interesting in their argument throughout *Remediation*, however, is the language of contestation and opposition in which they couch it, and its almost aggressive dependence on notions of a progressive faith in positive transformation through technological advance that would seem to imply that new and old media are involved in some kind of struggle for domination:

In our terms, new technologies of representation proceed by reforming or remediating earlier ones, while earlier technologies are struggling to maintain their legitimacy by remediating newer ones. The cyberenthusiasts argue that in remediating older media the new media are accomplishing social change. (94)

For more negative critics, video games remain a form of popular entertainment that are at best considered somewhat disreputable and immature, and at worst to be a form of consumption that prepares its players for actions and events in the world that are abhorrent and reduce the player not only to the naive and passive consumption of experience, but subject to something that resembles narcotic delusion. Although Paul Virilio (2002: 92) was concerned with a critique of those military-themed video games whose popularity increased during the first Gulf War, for example, he expressed the commonplace unease that many commentators feel when they consider the immersive potential of the video game that he described as a '"drug for the eyes" where virtual and actual realities are confused'.[9]

What this ignores is the concentration on action and agency in contemporary video-game play that is generated by the first encounter with the game space in its mobile state. The question of agency, of course, is at the heart of *The Lord of the Rings* in all its manifestations. It is certainly an issue explored through Frodo, who is only too aware that his choices are limited, and that his freedom to act is circumscribed. Conventional understandings of heroism, however, would insist upon the importance of exercising agency: it is not enough to act, one must also have been free to act in a different way. To be fated to be involved in the clash between great armies and the battle between good and evil is not sufficient. As sophisticated readers we are undoubtedly aware that there is little point to the asking questions of our cinematic or literary texts as if their protagonists had possession of some kind of extratextual agency. It is certainly worth spending some time, however, considering whether the freedom to act, and the imperative to act, in video game play marks a significant departure from our other textual forms, and whether it stands in direct opposition to those forms of play that provide the passivity of 'action without adventure'. To ask the question 'what if?' of the conventional narrative text, whether film or novel, makes little sense beyond making for a potentially interesting parlour game. To ask not only 'what if?', but 'what happens next if I?' is not only possible but crucial within video-game play. This is where the video game moves from re-enactment or rehearsal to allowing imaginative engagement with the game space, and this is the space in which future video games might fully push the boundaries of their still as yet unformed structures and conventions that are still too reliant on echoing the forms of film to provide a form of popular entertainment that goes beyond what either books or film have to offer to finally satisfy that desire to enter a fictional world that Tolkien's text has always provoked.

CHAPTER 12

IN THE TRADITION . . .

Roz Kaveney

It is almost a joke, certainly a cliché, that any large-scale multi-volume fantasy novel will be described on its dust jacket as being 'in the tradition of Tolkien at his best', regardless of its actual merits or the degree to which, if at all, it has been influenced by Tolkien. Such descriptions are an attempt to shill readers into purchasing books; they also, both for good and ill, reflect the immense influence Tolkien has had on his readers and especially perhaps on those of his readers who subsequently become writers. There is inevitably a close relationship between the desire of publishing houses to have new saleable products on their lists, the desire of many readers to buy something which at least superficially adheres to a much-loved formula and the ambition of writers to produce books which resemble those of a writer they admire. It should not be assumed that this relationship is entirely corrupt; life and literature are more complicated than that.

The creation of fantasy as a publishing genre, eventually a highly successful genre, was in large part a consequence of the successful issue of *The Lord of the Rings* in paperback, especially the various US editions, quasi-pirate and approved, of the mid-1960s. Ballantine, who produced the authorized paperbacks, followed this in due course with the Adult Fantasy line of reissues of classics such as the romances of William Morris, the Poictesme novels of James Branch, as well as some current works of High Fantasy such as the novels of Katherine Kurtz and Evangeline Walton. This list over-lapped – Lindsay's *A Voyage to Arcturus* (1968) – with earlier lists of fantasy classics such as that produced by Gollancz, and has been highly influential. Notably, the reissue by Ballantine of Hope Mirrlees' *Lud-in-the-Mist* in 1970 provided a whole generation of British writers – Neil Gaiman and Susanna Clarke to name but the most obvious – with a template for fantasy which quite specificially enabled them to avoid a debt to Tolkien. By the mid-1970s, declining sales and the simple fact that the series editor Lin Carter had acquired most of the material in which he was interested led to the cancellation of the line; Ballantine searched for a new strategy and partly found it in the issue of Terry Brooks' *The Sword of Shannara* perhaps the most obviously derivative of all post-Tolkien quest fantasies.[1] (One of their other answers was the less clearly Tolkien-derived Stephen Donaldson Thomas Covenant trilogy; another turned out to be Piers Anthony's *Xanth* novels. The fact that the series which started from it is charmless and gormless should not entirely blind us to what merits *A Spell for Chamelon* possessed.)

Another possible line was that pursued at roughly the same time by other publishers. In 1963 L. Sprague deCamp had produced for Pyramid Books an anthology *Swords and Sorcery* which drew on the extensive pulp literature of what we may as well call Low High Fantasy, which is to say fiction which is set in the same world as High Fantasy's epic quests but in general chooses to deal with the adventures of rogues who are looking for loot rather than plot tokens, aiming to survive rather than to cure the world's pain. (He produced a similar anthology *The Spell of Seven* in 1965.)

DeCamp reprinted in these books stories by both Robert E. Howard and Fritz Leiber; Low High Fantasy story cycles such as Howard's Conan stories, many of them completed by deCamp and his associates, and Leiber's Fafhrd and the Gray Mouser tales were reissued in paperback in the course of the late 1960s. (Leiber was encouraged by this to write more stories in the cycle, which reflected the preoccupations of his late phase with disillusion and recovery.) DeCamp's own original work in comic portal fantasy, including his collaborations with Fletcher Pratt, continued to be reissued during the 1960s and 1970s and were an influence on such minor writers as Marvin Kaye. It is important to remember that Howard, deCamp and Leiber were of a generation that were formed by the same influences – Dunsany, Eddison – as Tolkien himself; Howard died before Tolkien had published a word of fiction and Leiber and others read him as adults.

One of the most interesting fantasies of the early 1950s is Poul Anderson's *The Broken Sword* (1954) in that it draws on the Scandinavian material that was one of Tolkien's influences, but does so with a bleakness entirely alien to Tolkien. Though the universe Anderson shows us is one in which good has a role, possibly a primary role, there is never quite the sense that all will, in the end, be well that pervades *The Lord of the Rings* in spite of its effective portrayal of the possibility of universal jeopardy. The young Anderson had a tragic view of life – even a conservative like Anderson who found a measure of social hierarchy congenial was not necessarily sold on the essential optimism that, in Tolkien, goes with that sense of the restoration of order.

Those writers in the next generation who specifically rejected the theodicy of Tolkien's trilogy on ideological grounds were inevitably drawn to imitate Howard and Leiber in much of their actual work, even if the models they professed to draw on were more literary. Michael Moorcock was derisory in his attacks on Tolkien, referring to *The Lord of the Rings* as 'Epic Pooh' and claimed as his master the Mervyn Peake of the Gormenghast books (a trilogy only in the sense that Peake was only healthy long enough to write three of them). The various versions of the Eternal Champion which Moorcock wrote about from the early 1960s onwards were posher and more sensitive than Conan, less likely to wander into farce plots than Fafhrd and the Gray Mouser, but they recognizably inhabited the same moral universe even when compelled to save the world. Moorcock's dislike of Tolkien's Christianity resulted in his choosing to make his protagonists defenders of the Balance between Order and Chaos rather than, ultimately, partisans of either side.

It is also crucial that part of what made Moorcock reject Tolkien was the older man's politics around class and hierarchy; Moorcock, as a man of the Left, found the sentimental patrician conservatism espoused by *The Lord of the Rings* repellent. However, as a bohemian aesthete, Moorcock tended to produce protagonists who are antinomian aristocrats rather than working-class heroes. It has also to be noted that Tolkien's central characters, Bilbo and Frodo, are solid members of the rentier class rather than members of what passes for Hobbit aristocracy – Tolkien's Merry and Pippin, it needs remembering in the light of the particular shading of the Peter Jackson films in this respect, are feckless scions of landed gentry, sowing wild oats, rather than mere proletarians.

Moorcock and such associates as M. John Harrison actually wrote material influenced by the pulp Low High Fantasists, but their aspiration was higher than that. The model they professed to admire was Mervyn Peake, the visual precision of whose prose derived in part from his artist's eye for detail. At the same time, it can hardly be said that Peake influenced their plotting save through pessimism – Harrison's *The Pastel City* and *A Storm of Wings* remain firmly in the Low High Fantasy tradition, and even the later, more genre-crossing additions to the Viriconium cycle retain some links to pulp stories of warriors and maguses, even when they are mostly concerned with doomed decadent artists. Harrison has in turn inspired younger writers like China Mieville, whose rejection of Tolkien on political grounds is far more considered and intellectual, far less instinctual. In all of these writers, rejection of Tolkien is a rejection even of an antagonistic relationship with him, a collective view that his influence had been altogether bad.

One of the other strains of fantasy which grew up in the late 1960s was revisionist about gender and to a lesser extent race, but was far more involved with Tolkien and his legacy. Ursula LeGuin's *Earthsea Trilogy* (1968–72) was published in the first instance, like the reissues of Leiber, by Ace Books, who had been responsible for the unauthorized publication of *The Lord of the Rings*. This trilogy, subsequently expanded and auto-critiqued by later volumes such as *Tehanu* (1990), made a point of having its 'good' culture be brown-skinned and its unpleasant theocracy blond, taking quiet note of the tendency of other High Fantasies to be inhabited by the white-skinned. LeGuin's later criticism of herself and her readers in *Tehanu* for not being anti-sexist enough should not obscure the fact that even the male-centred *A Wizard of Earthsea* refused much of fantasy's standard ideological baggage about masculinity and its discontents – Ged is not merely a man who goes on learning, but one who is uneasily aware that there will never be any end to his need to learn more.

LeGuin's relationship with Tolkien is complex and uneasy; she is aware of his influence on her, critical of much of his ideological baggage and totally aware that killing the father, or walking away from him totally, is something boys do, and she need not. At the same time, she found his emphasis on the theme of return highly congenial, and some of her quasi-Taoist thinking about the appropriate use of magic derives from the differentiation made by Tolkien between the showy magical effects of his evil mages and the minimalist use of it in dire necessity by Gandalf, even after his transfiguration. She also welcomed Tolkien's decision to centre his narrative on the unconventional heroism of Bilbo, Frodo and Sam, whose virtues are those of endurance and nurture, and whose courage is more moral than physical. Tolkien was a very long way from being a feminist and yet there were emphases in his work that a feminist like LeGuin could make use of.

Both LeGuin and Tolkien are theoreticians of story. Again, Tolkien's metaphor of the stewpot into which elements are eclectically thrown was one clearly congenial to LeGuin, whose own preferred metaphor of the shopping bag into which the female gatherer puts what comes to hand without necessarily organizing it into something as phallocentric as a plot, with an ending, is to some degree an echo of it.

Much of LeGuin's highly considered and thoughtful relationship with Tolkien takes the form of a strategy of revisionism or refusal. Where Tolkien's plots are set in motion by individual criminality, albeit on the vastest of scales, LeGuin's have to do with the consequences of what is false within, or the tyranny of institutions like the Karhidish religion in which no one single person is specifically guilty of more than petty oppression. Where Tolkien's dragon Smaug is, while personable enough, a traditionalist one with a hoard and a taste for sarcasm and riddles, LeGuin's dragons are far more complexly Other, beings whose whole point is that communication with them is possible, but empathy harder. When, in later books, the relationship between humanity and dragons is shown metaphorically to reflect the complexities of that between men and women, it is a happy piece of ret-conning that never feels like a cheat.

Rather later on, there grew up a strain of High Fantasy which was explicitly feminist and therefore almost as entirely uninterested in having a critical relationship with Tolkien as the Moorcock group and its epigones. Marion Zimmer Bradley's *The Mists of Avalon* (1982) is an Arthuriad centred on the perception that Guenevere is a priestess of the Old Religion, a Celtic paganism back-projected from the works of Gerald Gardiner and Margaret Murray, rather than closely related to what we know of the actual history of Celtic religion, which seems to have been in most respects quite as patriarchal as its successful rivals. Many of Bradley's heirs and imitators avoid such issues by placing their pariah elites of witches, telepaths and elves in fantasy worlds untrammeled by the inconvenience of historical fact.

Much of what has been published as fantasy commercially derives at least as much from the Howard and Leiber tradition, or from

Moorcock, LeGuin and Bradley, as it does from Tolkien, even when its rogues are caught up in plots which oblige them to save the world. Mid-list fantasy is eclectic in its sources – one has only to look at writers like Martha Wells and Barbara Hambly to see all of these influences in full flower, and the same applies to better-selling writers like Robin Hobb (Megan Lindholm) and George R. R. Martin, who have demonstrated that it is possible to write large-scale best-selling novels of heroic fantasy whose debt to Tolkien is peripheral at best. However, most of the best-selling fantasies of the decades since Brooks have nonetheless been written in a mode that clearly derives from imitation of Tolkien and from a relationship with him which is one of endebtedness rather than primarily antagonism and it is this strain which we will now consider – such texts as Brooks *Shannara* books,[1] David Edding's *The Belgariad*,[2] Stephen Donaldson's *Chronicles of Thomas Covenant the Unbeliever*, Terry Goodkind's *The Sword of Truth*,[3] Robert Jordan's *The Wheel of Time*[4] and Tad William's *Memory, Sorrow and Thorn*.[5]

The post-Tolkien fantasy can be recognized partly through its scale – *The Lord of the Rings*'s three volumes have usually been exceeded both numerically and in terms of the size of individual volumes – and partly through the imitative use of recognizable tropes. As a general rule, and with variations that may take the form of deliberate refusal of the tropes, a Dark Lord who has attempted to take power on earlier occasions, often in the distant past, and been defeated, is returning to potency with the assistance of creatures he has warped and other allies. A group of the powerless is assembled, often under the tutelage of the wise, and they travel the threatened Land, gathering both the wisdom and the talismanic objects which are needed to defeat Evil. Martial valour is important to this victory, but so is a capacity for fine discrimination, and perhaps compassion. At story's end, to some degree, earlier falls from grace are partly compensated for, but at some terrible price.

Some of what is taken from Tolkien is what John Clute and I, in the *Encyclopaedia of Fantasy*, termed maggots – half-baked and offensive unexamined ideas about the importance of virginity, the role of women and the innate evil of certain groups that derive eclectically from religion, Victorian pseudo-science and Orientalism. Some of it is more interesting, if equally unexamined – an assumption, for example, that evil is less capable of understanding the motives of the good than vice versa, and a belief that Providence works through paradox. Another often-copied Tolkien mannerism is the interpolation of songs – where Tolkien was at least a minor poet of the Georgian school, few of his imitators are that competent.

Interpolated stories are one of the ways in which Tolkien gives his readers a sense of the deep abyss of time, which provides his narrative with roots. We know far better now how much *The Lord of the Rings* was merely one of a number of narratives which Tolkien had fleshed out in his mind on paper and the extent to which the interpolations and appendices are allusions to these other works. What this background does in the specific context of *The Lord of the Rings* is to provide the trilogy with a thickness of epic texture which has always been one of its major appeals – each reference slingshots the reader into a sense of the vastness of Tolkien's project. Most of Tolkien's imitators have at least attempted something of the sort, but without decades of rumination on their secondary world's back story – accordingly, the texture is liable to be significantly thinner. The chunks of mythology with which David Eddings starts each volume of the *Belgariad* are a good example of this limitation, as is the comparative slightness of his portrayal both there and in appended volumes like *Belgarath the Sorcerer* of the burden of an immortality that causes his mages to outlive everyone they care about.

An aspect of Tolkien which inspired his new readership of the 1960s was his distrust of technology and its effects. Pollution and environmental degradation are seen almost always in post-Tolkien fantasy as examples of debasement and desecration, as the outward signs of inner corruption. Mordor and the lands on its borders are a transmogrification of the industrial landscapes of Tolkien's childhood after he moved to the Midlands (UK) from South Africa, as well as the churned mud of World War One's trenches – one of his strengths as opposed to his imitators is that these were direct elements in his lived experience. Donaldson manages an effective portrayal of debasement by having evil inflict plagues and corruption on the Land somewhat in the manner of Jehovah. Williams restricts his portrayal of industrial debasement to the climactic scenes in which Simon undergoes ordeals by fire and water in Pyrates underground foundry; in scenes with malign giants, creeping squidlets and ravenous burrowers he derives from Tolkien's other perception of evil, that it represents a return of repressed elements never properly dealt with.

The first of the major imitators, Terry Brooks became, with the publication of *The Sword of Shannara* in 1977, and has remained, a highly successful author for as long as he has stayed at least notionally with the Shannara brand name, though later volumes have derived far less obviously from Tolkien. (His other lighter books, *Magic Kingdom for Sale* for example, have generally been rather less commercially successful.) For one thing, the main line of *The Sword of Shannara*'s plot uses up much of the cure for the world's pain, destruction of the Dark Lord, and metamorphosis of an ugly duckling hero to full heroic status that are part of the template for post-Tolkien fantasy. For another, where the world of *The Lord of the Rings* is one that has fallen away from close communication with the deity and with the natural world, the world of the Shannara books is one which has changed to a world of magic from one in which there was once advanced technology. Several of the later books deal in part with left-over pieces of such technology – *Antrax* (2001) has as a subsidiary villain a vast autonomous and self-aware computer. Generally speaking, Brooks is at his most interesting when his books derive least from Tolkien, while remaining within a world created originally in imitation of him.

What the success of *The Sword of Shannara* ensured was that one of the main strains of fantasy publishing would become and remain material which derived much of its material second hand from Tolkien. It would be a literature of comfort in which the ability of the reader to expect what a book or more probably a series of books would deliver would be at least as important as originality. Furthermore, where Tolkien was creating Middle-earth and its inhabitants out of his long fascination with dead and created languages, and with literature that demonstrated the potential of those languages for expression of thematic material he found congenial, and for sheer linguistic complexity, many of his imitators were mostly concerned with Tolkien and the more superficial of his techniques and themes. Many of them have a tendency to verbal infelicity which indicates a failure to pay attention to Tolkien's good ear for such things as names – Robert Jordan's footsoldiers of evil, for example, are called Trollocks.

To take but one example of much copied elements of *The Lord of the Rings*, Norman Cantor in his *Imagining the Middle Ages* (Morrow 1991) rightly points to the extent to which Tolkien's portrayal of the arduousness and duration of long journeys on foot and horseback has altered popular perception of the lived experience of pre-technological epochs. Tolkien disdained allegory, but his perception of the hardships of travel was inevitably informed by his Catholic sense of all mortification of the flesh as something which can be used as spiritual discipline. Hardship flenses Frodo of much of his earlier bourgeois taste for comfort and is part of what enables him to resist the temptation of the Ring for as long as he does.

In many of the imitative epics which derive from Tolkien, journeying is a plot device with little in the way of moral content. It is a mechanism for wandering among peoples who represent aspects of the moral universe far more schematically than Tolkien's ever did, for collecting plot tokens (Nick Lowe's useful term for the talismanic items often crucial to fantasy plots) and for collecting travelling companions. In David Eddings, in particular, it largely lacks emotional content – Tolkien was formed by his experiences in the trenches of World War One and all of his journeys into war and peril have to some degree that sense of the journey up the line to death. Where that sense of potential doom is lacking, as it is in Eddings' *Belgariad* sequence, it is not enough to be travelling through difficult terrain.

Tad Williams' Simon and Miriamele, in *Memory, Sorrow and Thorn* undergo journeyings that are a part of the moral education that will fit them for rule – it is important that both nearly die on journeys, he from starvation and exposure, she from storms at sea. The jeopardy is real and evocatively felt; it is also there for a purpose other than the requirements of the Tolkien template since the hardship and jeopardy that Simon and Miriamele undergo are there to equip them for monarchic rule. Where Frodo's hardship fits him for his mission, the mission Simon believes himself to be on is a colossal mistake; what saves the world is his capacity for compassion, a capacity that was present in him from the start.

In Stephen Donaldson's *Chronicles of Thomas Covenant, the Unbeliever*, Ballantine's other great fantasy investment of 1977, the journey is as much fever dream as steady plodding. Donaldson's debt and relationship to Tolkien is sufficiently marginal in most respects that he almost fails to belong in the group of Tolkien's heirs; what he does derive from Tolkien, while putting his own spin on it, is a sense of journeying as moral experience. In his case, there is the complication that Thomas, as a leper, dare not allow himself too much sense of the reality of the landscape through which he passes because he is compelled by the necessity of his condition to a brutal realism threatened by the possibility that he has wandered through a portal into some other realm. Hallucination is less of a threat to his moral universe than magic – journeying potentially regrounds him in the Land, whereas he needs to be grounded in his constant need to inspect his extremities for further signs of decay.

In the end, of course, Thomas finds his way to a balanced perception that allows him to perceive the Land as real enough to involve him in moral responsibility for the welfare of it and its inhabitants, while maintaining his distance from full commitment to its epistemo-logical status. Donaldson demonstrated that it is possible for the multi-decker fantasy novel to be a work of moral earnestness at a point where Brooks and Eddings were watering down Tolkien into a set of plot gestures and decorative descriptions, and ignoring part of the point of what epic is for. Unfortunately, this seriousness on Donaldson's part has been to some extent vitiated by his inability to leave the material alone – in 2004 he embarked on a third Thomas Covenant trilogy in spite of Thomas' death in the sixth volume – and by a style whose over-reliance on unusual vocabulary and set phrases many readers find alienating.

The other serious weakness of Donaldson's work is one he shares with other High Fantasists such as Brooks, Robert Jordan and Terry Goodkind. One of the strengths of *The Lord of the Rings* is Tolkien's creation of a cast of characters about all of whom we genuinely care – the emphasis placed by the title of the first volume *The Fellowship of the Ring* indicates that this is, among other things, a novel about comradeship in which the efforts of a large cast of characters are essential to the quest's success. It is possible to engage passionately with Thomas Covenant and his fate, but few readers feel as strongly about, say, the giant companion whose laughter in the face of defeat makes it possible for Thomas to defeat his adversary Lord Foul as they do about even a comparatively peripheral figure like Tolkien's Legolas.

Eddings' admirers often argue that he is an exception among his peers and point to characters like the princely thief Silk as examples of endearing characters; in this case, and arguably even with the dangerous virtuous wizard and sorceress Belgarath and Polgara, 'asserts these characters' lovableness so often that he wears the readers down. It is better to show than to tell, but sometimes telling often enough is reasonably effective.

The same is true of the characters met in chance encounters. Tolkien's Elf-lords and monsters are memorable; most of those of his imitators not. A partial exception can be made here for Jordan, in that his chance encounters are often with people or creatures whose status is at least intellectually interesting; Jordan's interminable *Wheel of Time* sequence is at its most interesting in side-bars to the conventional post-Tolkien plot where he creates, for example, a warrior people the motivating force of whose frenzied bravery is guilt at having abandoned their original pacifism.

There is a naive creativity to Jordan, a capacity for wondering 'what if?' about the cliches of fantasy which sometimes leads him into odd tangents like the obsession of his conspirator nuns with corporal punishment, and sometimes creates genuinely interesting plot strands like the need to find a way of operating magically around the contamination of all male magic. Unfortunately, this is the positive side of a tendency to proliferate, which means that the sequence has extended to so many volumes: each of Rand's original companions has acquired some sort of kingdom with the affairs of which we have to be so continually updated that the sequence's central topic – the battle against a Malign Sleeper Dark Lord and his various accomplices – has slowed down to a snail's pace.

Terry Goodkind's sidebar characters and plots are interesting primarily in terms of the way they fit into his overarching cynicism. We discover in *Wizard's First Rule* that 'People are stupid' and the various death cults and groups of the magically empowered that we encounter subsequently do nothing to change this perception. The utter ruthlessness of both good and bad characters makes for a depressing read – Goodkind starts cynical and becomes bleak. The weakness of the *Sword of Truth* sequence lies in just this – that its hero and heroine are only likable by comparison with the utterly murderous.

What Goodkind *does* bring to the post-Tolkien epic is a sense of evil that is genuinely disturbing, deriving from twentieth-century monsters like Hitler and Jim Jones. His use of sado-masochistic imagery is altogether more interesting than Jordan's slightly fetishistic use of spanking – there is a real sense of the perverse in Goodkind.

One of the weaknesses of his rivals is in this area. Eddings, for example, has Torak, a Cain-like fallen deity hideously marked by the presumption which damaged the world. Torak's minions are a cabal of evil mages, continually trying to outdo each other. All of which would be impressive enough were the felt experience of evil in the Belgariad even as intense as that in Jordan, whose evil enchanters sometimes have glamour to make them interesting, but the final encounter is as slight and bland as anything else in Eddings, whose charm and weakness is his fondness for pastel-coloured prose.

One of the many strengths of Williams' *Memory, Sorrow and Thorn* has to do with his refusal to deal in the moral absolutes of Tolkien. For one thing, Williams deals far more convincingly than Tolkien with redemption – where it is necessary for the salvation of the world that Gollum finally fall to his damnation, the brutal warrior Guthwulf is changed forever by the consequences of a single unselfish act. He intervenes to save the housekeeper Rachel from murder by the evil magician Pryrates and is blinded for his pains, and left wandering in the cellarage of the Hayholt, the edifice which dominates Williams' trilogy. In a particularly telling moment, starving, he decides not to kill a cat and we realize that he has changed. He helps Simon escape from the vast waterwheel to which the youth has been bound and dies of his efforts. Williams' world is one in which it is possible for the evil to change.

(The analogy between Guthwulf and Shakespeare's Gloucester is obvious, and points to the broader influence of *King Lear* on a tale of an old king and his younger heirs, one of them good and one of them bad. Williams' interest in the moral richness of quite minor characters is, in aspiration at least, Shakespearian. Given Tolkien's professed disdain for Shakespeare, it is relevant that one of his most interesting imitators should so clearly disagree.)

Williams' refusal of moral absolutes extends to his take on the figure of the Dark Lord; the principal adversary in *Memory, Sorrow and Thorn*, the Storm Lord Ineluki, is a being who has suffered great wrongs, though his principal ally, the Norn Queen, is more concerned with the effects of great age and stored-up grudges of a trivial, almost domestic kind. What Ineluki wants is not to have died, and he is prepared to destroy time and everything bound by it to return to the world – what he wants is something even more unjust than the human-on-elf genocide of which his death was part. This selfishness is what he shares with his pawns – Pryrates wants knowledge at the expense of all other value and the corrupted King Elias wants his wife not to have died.

What enables Simon and Miriamele to defeat them is in part a moral education which enables them to get past their own innate capacities for selfishness. Miriamele would like nothing better than to have her mad debased father restored to her as he once was – but the most merciful thing she can do for him is to kill him once Ineluki has possessed him body and soul. Simon would like back his carefree life as a kitchen-boy and scholar's apprentice – but he returns to the Hayholt as its lord. He would like back the simple affection he and Miriamele shared before he knew she was a princess – instead, they have a marriage based on acceptance of each other's sexual history with others and on the fact that, even if they did not in fact love each other, their marriage would be a necessity of state.

One of the reasons why *Memory, Sorrow and Thorn* is arguably the most interesting of the post-Tolkien narratives is that Williams is so questioning of some of Tolkien's unexamined values – there is a serious extent to which he is writing out of polemical engagement with Tolkien's positions on the role of women, or attitudes in *The Lord of the Rings* that are sufficiently cognate with racism to have appealed to neo-Nazis. In particular, and not without a certain dishonesty, he tries to have his cake and eat it – Simon is at once the lost heir of a rightful dynasty and a working-class lad rising on merit, he is at once a dragon slayer and warrior and someone whose principal claim to heroism derives from his endurance, and from the ecstatic bleak vision of reality he undergoes when bound to the wheel. (This picks up on experiences undergone by Gandalf and Frodo in *The Lord of the Rings* – Williams is not merely antagonistic and revisionist in his use of Tolkien.)

Another reason is that, far more than the other post-Tolkien narratives, *Memory, Sorrow and Thorn* shows the footprints of other influences. In the first volume *The Dragonbone Chair*, in particular, Simon derives from T. H. White's Wart as much as from Frodo; without realizing it, he undergoes the education of a future king, and gets it as much from the housekeeper Rachel (who gets the last word of the body of the trilogy) as from his Merlin, Doctor Morgenes. His self-education by clambering around the tunnels and roofs of the Hayholt, eavesdropping on secrets and catching sight of distant princesses, is reminiscent of the early phase of the career of Steerpike in Mervyn Peake's *Gormenghast* books, before that other young man on the make turns to evil. The Hayholt itself unites the influence of Tolkien with that of Peake – it is at once a gloriously complicated edifice, a haunted palace of the mind, and a repository of centuries of secrets, and repressed bad faith; it is a worthy successor of elements in both writers, because Williams learned, in this first of his major works, that the importance of an influence is to use it, and be transformed by it, not to be imprisoned by it.

NOTES

CHAPTER 1: TOWARDS A BETTER TOLKIEN CRITICISM

1   There is a good round-up of some of the most egregious in Shippey (1992: 1–5 and 292–5), and see also Curry (1997: 15–33). Rosebury is somewhat more forgiving (2003: 1–9 and 196–220). *J. R. R. Tolkien: This Far Land*, edited by Robert Giddings (1984), attempts to engage Tolkien with early post-modernist approaches, but it is so dogmatic and heavy-handed that it reads like a parody of early 1980s post-modernism. Just to choose one random bizarre text, Nick Otty's 'The Structuralist's Guide to Middle-earth' presents several long discussions in which the author uses the weakest form of folk-etymology (what the word sounds like to him); so we get 'Shagrat (strange sexual practices(?), hairy rat, aquatic bird rat), Sauron (sour one (!))' (Giddings 1984: 168).

2   For sections of *The Lord of the Rings* as a serial, see *FR*, Foreword, 6; *Letters* 103–6.

3   Documented in detail throughout *The History of Middle-earth* volumes VI–IX (*The Return of the Shadow, The Treason of Isengard, The War of the Ring, Sauron Defeated*) (Tolkien 2003).

4   For the difficulties of developing a clean text of *The Lord of the Rings*, see Anderson (1988) 'Note on the Text'. Even the clean text is problematic. Christopher Tolkien notes that 'bed-loft' (*FR*, II, vi, 359) should be 'bird-loft'; 'bird-loft' was in the fair copy manuscript but was left out of the typescript. Since the typescript and various later versions of the text were proofed by Tolkien, but 'bed-loft' was not changed, its status is not a simple matter (*Treason* 243 n. 47). Similarly, the description of the great hall in Minas Tirith appears to have been affected by a line-jumping error in the final typescript (*RK*, V, i, 26; *War* 288).

5   The source of the phrase 'mythology for England' is Humphrey Carpenter's 1977 biography of Tolkien; Anders Stenström argues convincingly that Carpenter spliced quotations from two different letters (1995: 310–11). For additional discussion, see Drout and Wynne (2000: 111–13). The influence of the letter to Milton Waldman (*Letters* 144–5)

is very great; this author has not been completely successful at resisting the temptation to quote it (Tolkien 2002: 13–14; Drout 2004a: 229).

6 I refer here to what Hilary Wynne and I termed the 'source study' school of criticism. Our listing was not exhaustive, and source study works have continued to proliferate since our article was published (Drout and Wynne 2000: 106–8 and *passim*). For more recent works see many of the essays in Chance 2003 and 2004.

7 For a more detailed discussion that acknowledges the ambiguities, see Christopher Tolkien's introduction to *Lost Tales I* (Tolkien 1983).

8 For *The Notion Club Papers*, see *Sauron* (145–327); for a discussion see Flieger, *A Question of Time*.

9 Keeping track of the changing narrators and frame narratives is exceptionally difficult, but Gergely Nagy has a clear discussion (2003: 250–2).

CHAPTER 2: TIME

1 Hereafter *LOTR: Fellowship*, *LOTR: Towers*, *LOTR: Return*.

2 At other times – and increasingly, it would appear, in later life as the novel's success and imaginative power to a wide audience became clear – his discussions of the moral and theological import of his work seem to qualify these claims.

3 However Tolkien readily admitted that, as comparatively thorough and dense as it might be, the cultural realization of Middle-earth was far from complete, and necessarily bounded by the limitations of his own competences (he confessed to particular sketchiness in his knowledge of the applied arts – clothes, architecture, pottery, etc. – and music): 'even a committee of experts in different branches could not complete the overall picture' (*Letters* 196).

4 In Erwin Segal's explanation, 'When one reads [or views, or hears] a narrative . . . he or she is often required to take a cognitive stance within the world of the narrative. A location within the world of the narrative serves as the center from which the sentences are interpreted' (quoted in Herman 2002: 13).

5 Dates and calculations are based on Tolkien's chronology in *The Lord of the Rings*, Appendix B. There is also material – notably at the Council of Elrond, for example, Gandalf's brief account of Saruman's earliest subversion of the work of the White Council some 90 years before his first meeting with Bilbo situated as it were at an outlying boundary of the contextual and the properly archaic, but as we shall see the Council is most importantly extended into the archaic dimension.

6 By contrast, Tolkien's frequent jocular asides to his juvenile readership in *The Hobbit* – which Tolkien subsequently regretted – draw repeated

(implicit) attention to the difference between the time/space of the fantasy narrative and that of its consumption. The issue of the novel's (non-allegorical) 'applicability' to contemporary world affairs (helpfully discussed by Shippey 2000: 164–71) also obviously relates to contemporary extension.

7   In fact, although Jackson blames Aragorn's enforced idleness on Tolkien, this is an occasion where Jackson's desire to streamline and intensify dramatic action has created a 'problem' where none existed in the text: in the novel, Aragorn sets out (with the Dunedain) for the Paths of the Dead separately from, but almost simultaneously with, Théoden's departure for Harrowdale. It is because in *LOTR* Aragorn attends the muster of Rohan – and is more importunately set on his way to the Paths of the Dead by Elrond's arrival with the reforged Anduril and news of Arwen's imminent demise – that he is compelled to 'hang around' at Edoras awaiting the lighting of the beacons.

8   *The Lord of the Rings* of course also employs parallel narration, in larger overlapping chunks, but another obvious source of Jackson's narrative strategy for *LOTR* is the parallel montage of *Return of the Jedi* (1984).

CHAPTER 3: GOTHIC ECHOES

1   Jane Chance in her 2001 study of *The Lord of the Rings* observes that the essential institutional model of Bentham's 'panoptican' identified by Foucault in 'The Eye of Power' is 'the same model used by Tolkien to locate the nature of Sauron's power, Saruman's power, Shelob's power, and even the Sackville Bagginses' power' (Chance 2001: 21).

2   For a useful brief account of the use of the term 'Gothic', see Robin Sowerby, 'The Goths in History and Pre-Gothic Gothic' in Punter 2000: 15–26.

3   See Jerrold E. Hogle, 'The Gothic Ghost of the Counterfeit and the Progress of Abjection' in Punter 2000: 293–304 and Jerrold E. Hogle, 'Introduction: The Gothic in Western Culture' in Hogle 2002: 1–20.

4   John Ellison in 1991 made the connection between *The Lord of the Rings* and those 'horrid novels' apparently satirized in Jane Austen's *Northanger Abbey*, seeing echoes of Ann Radcliffe's work in Tolkien's descriptive detail.

5   See, for example, Kenneth McLeish, 'The Rippingest Yarn of All' in Giddings 1983: 125–36.

6   The influence of Tolkien's boyhood reading of Rider Haggard on the creation of Gollum has been discussed by William Rogers II and Michael R. Underwood in an essay that compares Gollum with the 'Gagool' of *King Solomon's Mines* as examples of degeneration (Clark and Timmons 2000: 122–31).

7 Jay D. Salisbury suggests that 'when the Wanderer appears in the Gothic novel it embodies the dreadful uncertainty upon which subjects and structures of meaning found their epistemologies' (Salisbury 2001: 46).

8 'Another highly theological bit is Galadriel and the land of Lórien, almost transparently a vision of the Immaculate ... There is no stain over Lórien.' Father Charles Dilke, cited in Pearce 1998: 151.

9 Jane Chance suggests that Gollum is Cain-like in his murder of his cousin to secure the Ring and that 'the two names of Gollum-Sméagol dramatize the fragmenting and divisive consequences of his fall into vice, the "Gollum" the bestial sound of his swallowing as an expression of his gluttony and his greed, the "Sméagol" in its homonymic similarity to Déagol as a sound relating him to a group of others like him to establish his common hobbitness' (Nitzche 1979: 101).

CHAPTER 4: THE ONE RING

1 Carter lists eight points of similarity between Tolkien's Ring and Wagner's opera-cycle, and quotes from *Seigfried* Act III: 'And could he discover the Ring,/It would make him the lord of the world!' (Carter 2003: 128). Tolkien, however, was angered by a Swedish translator's assumption that 'the Ring is in a certain way "der Nibelungen Ring" ', writing to Allen and Unwin on 23 February 1961, that 'both rings were round and there the resemblance ceases' and adding that 'the "Nibelung" traditions ... [have] nothing whatsoever to do with *The Lord of the Rings*' (*Letters* 306–7)

2 In one of the weaker moments of visual realization in Peter Jackson's generally impressive movie version, Sauron is shown wielding the Ring in a manner not derived from the book: he strides into battle wielding a giant mace, and the Ring seems to augment the power of the blow of this club, scattering dozens of Men and Elves with each sweep. But this is, when you think about it, a rather feeble manifestation of what amounts to – in modern parlance – a weapon of mass destruction.

3 Relatively few critical studies have addressed the novel in these terms, although one exception is Stratford Caldecott's *Secret Fire: The Spiritual Vision of J. R. R. Tolkien* (2003). Caldecott quotes from the Catholic catechism (para 1147: 'God speaks to man through the visible creation') and argues that 'a sense of divine providence, of things meaning more than we know, of coincidences needing to be understood, is of course one of the strongest and most lasting impressions one receives from *The Lord of the Rings*' (63). Caldecott has a different reading of the Ring to mine, however; seeing it as 'the archetypal "Machine" ' which 'exemplifies the dark magic of the corrupted will' (60).

4　'The theological significance of the sacraments lies in: (1) the exhibition of the principle of Incarnation. By the embodiment of spiritual reality in material form an appropriate counterpart of the union of God with man in the Person of Christ is made patent; (2) Their expression of the objectivity of God's action on the human soul . . .; (3) As ordinances mediated through the Church, their essentially social structure (Cross 1997: 1435). Sacraments work *ex opere operato*, which is to say it is the Grace itself, and not the person administrating them, that validates them: a sacrament administered by a priest is not invalidated should it transpire that the particular priest was married, a murderer or mad.

5　See for instance Shippey 1992: 177–84.

6　Something similar was the case with Hobbits as well: 'As far as I know Hobbits were universally monogamous (indeed they very seldom married a second time, even if wife or husband died very young)' (Letter to A. C. Nunn, drafted prob. late 1958–early 1959; *Letters* 293).

7　Tolkien stresses the sense of Tom's house as a safe circle through which the Hobbits pass. They enjoy their only contented nights' sleep in Tom's beds. His house has windows 'at either end . . . one looking east and the other looking west' (*FR*, I, vii, 169). It is repeatedly described as suffused with golden light.

CHAPTER 6: HOME

1　It is not a question here of giving a precise date at which the modern begins; instead, as Fredric Jameson argues, 'Modernity is not a concept but rather a narrative category' (2002: 94) that comes to form and express the processes of continual transformation that people and societies experience.

2　J. R. R. Tolkien, letter to Milton Walshman, 1951, reprinted in Tolkien (1999: xiii–xvi).

3　It is only perhaps in the light of the transformation at the end of *The Lord of the Rings* that Tolkien's description of Hobbits at the beginning of *The Hobbit* takes on its full significance: 'what is a Hobbit? I suppose Hobbits need some description nowadays, since they have become rare and shy of the Big People, as they call us. They are (or were) a little people, about half our height, and smaller than the bearded dwarves' (Tolkien 1995: 4).

4　It is for this reason that the process of 'scouring' and rebuilding the Shire is vital to the novel, and its omission from Peter Jackson's otherwise entirely remarkable film trilogy was so problematic.

5　This equation of 'revealing' and 'truth' develops from Heidegger's earlier argument that the ideas of truth as a correspondence between a statement and the world or as a coherence between statements are founded upon a prior process of the statement's 'revealing' or 'unconcealing' the state of affairs that exists, for which he uses the Greek term *alētheia*. For his exposition of this, see Heidegger (1962: 256–73).

6   The German-language text of this lecture can be found in Martin Heidegger's *Gesamtausgabe*, vol. 7, p. 61; the translation of this passage is from Pattison (2000: 60).

7   This redefinition of home, which transforms its ontological force, is central to Sigmund Freud's discussion of 'the uncanny' (*das Unheimliche*) in his essay of the same name (Freud 1985), which has been taken by a number of thinkers as a key trope through which contemporary experience can be thought. There is not enough space here to engage with Freud's argument, but a detailed and nuanced reading that develops some of the ideas presented here can be found in Royle (2003).

CHAPTER 7: WOMEN

1   This is 'common knowledge' in *Beowulf* studies (Glosecki 1999: 44 n.63). For discussion see Bremmer (1980).

2   *Beowulf* 3065b. Citations from *Beowulf* are taken from Mitchell et al. (1998) and will be cited parenthetically by line number. All translations are my own.

3   More than 90 per cent of the glosses and emendations accepted today are Klaeber's own or accepted by Klaeber (Kelly 1983).

4   For major discussions of these roles, see Enright (1996), Sklute (1990), Bennett (1989), Welsh (1991), Mustanoja (1967) and Bennett (1992).

5   His protective role is repeatedly, perhaps ironically, stated at *Beowulf* 371b, 428a, 456b, 663a, 1044a and 1321b.

6   Cf. Lees (1997: 152) 'women, as well as men, produce and use culture, sometimes in similar ways, more often in quite different ones'.

7   Cf. the very negative reading of Hrothgar in Irving (1989: 52).

8   Richard North has argued that the offer which Wealhtheow contests is the adoption of Beowulf via the hand of his daughter in marriage: '*Beowulf* and the *Aeneid*: Four Episodes', paper given to the London Old and Middle English Research Seminar, 24 November 2004.

CHAPTER 8: MASCULINITY

I would like to thank the Charles Phelps Taft Memorial Fund and the Department of English and Comparative Literature at the University of Cincinnati for providing the funds and leave that allowed me to conduct the initial research leading to this essay. Special thanks also to Jana

Evans Braziel, whose work on Haitian diasporic masculinities deeply influenced my thinking in what follows.

1 See Jonathan Evans (2003: 194–224), who claims that Tolkien's race of 'Men' 'includes other kinds of people', though he suggests that in their common fallen condition, 'each of Tolkien's races symbolizes a particular facet of *human* beings in the real world' (197–8). Though I am not as interested in upholding Tolkien's theological view of humankind, Evans's focus is extremely useful in thinking about the purposes to which a unifying masculinity may be put.

2 It is clear from some of his writings that Tolkien meant to be anti-racist, especially as racism was inflected by the biological theories propounded in the late nineteenth and early twentieth centuries (and propagated by the Nazi government). See Christine Chism (2003: 63–92), who reads the ultimate destruction of the Ring as Tolkien's confrontation with the politics and ethics of mythmaking, arguing that 'Each of Tolkien's created peoples opens a different set of ethical questions about the aesthetic' (66). His *moral cartography* causes some rather awkward defenses against racism, however. See Patrick Curry (1995: 126–38), who claims that 'it is grossly insulting to his readers to assume they automatically transfer their feelings about Orcs to all the swart or slant-eyed people they encounter in the street' (127). Virginia Luling (1995) seeks to counter her acknowledgment that the Southrons, outside of a single moment of individuation when Sam wonders about the identity of a fallen warrior, 'remain vague, undeveloped figures, swarthy, in scarlet, and waving scimitars, or bearded and axe-wielding, never moving beyond the derived stereotype' (56), finally with a thought experiment that writes the blank pages of the Red Book to include a story of King Elessar's recognition of a man of the South as an old friend from his days as a Ranger (57).

3 In her *Crossing the Line: Racial Passing in Twentieth-Century U.S. Literature and Culture* (2000), Gayle Wald pithily sums up much thinking in critical race studies by noting, 'although race is a fiction, racial identities are both substantive and "real" '(187). The two volumes *Race Critical Theories: Text and Context*, ed. Philomena Essed and David Theo Goldberg (2002); and *Theories of Race and Racism: A Reader*, ed. Leo Back and John Solomos (2000), do a very good job of gathering together key voices in outlining the relation of race as a moral and social category to constructions of bodily and geographical difference. Particularly important to the concerns of this essay, articles in the collection *Race and the Subject of Masculinities*, ed. Harry Stecopoulos and Michael Uebel (1997), challenge the invisible privileges assumed by (white) masculinities.

4 Traditional imperialist practices are often associated with a need for

history, since, as Clare Lees and Gillian Overing remark in their essay, 'Signifying gender and empire' (2004: 1–16): 'Empires are marked by chronologies as much as geographies' (2). See Verlyn Flieger, *A Question of Time: J.R.R. Tolkien's Road to Faërie* (1997), who traces the temporal tension in Tolkien between history and mythos. Tolkien's conception of time in *The Lord of the Rings* is widely thought to follow a grand chronology that figures legend by incorporating whiffs of nostalgia and feelings of loss. Chism (2003: 86) sees the destruction of the Ring as a retreat from myth into history. Yet with the return to mortality in the Age of Men, it should be added, there is also a suspension of history proper: Aragorn's accession is the culmination of a history that has no future. As Tolkien himself acknowledged in a late letter of 1972 (Carpenter 1981: 419), he was left with little to say about Aragorn's actual rule: 'Then I of course discovered that the King's Peace would contain no tales worth recounting; and his wars would have little interest after the overthrow of Sauron'.

5 This 'crisis' theory of masculinity, wherein phallic, hegemonic or dominant masculinities are always on the verge of falling to pieces, suggests that Tolkien is indeed a post-war writer, as different critics have claimed (though citing different wars). Arthur Brittan, in *Masculinity and Power* (1989), points out that this theory assumes men in previous centuries knew who they were, suggesting the appeal of historicized myths that unify heroic formations of masculinity. See Steven Cohan, *Masked Men: Masculinity and the Movies in the Fifties* (1997), who investigates the crisis that increased domesticity produced in masculinities after World War Two. Peter Middleton (1992), connects Superman's appeal in the Cold War to his 'defensive masculinity', which is related to an ever-impending threat of crisis (6). In defending Tolkien against his critics, Thomas Shippey (1995) invokes a similar binary to put masculinity in crisis, characterizing the literary world that received Tolkien's fiction as dominated by 'privileged young men, often homosexuals, often Old Etonians, deeply contemptuous of the older generation, and classifiable as Naifs, Dandies, or Rogues' (91). Tolkien, like C.S. Lewis and others who would have felt the 'deepest distaste' for such men, 'dropped out . . . creating a cult of self-conscious simplicity, heartiness, even Philistinism, as a kind of protection' (91).

6 See Nick Otty (1984: 154–77), who notes in his entry on 'Race' that 'there are some curiously contradictory judgments concerning cross-breeding between "races". It is evidently acceptable for Aragorn to wed Arwen, an Elf . . . But Treebeard is shocked to his roots at the idea that there has been any blending of the "races of Orcs and Men" ' (173).

7 See Alasdair MacIntyre's *After Virtue* (1984). Although MacIntyre only obliquely acknowledges that the Latin *virtus* vests the qualities extolled

in the tradition he traces solely in men, he more broadly suggests that these characteristics depend upon their visible performance, 'A man in heroic society is what he does' (122). See Guy Halsall (2004: 18–39), who traces the multiplicity of masculinities emerging during the late Roman era even as he acknowledges the unifying idea that 'A dominant form of masculinity was based upon notions of civic virtue' (21).

8 Since the 'New Age' of Men is 'characterized fundamentally by a lack of boundaries', Tolkien's trilogy can be said to figure what Michael Hardt and Antonio Negri (2000) identify as the 'concept of Empire' (as opposed to imperialism) (xiv). Besides erecting a 'spatial totality', Empire so-defined is also 'an order that effectively suspends history' (xiv), eerily matching Aragorn's ability to master an enduring epoch in his ascension to the throne. These correspondences are important to this essay only to the extent that Tolkien's trilogy points to masculinity as a troubling blind-spot in contemporary theorizations of globalization and resistance. Even as critics including Anne McClintock (1995), Ania Loomba (1998), and Chandra Mohanty (1991: 51–80) problematize post-colonialism's effacement of women's experience in its elision of gendered perspectives, most calls to consider gender's effect on potential for resistance do not consider the pull that universalized – really *globalized* – modes of masculinity exert over subjects, particularly but not exclusively males. Such calls to 'act as/for men' often encourage individuals to assent to nationalized interests in ways that run counter to their more locally and personally defined investments. Important exceptions are the volumes published in the *Global Masculinities Series*, Series Editor Michael S. Kimmel, at Zed books, which counter the trend of looking at masculinities in development discourse as either effeminized or patriarchized.

9 See Tolkien's 1951 letter, in which he claims that Hobbits are part of the '*human* race' (Carpenter 1981: 158; emphasis original).

10 Jane Chance (2001: 26–59) argues that Tolkien problematizes the provincialism of the Hobbits, and that the tolerance for cultural difference that the trilogy promotes is illustrated through the 'queer' Hobbits, Bilbo and Frodo, who seek larger adventures outside the Shire. While I strongly agree that Tolkien illustrates the detrimental limits of cultural isolation, his portrayal of Frodo and Bilbo's corruption through their 'queerness' would suggest that a degree of provincialism is desirable in kinds other than Men. Samwise, for example, is enriched by his experiences outside the Shire, because these wanderings give him an important appreciation for the cultivated simplicity that others have taken for granted.

11 Jane Chance (2001: 19–35) investigates resistance to Sauron's brand of visible power using Foucault's analysis.

12 Catherine R. Stimpson (1969), who critiques Tolkien for being 'irritatingly, blandly, traditionally masculine', on the one hand, and 'An incorrigible nationalist', on the other, is perhaps less reductive than later defenders of Tolkien would like to admit, since many would agree a collection of traits associated with Men emerge from the trilogy, and that these traits, no matter who assumes them, forge a unified nation ruled by Men. Indeed, Thomas Shippey (1992: 268–72) argues for the positive potential of Tolkien's construction of a form of patriotism, as opposed to nationalism.

CHAPTER 9: HOMOEROTICISM

1 My thanks to Will Smith for allowing me to record this incident. (www.theotherwillsmith.co.uk)
2 See Marion Perret for more on the symbolism of hands: 'Rings off Their Fingers: Hands in *The Lord of the Rings*'. *Ariel* 6.4 (1975).

CHAPTER 10: SERVICE

1 Medieval literature gives a more complicated picture of social relations than can be treated here, and, in any event, Tolkien's understanding of medieval literature differs in important ways from our understanding today. Likewise, literary depictions of social relations are themselves often simplifications of the historical reality. It is not my intention to show that Tolkien accurately reproduces literary or historical models in their entirety, only that he draws on them in depicting service relationships in his fictional settings.
2 The results can be troubling for today's readers, as the recent film adaptations by Peter Jackson often reveal, and I will refer below to some of the ways in which the films respond to Tolkien's depiction of service relationships.
3 Théoden's attachment to his servants is clear when he resists the temptation of Saruman's voice by recalling the desecration of his door-warden by Saruman's troops: 'And they hewed Háma's body before the gates of Hornburg, after he was dead' (*TT*, III, x, 225).
4 It is impossible in so small a space to give a full account of the complexities historical developments of the later Middle Ages, and I aim here only to summarize broad patterns relevant to my discussion. For a succinct account of the transformation of personal loyalties during this period, see Barber (1995: 17–18).
5 Service was, in the Middle Ages, an expected part of the relationship between aristocratic fathers and sons; one thinks, for example, of

Chaucer's Squire, who 'carf beforn his fader at the table'. See Benson (1987: line 100).

6 Nevertheless, Denethor hints at his potential for exploitation in his admiring assessment of Sauron's philosophy of leadership: 'He uses others as weapons. So do all great lords, if they are wise, Master Halfling' (*RK*, V, iv, 99).

7 Tolkien described the Shire as 'more or less a Warwickshire village of about the period of the Diamond Jubilee'. See letter 178 in Carpenter (1981).

8 For the calquing of Marcho and Blanco on Hengest and Horsa, see Shippey (1992: 92–3). For Jefferson's plan for the Great Seal, see Frantzen (1990: 15–18).

9 In the speculations about the origins of smoking, the Bree-folk, like the Native Americans, claim to have been first, before the 'colonists' of the Shire.

10 We are told in Appendix F that, both in Isengard and Mordor, the 'lesser kinds' of Orcs are referred to as *snaga* 'slave'.

11 Between 1881 and 1911, the number of gardeners went from 74,503 to 118,739 (Horn 1975: 72).

12 Interest in *The Prisoner of Zenda* was fairly continuous throughout Tolkien's childhood – it was made into a play in 1896 and a silent film in 1922. The novel shares a number of themes with *The Lord of the Rings*, notably an interest in the significance of noble lineage.

13 Tolkien approved of deference to one's superiors on moral grounds. As he put it, 'Touching your cap to the Squire may be damn bad for the Squire but it's damn good for you'. See Carpenter 1981: 133.

CHAPTER 11: GAMES

1 A sensitive and intelligent discussion of both immersion and agency can, however, be found in Murray 1997.

2 For a discussion of how possible immersion in this space can be overstated see Atkins 2003: 138–43.

3 As the academic and journalist David Thomas noted in 'Video Game Vocabulary: A Lexicon of Experiental Anchors', an unpublished paper presented at the Form, Culture and Videogame Criticism conference at Princeton University in March 2004, it is as difficult to define what is meant when it is claimed that a game is 'immersive' in the same way that it is difficult to comprehend what is meant when a song is defined as 'cool'. The relative immaturity of the language of game criticism remains a barrier to sophisticated analysis.

4 The first games that had a direct (and licensed) association with the works were *The Hobbit* (1983), a text adventure with crude graphics for

the ZX Spectrum platform that is still remembered with some affection by many games players, and a far less well known arcade-style action game for the Amiga, *Shadowfax*, released in 1982. Until there was a split in the licensed properties available for games development into the separate exploitation of the intellectual properties related to the books and that of Peter Jackson and New Line Cinema's films, directly licensed games were surprisingly few, with two games based on the first two books of *The Lord of the Rings* trilogy appearing in the 1990s. This chapter will deal directly with the games that are directly associated with the films, but it is worth noting that titles licensed from the books were also produced during the same period, and these are listed at the end of this chapter.

5   The claim made by New Zealand Tourism Online is that 'Middle-earth is New Zealand.' See http://www.tourism.net.nz/lord-of-the-rings.html. Accessed November 2004.

6   See Atkins (2004), where this public debate of opposition is examined in some detail.

7   There is a still formidable hurdle to jump before there is a flattening of difference between what can be realized in a video game and what can be realized in a game. In a game the calculations that actually put the image on the screen have to be working at in real-time, while the game engine is also busy with all the other calculations that bring the game into being. In the case of film many hours can be devoted to processing a single image.

8   I am grateful to the 2004–5 cohort of the MA Digital Games course at the International Centre for Digital Content at Liverpool John Moores University for the complex discussions of the experience of play that have informed my understanding of these games.

9   Curiously enough, we can see the same sense of anxiety at the heart of the film trilogy. What begins as a celebration of the ways in which the real and the virtual cohabit the screen in as seamless a way as possible moves towards a point at which the audience is not only asked to wake from the stupor caused by its own form of 'drug for the eyes' of cinematic spectacle, but to endorse its eradication. The audience may be enthralled by the spectacle of the previously unseen in the form of the Nazgûl, the Mumakils or the Army of the Dead, but the actions of the Fellowship must lead to their erasure from Middle-earth, to be replaced only with the mundane and the material. The anxiety that attends this contestation between virtual and material is perhaps most obvious in the final confrontation at the Crack of Doom, where the CGI Gollum fights with a Frodo who has moved from the material to the virtual by slipping on the Ring and becoming a CGI construct himself, albeit one that is subject to the simultaneous erasure of invisibility.

CHAPTER 12: IN THE TRADITION . . .

1   *Shannara* sequence, beginning with:
    Brooks, T. (1977), *The Sword of Shannara*. New York; Ballantine.
2   The *Belgariad* sequence, beginning with:
    Eddings, D. (1982), *The Pawn of Prophecy*. New York: Del Rey.
3   *The Sword of Truth* sequence beginning with:
    Goodkind, T. (1994), *Wizard's First Rule*. New York: Tor.
4   *The Wheel of Time* sequence, beginning with:
    Jordan, R. (1990), *The Eye of the World*. New York: Tor.
5   *Memory Sorrow and Thorn* sequence, beginning with:
    Williams, T. (1988), *The Dragonbone Chair*. New York: DAW.

REFERENCES

INTRODUCTION

Curry, P. (1998), *Defending Middle-Earth*. London: HarperCollins.
Fussell, P. (1975), *The Great War and Modern Memory*. Oxford: Oxford University Press.
Fussell, P. (1988), *Killing in Verse and Prose*. London: Bellew Publishing.
Fussell, P. (1989), *Wartime*. Oxford: Oxford University Press.
Shippey, T. (2000), *J. R. R. Tolkien: Author of the Century*. London: HarperCollins.
Shippey, T. (2003), *The Road to Middle Earth* (revised and expanded edn). Boston and New York: Houghton Mifflin.

CHAPTER 1: TOWARDS A BETTER TOLKIEN CRITICISM

Anderson, D. A. (1988), 'Note on the Text' in all editions of *The Lord of the Rings* since 1988.
Anderson, D. A. (2002), *The Annotated Hobbit* (2nd edn, revised). Boston: Houghton Mifflin.
Barthes, R. (1977), 'The Death of the Author', in *Image, Music, Text*, trans. Stephen Heath. New York: Hill, pp. 142–8.
Carpenter, H. (1977), *Tolkien: The Authorized Biography*. Boston: Houghton Mifflin.
Carpenter, H. (ed.) (1981), *Letters of J. R. R. Tolkien*. London: Allen and Unwin.
Chance, J. (2001a), *The Lord of the Rings: The Mythology of Power* (revised edn). Lexington, KY: University Press of Kentucky.
Chance, J. (2001b), *Tolkien's Art: A Mythology for England* (revised edn). Lexington, KY: University Press of Kentucky.
Chance, J. (ed.) (2003), *Tolkien the Medievalist*. New York: Routledge.
Chance, J. (ed.) (2004), *J. R. R. Tolkien and the Invention of Myth*. Lexington, KY: University Press of Kentucky.

Clark, G. (1990), *Beowulf*. Boston: Twayne Publishers.

Curry, P. (1997), *Defending Middle-earth*. New York: St. Martins.

Drout, M. D. C. and H. Wynne (2000), 'Tom Shippey's *J. R. R. Tolkien: Author of the Century* and a look back at Tolkien criticism since 1982'. *Envoi* 9, (2), 101–34.

Drout, M. D. C., H. Wynne and M. Higgins (2000), 'Scholarly Studies of J.R.R. Tolkien and His Work (In English): 1984–2000'. *Envoi* 9, (2), 135–65; Web pre-print at http://members.aol.com/ENVOIjrnl

Drout, M. D. C. (2004a), 'A Mythology for Anglo-Saxon England', in Jane Chance (ed.), *J. R. R. Tolkien and the Invention of Myth*. Lexington, KY: University Press of Kentucky, pp. 335–62.

Drout, M. D. C. (2004b), 'The Problem of Transformation: The Use of Medieval Sources in Fantasy Literature'. *Literature Compass* 1 ME 101, 1–22. http://www.literature-compass.com/viewpoint.asp?section=1&ref=437

Drout, M. D. C. (2004c), 'Tolkien's Prose Style and its Literary and Rhetorical Effects'. *Tolkien Studies* 1, 139–63.

Drout, M. D. C. (forthcoming 2005), *How Tradition Works: A Meme-Based Poetics of the Anglo-Saxon Tenth Century*. Tempe, AZ: Arizona Medieval and Renaissance Texts and Studies.

Drout, M. D. C. (forthcoming 2006), 'The Rhetorical Evolution of "*Beowulf*: The Monsters and the Critics" ', in Wayne Hammond and Christina Scull (eds), *Scholarship in Honor of Richard E. Blackwelder*. Milwaukee, WI: University Press Marquette.

Ellison, J. and P. Reynolds (1994), 'Editorial'. *Mallorn* 31, 6.

Fish, S. (1980), *Is there a Text in This Class? The Authority of Interpretive Communities*. Cambridge, MA: Harvard University Press.

Fernandez-Armesto, F. (2002), 'Fantasy is the Opium of the Ignorant and Indolent'. *TimesOnLine.com*, 18 December 2002 http://www.timesonline.co.uk/article/0,,1072-517489,00.html

Foucault, M. (1984), 'What is an Author', in Paul Rabinow (ed.), *The Foucault Reader*. New York: Pantheon, 101–20.

Giddings, R. (ed.) (1984), *J. R. R. Tolkien: This Far Land*. New York: Barnes & Noble.

Haber, K. (ed) (2001), *Meditations on Middle-Earth*. New York: St. Martin's Press.

Horobin, S. C. P. (2001), 'J. R. R. Tolkien as a Philologist: A Reconsideration of the Northernisms In Chaucer's Reeve's Tale'. *English Studies* 82, (2), 97–105.

Iser, W. (1981), 'The Reading Process: A Phenomenological Approach', in Jane P. Tompkins (ed.), *Reader Response Criticism: From Formalism to Post-Structuralism*. Baltimore: Johns Hopkins University Press.

REFERENCES

Klaeber, F. (1950), *Beowulf and the Fight at Finnsburg* (3rd edn). Lexington, MA: D. C. Heath.

Lane, A. (2001), 'The Hobbit Habit: Reading *The Lord of the Rings*'. *The New Yorker* 10 December: 98–105.

Nagy, G. (2003), 'The Great Chain of Reading: (Inter-)textual Relations and the Technique of Mythopoesis in the Túrin Story, in Jane Chance (ed.), *Tolkien the Medievalist*, New York: Routledge, pp. 239–58.

Orchard, A. (2003), *A Critical Companion to Beowulf*. Cambridge: D. S. Brewer.

Pearce, J. (1998), *Tolkien: Man and Myth*. London: Harper Collins.

Robinson, F. C. (1974), 'Elements of the Marvelous in the Characterization of Beowulf: A Reconsideration of the Textual Evidence', in Robert B. Burlin and Edward B. Irving, Jr. (eds), *Old English Studies in Honour of John C. Pope*. Toronto: University of Toronto Press, pp. 119–37.

Rosebury, B. (2003), *Tolkien: A Cultural Phenomenon*. London: Palgrave Macmillan.

Rushdie, S. (2003), 'Arms and the men and hobbits'. *The Guardian*, 4 January 2003.

Shippey, T. (1991), 'Tolkien and "The Homecoming of Beorhtnoth"' in Shippey, et. al. (eds), *Leaves from the Tree: J. R. R. Tolkien's Shorter Fiction*. London: The Tolkien Society, pp. 5–16.

Shippey, T. (1992), *The Road to Middle-earth* (revised edn). London: HarperCollins.

Shippey, T. (2000), *J. R. R. Tolkien: Author of the Century*. Boston: Houghton Mifflin.

Shulevitz, J. (2001), 'Hobbits in Hollywood'. *New York Times*, 22 April 2001.

Stenström, A. (1995), 'A Mythology? For England?', in Patricia Reynolds and Glen H. Goodknight (eds), *Proceedings of the J. R. R. Tolkien Centenary Conference, Keble College, Oxford, 1992. Mythlore* 80/ *Mallorn* 30. Milton Keynes, England: Tolkien Society; Altadena, CA: Mythopoeic Press.

Tolkien, C. (2003), The Complete History of Middle-Earth. London: HarperCollins.

Tolkien, J. R. R. (1983), *The Book of Lost Tales, Part 1*, edited by Christopher Tolkien. London: Allen and Unwin.

Tolkien, J. R. R. (1992), *The Silmarillion*, edited by Christopher Tolkien. London: HarperCollins.

Tolkien, J. R. R. (1998), *Unfinished Tales*, edited by Christopher Tolkien. London: HarperCollins.

Tolkien, J. R. R. (2002), *Beowulf and the Critics*, edited by Michael Drout. Arizona Center for Medieval and Renaissance Studies.

Turner, J. (2001), 'Reasons for liking Tolkien'. *London Review of Books*, 15 November, 2001: 15–24.

CHAPTER 2: TIME

Aldrich, K. (1988), 'The Sense of Time in Tolkien's *The Lord of the Rings*'. *Mythlore* 15, 5–9.

Bal, M. (1985), *Narratology: Introduction to the Theory of Narrative*, trans. van Boheemen, C. Toronto: University of Toronto Press.

Carpenter, H. (1977), *J. R. R. Tolkien: The Authorised Biography*. London: Allen and Unwin.

Carpenter, H. (ed.) (1981), *Letters of J.R.R. Tolkien*. London: Allen and Unwin.

Deleuze, G. (1989a), *Cinema 1: The Movement-Image*, trans. Tomlonson, H. and Galeta, R. London: Athlone.

Deleuze, G. (1989b), *Cinema 2: The Time-Image*, trans. Tomlonson, H. and Galeta, R. London: Athlone.

Flieger, V. (1997), *A Question of Time: J. R. R. Tolkien's Road to Faërie*. Kent, OH: Kent State University Press.

Menand, L. (2002), 'Goblin Market'. *New York Review of Books*, 17 January 2002, 8–9.

Ricoeur, P. (1985), *Time and Narrative*, 3 vols, trans. McLaughlin, K. and Pellauer, D. Chicago: University of Chicago Press.

Roseberry, B. (1992), *Tolkien: A Critical Assessment*. Basingstoke: Macmillan.

Smith, J. and Matthews, J. C. (2004), *The Lord of the Rings: The Films, the Books, the Radio Series*. London: Virgin.

Shippey, T. (2000), *J. R. R. Tolkien: Author of the Century*. London: HarperCollins.

Stringer, J. (ed.) (2003), *Movie Blockbusters*. London: Routledge.

Thompson, K. (2003), 'Fantasy, Franchises, and Frodo Baggins: *The Lord of the Rings* and Modern Hollywood'. *The Velvet Light Trap* 52, 45–63.

Tolkien, J. R. R. [1954] (1965), *The Lord of the Rings*, 3 vols. New York: Houghton Mifflin.

CHAPTER 3: GOTHIC ECHOES

Brooke-Rose, C. (1980), 'The Evil Ring: Realism and the Marvellous'. *Poetics Today* 1 (4), 67–90.

Carpenter, H. (1977), *J. R. R. Tolkien: A Biography*. London: George Allen & Unwin.

Chance, J. (2001), *The Lord of the Rings: The Mythology of Power*. Lexington: University Press of Kentucky.

Clark, G. and D. Timmons (2000), *J. R. R. Tolkien and his Literary Resonances*. Westport CT: Greenwood Press.

Curry, P. (1997), *Defending Middle-earth*. London: HarperCollins.

Dickson, A. (ed.) (1985), *Sigmund Freud: The Penguin Freud Library.* Harmondsworth: Penguin Books, Vol. 14 'Art and Literature'.

Du Maurier, G. (1992), *Trilby* (1894), Leonee Ormond (ed.). London: Dent.

Ellison, J. (1991), 'Sublime Scenes and Horrid Novels: Milestones along the Road to Middle-earth'. *Mallorn* 28, 23–8.

Fairclough, P. (ed.) (1968), *Three Gothic Novels.* Harmondsworth: Penguin.

Friedman, B. (1982), 'Tolkien and David Jones: The Great War and the War of the Ring'. *Clio: A Journal of Literature, History and the Philosophy of History*, 11, (2), 115–35.

Gelder, K. (2003), 'Epic Fantasy and Global Terrorism'. *Overland* 173, 21–7.

Giddings, R. (ed.) (1983), *J. R. R. Tolkien: This Far Land.* London and Towota, NJ: Vision.

Hogle, J. E. (1996), 'The Gothic and the "Otherings" of Ascendant Culture: The Original *Phantom of the Opera*'. *South Atlantic Quarterly*, 95, (3), 157–171.

Hogle, J. E. (ed.) (2002), *Gothic Fiction.* Cambridge: Cambridge University Press.

Hood, G. (1987), 'Sauron and Dracula', in *Mythlore: A Journal of J. R. R. Tolkien, C. S. Lewis, Charles Williams and The Genres of Myth and Fantasy Studies.* 14 (2(52)), 11–17.

Hurley, K. (1996), *The Gothic Body: Sexuality, Materialism and Degeneration at the Fin de Siècle.* Cambridge: Cambridge University Press.

Kocher, P. (1974), *Master of Middle-earth: The Achievement of J. R. R. Tolkien* (1972). Harmondsworth: Penguin Books.

Kristeva, J. (1982), *Powers of Horror: An Essay on Abjection*, trans. L. S. Roudiez. New York: Columbia University Press.

Nitzche, J. Chance (1979), *Tolkien's Art: A Mythology for England.* Basingstoke: Macmillan.

Partridge, B. (1983), 'No Sex Please – We're Hobbits: The Construction of Female Sexuality in *The Lord of the Rings*', in R. Giddings (ed.), *J. R. R. Tolkien: This FarLand.* London and Towota, NJ: Vision.

Pearce, J. (1998), *Tolkien: Man and Myth.* London: HarperCollins.

Pick, D. (1993), *Faces of Degeneration: A European Disorder, c.1848–c.1918* (1989). Cambridge: Cambridge University Press.

Pick, D. (2000), *Svengali's Web: The Alien Enchanter in Modern Culture.* New Haven and London: Yale University Press.

Punter, D. (ed.) (2000), *A Companion to the Gothic.* Oxford: Blackwell.

Robbins R. and J. Wolfreys (eds) (2000), *Victorian Gothic: Literary and Cultural Manifestations in the Nineteenth Century.* Basingstoke: Palgrave.

Salisbury, J. D. (2001). 'Gothic and Romantic Wandering: The Epistemology of Oscillation'. *Gothic Studies* 3, (1), 45–59.

Sedgwick, E. Kosofsky (1985), *Between Men: English Literature and Male Homosocial Desire*. New York: Columbia University Press.

Shippey, T. (1992), *The Road to Middle-earth* (1982). London: HarperCollins.

Shippey, T. (2000), *J. R. R. Tolkien: Author of the Century*. London: HarperCollins.

Showalter, E. (1987), *The Female Malady: Women, Madness, and English Culture, 1830–1980*. London: Virago.

Showalter, E. (1991), *Sexual Anarchy: Gender and Culture at the Fin de Siècle*. London: Bloomsbury.

Stoker, B. (1996), *Dracula* (1897), Maud Ellmann (ed.), Oxford: Oxford University Press World's Classics.

Tolkien, J. R. R. (1964), *Tree and Leaf*. London: George Allen & Unwin.

Tolkien, J. R. R. (2003), *The Lord of the Rings*. London: HarperCollins.

CHAPTER 4: THE ONE RING

Bergonzi, B. (1986), 'The Decline and Fall of the Catholic Novel', in *The Myth of Modernism and the Twentieth Century*. Brighton: Harvester Press, 172–87.

Caldecott, S. (2003), *Secret Fire: The Spiritual Vision of J. R. R. Tolkien*. London: Darton, Longman and Todd.

Carpenter, H. (ed.) (1995), *Letters: The Letters of J.R.R. Tolkien*. London: HarperCollins.

Carter, L. (2003), *Tolkien: A Look Behind The Lord of the Rings* 1969 (updated edn). London: Gollancz.

Cross, F. L. (1997), *The Oxford Dictionary of the Christian Church* (3rd edn), ed. E. A. Livingstone. Oxford: Oxford University Press.

Davies, B. (2002), *Aquinas: An Introduction*. London: Continuum.

DiGaetani, J. L. (1978), *Richard Wagner and the Modern British Novel*. London: Associated University Presses.

Manlove, C. (1975), *Modern Fantasy: Five Studies*. Cambridge: Cambridge University Press.

Shippey, T. (1992), *The Road to Middle-Earth* (2nd edn). London: Grafton.

Shippey, T. (2000), *J. R. R. Tolkien: Author of the Century*. London: HarperCollins.

Tolkien, J. R. R. (1992), *The Silmarillion*, edited by Christopher Tolkien. London: HarperCollins.

Tolkien, J. R. R. (1994), *Morgoth's Ring*, edited by Christopher Tolkien; *The History of Middle Earth, vol. x: Morgoth's Ring*. London: HarperCollins.

CHAPTER 5: INVISIBILITY

Caldecott, S. (2003), *Secret Fire: The Spiritual Vision of J. R. R. Tolkien*. London: Darton, Longman and Todd.

Caygill, H. (1995), *A Kant Dictionary*. Blackwell: Oxford.

Chance, J. (2001), *Tolkien's Art: A mythology for England* (revised edn). Lexington, KY: University Press of Kentucky.

Herodotus, (2003), *The Histories*, trans. Aubrey de Sélincourt, rev. John Marincola. London: Penguin.

Holt, P. (1992), 'H. G. Wells and the Ring of Gyges'. *Science Fiction Studies* 57.

Kant, I. (1998), *Religion Within the Boundaries of Mere Reason*, trans. and ed. Allen Wood and George di Giovanni. Cambridge: Cambridge University Press.

Levinas, E. (1991), *Totality and Infinity*, trans. Alphonso Lingis. London: Kluwer Academic Publishers.

MacIntyre, A. (1985), *After Virtue* (2nd edn). London: Duckworth.

Plato (1993), *The Republic*, trans. Robin Waterfield. Oxford: Oxford University Press.

Shippey, T. (2000), *J. R. R. Tolkien: Author of the Century*. London: HarperCollins.

Shippey, T. (2003), *The Road to Middle Earth* (revised and expanded edn). Boston and New York: Houghton Mifflin.

CHAPTER 6: HOME

Berman, M. (1983), *All that is Solid Melts into Air: The Experience of Modernity*. London: Verso.

Coleridge, S. T. (1993), *Poems*, ed. John Beer. London: J.M. Dent.

Coupe, L. (ed.) (2000), *The Green Studies Reader: From Romanticism to Ecocriticism*. London: Routledge.

Curry, P. (2000), 'Defending Middle-Earth', in Laurence Coupe (ed.), *The Green Studies Reader: From Romanticism to Ecocriticism*. London: Routledge.

Freud, S. (1985), 'The uncanny', in *The Pelican Freud Library*, 14, trans. James Strachey. Harmondsworth: Penguin, pp. 335–76.

Heidegger, M. (1962), *Being and Time*, trans. John Macquarrie and Edward Robinson. Oxford: Blackwell.

Heidegger, M. (1975), 'The origin of the work of art', in *Poetry, Language, Thought*, trans. Albert Hofstadter. London: Harper and Row, pp. 15–87.

Heidegger, M. (1977a), 'The question concerning technology', in *The Question Concerning Technology and Other Essays*, trans. William Lovitt. New York and London: Harper Torchbooks, pp. 3–35.

Heidegger, M. (1977b), 'The turning', in *The Question Concerning Technology and Other Essays*, trans. William Lovitt. New York and London: Harper Torchbooks, pp. 36–49.

Heidegger, M. (1996), *Hölderlin's Hymn 'The Ister'*, trans. William McNeill and Julia Davis. Bloomington and Indianapolis: Indiana University Press.

Hölderlin, F. (1998), 'Home', in *Selected Poems and Fragments*, trans. Michael Hamburger, ed. Jeremy Adler. Harmondsworth: Penguin, p. 13.

Jameson, F. (2002), *A Singular Modernity: Essays on the Ontology of the Present*. London: Verso.

Pattison, G. (2000), *The Later Heidegger*. London: Routledge.

Royle, N. (2003), *The Uncanny*. Manchester: Manchester University Press.

Tolkien, J. R. R. (1994), *The Lord of the Rings*. London: HarperCollins.

Tolkien, J. R. R. (1995), *The Hobbit, or There and Back Again*. London: HarperCollins.

Tolkien, J. R. R. (1999), *The Silmarillion*, edited by Christopher Tolkien. London: HarperCollins.

Žižek, S. (2002), 'I plead guilty – but where is the judgement?'. *Nepantla: Views from the South*, 3, (3), 579–83.

CHAPTER 7: WOMEN

Bennett, H. (1989), 'From peace weaver to text weaver: Feminist approaches to Old English studies'. *Old English Newsletter*, 15, 23–42.

Bennett, H. (1992), 'The female mourner at Beowulf's funeral: Filling in the blanks / hearing the spaces'. *Exemplaria*, 4, (1), 35–50.

Bloomfield, J. (1994), 'Diminished by kindness: Frederick Klaeber's rewriting of Wealhtheow'. *Journal of English and Germanic Philology*, 93, 183–203.

Bloomfield, J. (1999), 'Benevolent authoritarianism in Klaeber's *Beowulf*: An editorial translation of kingship'. *Modern Language Quarterly*, 60, 129–59.

Bremmer, R. H. (1980), 'The importance of kinship: Uncle and nephew in *Beowulf*'. *Amsterdam Beitreage zur Alteren Germanistik*, 15, 21–38.

Chance, J. (1990), 'The structural unity of *Beowulf*: The problem of Grendel's Mother', in Helen Damico and Alexandra Hennessey Olsen (eds), *New Readings on Women in Old English Literature*. Bloomington, IN: Indiana University Press, pp. 248–61.

Chance, J. (2001), *The Lord of the Rings: The Mythology of Power* (revised edn). Lexington, KY: University Press of Kentucky.

Crowe, E. L. (1995), 'Power in Arda: sources, uses, and misuses', in Patricia Reynolds and Glen H. GoodKnight (eds), *Proceedings of the J. R. R. Tolkien Centenary Conference, Keble College, Oxford, 1992* (combined issue of *Mythlore* 80 and *Mallorn* 30). Milton Keynes: Tolkien Society; Altadena, CA: Mythopeoic Press, pp. 272–7.

Damico, H. (1984), *Beowulf's Wealhtheow and the Valkyrie Tradition*. Madison: University of Wisconsin Press.

Donovan, L. A. (2003), 'The valkyrie reflex in J. R. R. Tolkien's *The Lord of the Rings*: Galadriel, Shelob, Éowyn, and Arwen', in Jane Chance (ed.), *Tolkien the Medievalist*. London and New York: Routledge, pp. 106–32.

Drout, M. (1996), 'Reading Tolkien reading *Beowulf*: Is a "masculinist" interpretation necessary?' *Old English Newsletter*, 29, A34–A35.

Drout, M. D. C. (ed.) (2002), *Beowulf and the Critics by J. R. R. Tolkien*. Medieval and Renaissance Texts and Studies 248. Tempe, AZ: Arizona Centre for Medieval and Renaissance Studies.

Enright, M. J. (1996), *Lady with a Mead Cup: Ritual, Prophecy, and Lordship in the European Warband from La Tene to the Viking Age*. Dublin: Four Courts Press.

Fee, C. (1996), 'Beag and beaghroden: women, treasure, and the language of social structure in *Beowulf*'. *Neuphilologische Mitteilungen*, 97, 285–94.

Frederick, C. and S. McBride (2001), *Women among the Inklings: Gender in C. S. Lewis, J. R. R. Tolkien, and Charles Williams*. Contributions in Women's Studies 191. Westport, CT: Greenwood.

Glosecki, S. O. (1999), '*Beowulf* and the wills: traces of totemism?' *Philological Quarterly*, 78, 15–47.

Hill, J. (1990), ' "Þæt wæs geomuru ides!" A female stereotype examined', in Helen Damico and Alexandra Hennessey Olsen (eds), *New Readings on Women in Old English Literature*. Bloomington, IN: Indiana University Press, pp. 235–47.

Horner, S. (2001), *The Discourse of Enclosure: Representing Women in Old English Literature*. Albany: State University of New York Press.

Irving, E. B., Jr (1989), *Rereading Beowulf*. Philadelphia: University of Pennsylvania Press.

Kelly, B. (1983), 'The formative stages of *Beowulf* textual scholarship: part II'. *Anglo-Saxon England*, 12, 239–75.

Koppinen, P. (2003), 'Judith Masquerading as a Man: Mimickery as an Empowering Force in the Old English Poem *Judith*'. Paper given to the Leeds International Medieval Congress. 17 July 2003.

Lees, C. A. (1997), 'At the crossroads: Old English and feminist criticism', in Katherine O'Brien O'Keeffe (ed.), *Reading Old English Texts*. Cambridge: Cambridge University Press, pp. 146–69.

Mitchell, B. and F. C. Robinson (eds) (1998), *Beowulf: An Edition*. Oxford: Blackwell.

Mustanoja, T. F. (1967), 'The unnamed woman's song of mourning over Beowulf and the tradition of ritual lamentation'. *Neuphilologische Mitteilungen*, 68, 1–27.

North, R. (2004), '*Beowulf* and the *Aeneid*: four episodes'. Paper given to the London Old and Middle English Research Seminar, 24 November 2004.

Overing, G. R. (1990), *Language, Sign, and Gender in Beowulf*. Carbondale: Southern Illinois University Press.

Partridge, B. (1983), 'No sex please – we're hobbits: the construction of female sexuality in *The Lord of the Rings*', in Robert Giddings (ed.), *J. R. R. Tolkien: This Far Land*. London: Vision; Totowa, NJ: Barnes & Noble, pp. 179–97.

Renoir, A. (1975), 'A reading context for *The Wife's Lament*', in Lewis E. Nicholson and Dolores Warwick Frese (eds), *Anglo-Saxon Poetry: Essays in Appreciation*. Notre Dame: Notre Dame University Press, pp. 224–41.

Ringel, F. (2000), 'Women fantasists: in the shadow of the ring', in George Clark and Daniel Timmons (eds), *J. R. R. Tolkien and His Literary Resonances: Views of Middle-earth*. Westport, CT and London: Greenwood, pp. 159–71.

Robinson, F. C. (1985), *Beowulf and the Appositive Style*. Knoxville, TN: University of Tennessee Press.

Rubin, G. (1975), 'The traffic in women', in Rayna B. Reiter (ed.), *Toward an Anthropology of Women*. New York and London: Monthly Review Press, pp. 157–210.

Shippey, T. (2003), *The Road to Middle Earth* (revised and expanded edn). Boston and New York: Houghton Mifflin.

Sklute, L. John (1990), '*Freoðuwebbe* in Old English poetry', in Helen Damico and Alexandra Hennessey Olsen (eds), *New Readings on Women in Old English Literature*. Bloomington, IN: Indiana University Press, pp. 204–10.

Tolkien, J. R. R. (2001), *The Lord of the Rings*. London: Collins Modern Classics.

Welsh, A. (1991), 'Branwen, Beowulf, and the tragic peaceweaver tale'. *Viator*, 22, 1–13.

Wood, T. C. (2000), 'Is Tolkien a Renaissance Man? Sir Philip Sidney's *Defense of Poesy* and J. R. R. Tolkien's "On Fairy Stories" ', in George Clark and Daniel Timmons (eds), *J. R. R. Tolkien and His Literary Resonances: Views of Middle-earth*. Westport, CT and London: Greenwood, pp. 95–108.

CHAPTER 8: MASCULINITY

Back, L. and J. Solomos (eds) (2000), *Theories of Race and Racism: A Reader*. New York: Routledge.

Bernasconi, R. (2000), 'The invisibility of racial minorities in the public realm of appearances', in Walter Brogan and James Risser (eds),

American Continental Philosophy: A Reader. Bloomington, IN: Indiana University Press, pp. 352–71.

Bhabha, H. K. (1995), 'Are you a man or a mouse?', in Maurice Berger, Brian Wallis and Simon Watson (eds), *Constructing Masculinity*. New York: Routledge, pp. 57–65.

Brittan, A. (1989), *Masculinity and Power*. Oxford and New York: Basil Blackwell.

Carpenter, H. (ed.), with the assistance of Christopher Tolkien (1981), *The Letters of J. R. R. Tolkien*. Boston: Houghton Mifflin.

Chance, J. (2001), *'The Lord of the Rings': The Mythology of Power* (revised edn). Lexington, KY: University Press of Kentucky.

Chism, C. (2003), 'Middle-earth, the Middle Ages, and the Aryan nation: Myth and history in World War II', in Jane Chance (ed.), *Tolkien the Medievalist*. New York: Routledge, pp. 63–92.

Cohan, S. (1997), *Masked Men: Masculinity and the Movies in the Fifties*. Bloomington and Indianapolis: Indiana UP.

Curry, P. (1995), ' "Less noise and more green": Tolkien's ideology for England', in Patricia Reynolds and Glen H. GoodKnight (eds), *Proceedings of the J.R.R. Tolkien Centenary Conference, Keble College, Oxford, 1992* (combined Issue of *Mythlore* 80 and *Mallorn* 30). Tolkien Society; Altadena, CA: Mythopoetic Press, pp. 126–38.

Essed, P. and D. T. Goldberg (eds) (2002), *Race Critical Theories: Text and Context*. London: Blackwell.

Evans, J. (2003), 'The anthropology of Arda: creation, theology, and the race of Men', in Jane Chance (ed.), *Tolkien the Medievalist*. New York: Routledge, pp. 194–224.

Flieger, V. (1997), *A Question of Time: J. R. R. Tolkien's Road to Faërie*. Kent, OH: Kent State University Press.

Foucault, M. (1995), *Discipline and Punish: The Birth of the Prison*, trans. Alan Sheridan. New York: Vintage.

Halsall, G. (2004), 'Gender and the end of empire'. *Journal of Medieval and Early Modern Studies*, 34, 18–39.

Hardt, M. and A. Negri (2000), *Empire*. Cambridge, MA: Harvard University Press.

Lees, C. and G. Overing (2004), 'Signifying gender and empire'. *Journal of Medieval and Early Modern Studies*, 34, 1–16.

Loomba, A. (1998), *Colonialism/Postcolonialism*. London and New York: Routledge.

Luling, V. (1995), 'An anthropologist in Middle-earth', in Patricia Reynolds and Glen H. GoodKnight (eds), *Proceedings of the J. R. R. Tolkien Centenary Conference, Keble College, Oxford, 1992* (combined Issue of *Mythlore* 80 and *Mallorn* 30). Tolkien Society; Altadena, CA: Mythopoetic Press, pp. 52–7.

MacIntyre, A. (1984), *After Virtue* (2nd edn). Notre Dame, IN: Notre Dame University Press.

McClintock, A. (1995), *Imperial Leather: Race, Gender, and Sexuality in the Colonial Contest*. New York: Routledge.

Middleton, P. (1992), *The Inward Gaze: Masculinity and Subjectivity in Modern Culture*. New York: Routledge.

Mohanty, C. T. (1991), 'Under western eyes: Feminist scholarship and colonial discourses', in Chandra Talpade Mohanty, Ann Russo and Lourdes Torres (eds), *Third World Women and the Politics of Feminism*. Bloomington: Indiana University Press pp. 51–80.

Otty, N. (1984), 'The structuralist's guide to Middle-earth', in Robert Giddings (ed.), *J. R. R. Tolkien: This Far Land*. New York: Barnes and Noble, pp. 154–77.

Shippey, T. (1992), *The Road to Middle-earth* (revised edn). Hammersmith: Grafton.

Shippey, T. (1995), 'Tolkein as a post-war writer', in Patricia Reynolds and Glen H. GoodKnight (eds), *Proceedings of the J. R. R. Tolkien Centenary Conference, Keble College, Oxford, 1992* (combined Issue of *Mythlore* 80 and *Mallorn* 30). Tolkien Society; Altadena, CA: Mythopoetic Press, pp. 84–93.

Solomon-Godeau, A. (1995), 'Male trouble', in Maurice Berger, Brian Wallis and Simon Watson (eds), *Constructing Masculinity*. New York: Routledge, pp. 68–76.

Stecopoulos, H. and M. Uebel (eds) (1997), *Race and the Subject of Masculinities*. Durham: Duke University Press.

Stimpson, C. R. (1969), *J. R. R. Tolkien*. Columbia Essays on Modern Writers, no. 41. New York: Columbia University Press.

Wald, G. (2000), *Crossing the Line: Racial Passing in Twentieth-Century U.S. Literature and Culture*. Durham: Duke University Press.

CHAPTER 9: HOMOEROTICISM

Behrens, W. (2002), 'A gay telling of Lord of the Rings.' *Bay Windows Online*. Available at: http://www.baywindows.com/news/2002/12/12/Fun/A.Gay.Telling.Of.Lord.Of.The.Rings–341243.html

Craig, D. M. (2001), 'Queer lodgings'. *Mallorn: The Journal of the Tolkien Society* January, (38), 11–18.

Doty, M. (1993) *Making Things Perfectly Queer*. Minnesota: University of Minnesota Press.

Helford, E. R. (2000), 'Feminism, queer studies and the sexual politics of *Xena, Warrior Princess*', in Elyce Rae Helford (ed.) *Fantasy Girls*. Lanham, MD: Rowman and Littlefield, pp. 135–62.

REFERENCES

Muir, E. (1955), 'A Boy's World.' *Sunday Observer* (London) 27 November, 11.

Nelson, C. W. (1994), 'But who is Rose Cotton?: Love and romance in *The Lord of the Rings*'. *Journal of the Fantastic in the Arts*, 3, (3), 6–20.

Perret, M. (1975), 'Rings Off Their Fingers: Hands in The Lord of the Rings.' *Ariel: A Review of International English Literature*, 6, (4), 52–66.

Stimpson, C. (1969), *J. R. R. Tolkien*. London: Columbia University Press.

Patridge, B. (1983), 'No sex please, we're hobbits: The Construction of Female Sexuality in *The Lord of the Rings*', in R. Giddings (ed.), *J. R. R. Tolkien: This Far Land*. London: Vision Press Limited.

'Peter Jackson answers THE GEEKS!!! 20 questions about Lord Of The Rings!!!' (1998) *Ain't It Cool News*. Available at: http://www.aint-it-cool-news.com/lordoftherings.html

Timmons, D. (2001), 'Hobbit Sex and Sensuality in Lord of the Rings'. *MythLore: A Journal of J. R. R. Tolkien, C.S. Lewis, Charles Williams*, 23, (3), 70–9.

Whatling, C. (1997), *Screen Dreams: Fantasising Lesbians in Film*. Manchester: Manchester University Press.

CHAPTER 10: SERVICE

Barber, R. (1995), *The Knight and Chivalry* (revised edn). Woodbridge: Boydell.

Benson, L. D. (ed) (1987), *The Riverside Chaucer*. Oxford: Oxford University Press.

Carpenter, H. (ed) (1981), *The Letters of J. R. R. Tolkien*. London: Allen & Unwin.

Chance, J. (1992), *The Lord of the Rings: The Mythology of Power*. New York: Twayne.

Chance, J. (2001), *Tolkien's Art: A Mythology for England* (revised edn). Lexington, KY: University Press of Kentucky.

Frantzen, Allen J. (1990), *Desire for Origins: New Language, Old English, and Teaching the Tradition*. New Brunswick, NJ: Rutgers University Press.

Given-Wilson, C. (1986), *The Royal Household and the King's Affinity: Service, Politics and Finance in England 1360–1413*. London: Yale University Press.

Horn, P. (1975), *The Rise and Fall of the Domestic Servant*. New York: St Martin's Press.

Shippey, T. A. (1992), *The Road to Middle-Earth* (2nd edn). London: Grafton.

Thomas, S. S. (2002), 'Promise, Threat, Joke, or Wager? The Legal (In)determinacy of the Oaths of *Sir Gawain and the Green Knight*'. *Exemplaria*, 10.2, 287–305.

Tolkien, J. R. R. (1953), 'The Homecoming of Beorhtnoth Beorhthelm's Son'. *Essays and Studies by Members of the English Association*, ns, 6, 1–18.

Turville-Petre, T. P. (1995), *England the Nation*. Oxford: Oxford University Press.

CHAPTER 11: GAMES

Atkins, B. (2004), 'To infinity, and beyond: Dialogue and critique in popular film's portrayal of video games'. *Text/Technology* 13, (1), 35–51.

Atkins, B. (2003), *More Than a Game: The Computer Game as Fictional Form*. Manchester: Manchester University Press.

Barthes, R. (1972), 'Toys'. *Mythologies*, trans. Annette Lavers. London: Cape.

Bolter, J. D. and Grusin, R. (1999), *Remediation: Understanding New Media*. Cambridge, MA: MIT.

Jenkins, H. (2004), 'Computer games as narrative architecture', in *First Person: New Media as Story, Performance and Game*, N. Wardrip-Fruin and P. Harrigan (eds). Cambridge, MA: MIT. Available online at http://www.electronicbookreview.com/v3/servlet/ebr?command=view_essay&essay_id=jenkins. Accessed November 2004.

Murray, J. (1997), *Hamlet on the Holodeck: The Future of Narrative in Cyberspace*. New York: Free Press.

Ryan, M.-L. (2001), *Narrative as Virtual Reality: Immersion and Interactivity in Literature and Electronic Media*. Baltimore: Johns Hopkins.

Salen, K. and Zimmerman, E. (2003), *Rules of Play: Game Design Fundamentals*. Cambridge, MA: MIT.

Tolkien, J. R. R. (1977), *The Silmarillion*. London: Allen and Unwin.

Tolkien, J. R. R. (1980), *Unfinished Tales of Numenor and Middle-earth*, edited by Christopher Tolkien. London: Allen and Unwin.

Virilio, P. (2002), *Desert Screen: War at the Speed of Light*, trans. Michael Degener. London: Continuum.

GAMES LICENSED FROM THE FILMS

The Lord of the Rings: The Third Age (2004), Electronic Arts.

The Lord of the Rings: The Battle for Middle Earth (2004), Electronic Arts.

The Lord of the Rings: The Two Towers (2002), Electronic Arts.

The Lord of the Rings: The Return of the King (2003), Electronic Arts.

REFERENCES

OTHER LICENSED TOLKIEN GAMES

The Hobbit (1983), Melbourne House.

The Hobbit (2003), Sierra, Inevitable Entertainment.

The Lord of the Rings: The Fellowship of the Ring (2002), Universal Interactive Studios.

J. R. R. Tolkien's The Lord of the Rings, Volume Two: The Two Towers (1991), Interplay.

J. R. R. Tolkien's The Lord of the Rings, Volume One: The Fellowship of the Ring (1990), Interplay.

Shadowfax (1982), Postern.

FURTHER READING

While it is true that Tolkien has not, in general, been terribly well treated by critics, there is a growing body of serious work on his writing. A very full bibliography and discussion is

Michael D. C. Drout and Hilary Wynne (2000), 'Tom Shippey's *J. R. R. Tolkien: Author of the Century* and a Look Back at Tolkien Criticism since 1982'. *Envoi* 9, (2).

This, which is available online at time of writing, and the online bibliography maintained by Michael Drout, should be the first point of call for serious work on Tolkien. Michael Drout is also the editor of *Tolkien Studies*, a journal from West Virginia University Press.

Tom Shippey could rightly claim to the leading expert on Tolkien. His two main books are

Tom Shippey (2003), *The Road to Middle Earth: How J. R. R. Tolkien Created a New Mythology* (revised and expanded edn). Boston and New York: Houghton Mifflin Company.

Tom Shippey (2000), *J. R. R. Tolkien: Author of the Century*. London: HarperCollins.

While these books do overlap a little in content, they also have distinct objectives. The first is a detailed account of the development and structure of Tolkien's work; the second argues that Tolkien is a quintessential 'author of the Twentieth Century'. Both are characterized by excellent readings, a wide knowledge of the medieval and Anglo-Saxon background and a sensitivity to Tolkien's context and ostensive aims.

For obvious reasons, Tolkien's work has also been very popular with medievalists. One of the chief among these is Jane Chance. She is the author of

Jane Chance (2001), *The Lord of the Rings: The Mythology of Power*. Lexington, KY: University Press of Kentucky, and

Jane Chance (2001), *Tolkien's art : A Mythology for England*. Lexington, KY: University Press of Kentucky.

Both of these are interesting accounts of his work. The first concerns the role of power, and, while claiming to be influenced by the work of Michel Foucault, does not really display this influence in depth and ends with a rather banal series of conclusions. The second is shaped by the (tendentious) claim that Tolkien wanted to create mythology for England (rather than one dedicated to England, as his letters imply) but covers a great deal of ground interestingly. She is also the editor of two collections of essays

Jane Chance (2004), *Tolkien and the Invention of Myth: A Reader*. Lexington, KY: University Press of Kentucky, and

Jane Chance (2003), *Tolkien the Medievalist*. London: Routledge.

Both are detailed collections of essays, mainly by medievalists: the latter contains an essay by Gergely Nagy on 'The Great Chain of Reading: (Inter-) textual relations and the technique of mythopoesis in the Túrin story' which Michael Drout argues is 'the single most important essay published on Tolkien in the past decade'. A collection of academic essays that is slightly broader in scope is

George Clark and Daniel Timmons (eds) (2000), *J.R.R. Tolkien and his Literary Resonances: Views of Middle-earth*. London: Greenwood Press.

Here, a range of writers outline other literary influences on Tolkien, including that of Shakespeare, Tennyson and Dickens.

There are a number of works that offer wide-ranging assessments of Tolkien's work

Brian Rosebury (2003), *Tolkien: A Cultural Phenomenon*. Basingstoke: Palgrave Macmillan,

is a good all round survey, though rather meandering at times.

Charles Moseley (1997), *J.R.R. Tolkien*. Plymouth: Northcote House/ British Council.

This 'writers and their work' series book is quite short, but very good on the interaction between Tolkien's creative and critical writings. There are of course many 'biographical' readings of Tolkien's work, based on his life and times. One of the more detailed, and rewarding, is

John Garth (2003), *Tolkien and the Great War: The Threshold of Middle-Earth*. Boston: Houghton-Mifflin,

which is detailed and readable biography of Tolkien's early life.

Among the number of religious readings of Tolkien,

Stratford Caldecott (2003), *Secret Fire: The Spiritual Vision of J.R.R. Tolkien*. London: Darton Longman and Todd,

stands out. Though insightful in places, his focus on the religious dimension swamps the complexities of the text and offers tempting easy answers to its problems. In a similar vein is

Joseph Pearce (1998), *Tolkien: Man and Myth*. London: HarperCollins,

which is perhaps rather over reliant on Tolkien letters.

Patrick Curry (1998), *Defending Middle-Earth*. London: HarperCollins,

is a lively thoughtful ecologically-minded work arguing that Tolkien aimed for a resacralization of nature in a contemporary cultural idiom. However, the book is torn between two audiences (the popular and the more scholarly) and so lacks a detailed critical rigour, while hinting at more complex ideas.

Another book with one key issue in mind is

Verlyn Flieger (2002), *Splintered Light: Logos and Language in Tolkien's World*. London: Kent State University Press.

While it focuses mainly on *The Silmarillion*, and veers close to psycho-biography at times, it draws on the work of Tolkien's friend Owen Barfield to offer one particular and unified view of what Tolkien aimed to achieve.

Of course, texts are open to an enormous – some have argued infinite – number of interpretations. Because *The Lord of the Rings* has been so popular, there are a huge number of readings of the novel available. While it behoves critics to let a thousand flowers bloom, it is also possible to note that readings like the theosophicial one offered in

Robert Ellwood (2002), *Frodo's Quest: Living the Myth in The Lord of the Rings*. Wheaton, IL: Quest Books,

are not really about Tolkien at all. If, as these sorts of books argue, all the stories we tell betray mythic, or unconscious, or divine structures, then these will be manifest in all stories, or indeed other texts. The creation of a lasagne from raw ingredients to final dish is as much an allegory for (say) the movement from ignorance to wisdom as *The Lord of the Rings*. Cashing in on the success of a particular book to sell a certain ideology is all very well – but it's also fine to critique a reading of this sort as crass and simplistic.

NOTES ON CONTRIBUTORS

Barry Atkins (Liverpool John Moores University) teaches popular genre fiction and narrative theory. He has published in the areas of Modernist American literature and computer games and narrative theory, including *More than a Game: The Computer Game as Fictional Form* (Manchester University Press, 2003) and 'To infinity and beyond?': Dialogue and critique in popular film's portrayal of videogames' *Text Technology*, 2003.

Holly A. Crocker is Assistant Professor of English at the University of South Carolina. She has published articles exploring gender's dependence on performances of passing in *Shakespeare Quarterly*, *Chaucer Review*, *MFF* and a number of essay collections. Currently, she is editing a collection of essays entitled *Comic Provocations: Exposing the Corpus of Old French Fabliaux* (Palgrave), and completing a book entitled *Chaucer's Visions* (Palgrave).

Michael D. C. Drout holds the William and Elsie Prentice Professorship at Wheaton College (Norton, MA) and is the editor of J. R. R. Tolkien's *Beowulf and the Critics* (Winner of the Mythopoeic Scholarship Award in Inkling Studies, 2003) and *How Tradition Works: A Descriptive Cultural Poetics of the Anglo-Saxon Tenth Century* (Arizona MRTS, 2005). He has published in *The Journal of English and Germanic Philology*, *Anglo-Saxon England*, *Studies in Philology*, *Modern Philology*, *Neophilologus* and *Children's Literature*. Drout is one of the founding editors of the new academic journal *Tolkien Studies* and is editor of *The J. R. R. Tolkien Encyclopaedia* (Routledge, 2006). He has spoken widely on Tolkien on TV and radio in the North American media.

Robert Eaglestone (Royal Holloway, University of London) works on contemporary and twentieth-century literature, literary theory and philosophy. His publications include *Ethical Criticism: Reading after Levinas* (1997), *Doing English* (1999, 2nd edn 2002), *Postmodernism and Holocaust Denial* (2001) and *The Holocaust and the Postmodern* (2004). He is the series editor of Routledge Critical Thinkers.

Roz Kaveney is a novelist, short-story writer and critic, published in the national press. She edited the two *Tales from the Forbidden Planet* (1987, 1990) anthologies, and co-edited both volumes of *The Weerde* (1992, 1993) and *Villains*. She also edited and co-wrote *Reading the Vampire Slayer* (2001), a critical book, and is the author of *From Alien to the Matrix: Reading Science Fiction Film* (2005). She was a contributing editor of the *Encyclopaedia of Fantasy* and wrote exensively for the *Cambridge Guide to Women Writing in English*, as well as being widely involved in civil liberties work.

Scott Kleinman is Associate Professor of English at California State University, Northridge. He works on Old and Middle English language and literature and has published articles in *Neuphilologische Mitteilungen*, *Studies in Philology*, *Exemplaria* and *Viator*. He is currently at work on a book on regionalism and ethnic identity in Middle English romances and chronicles.

Barry Langford (Royal Holloway, University of London) lectures in Film Studies and Critical Theory and has published articles on subjects including Holocaust film, Siegfried Kracauer and Walter Benjamin's film writings, maverick French documentary maker Chris Marker, and suburban sexuality, and is the author of *Film Genre: Hollywood and Beyond* (Edinburgh UP, forthcoming).

Simon Malpas (Edinburgh University) works on aesthetics, Romanticism, continental philosophy and the postmodern. He is the author of *The Postmodern* (Routledge, 2005) and *Jean-François Lyotard* (Routledge, 2003), and has edited Postmodern Debates (Palgrave, 2001), *William Cowper: The Centenary Letters* (Carcanet, 2000) and, with John Joughin, *The New Aestheticism* (Manchester University Press, 2003).

Jennifer Neville (Royal Holloway, University of London) specializes in Old English poetry in the department of English at Royal Holloway, University of London. Her publications include *Representations of the Natural World in Old English Poetry* (Cambridge University Press, 1999) and articles upon various topics such as monsters, chronicles, law codes, saints' lives, and seasons. She was short-listed for a National Teaching Fellowship in 2001.

Adam Roberts (Royal Holloway, University of London) is a novelist, writer and critic. He is the author of five novels: *Salt* (2000), *On* (2001), *Stone* (2002), *Polystom* (2003) and *The Snow* (2004), as well as two parodies of Tolkien *The Soddit* (2004) and *The Sellamillion* (2004). He has also written a number of critical books, mostly on nineteenth-century topics, including *Browning* (OUP, 1997, with Daniel Karlin) and *Tennyson* (OUP, 2000), as well as updating Lin Carter's *Tolkien: A Look Behind the Lord of the Rings* for Gollancz (2003). His *Palgrave History of Science Fiction* was published in 2005.

Esther Saxey (University of Sussex) works on queer theory, literature and popular culture, and has published on fan culture in *Reading the Vampire Slayer* and lesbian illegitimate heroines in *Women: A Cultural Review*.

Sue Zlosnik (Manchester Metropolitan University) is Professor of English and Head of Department. She works on nineteenth- and twentieth-century narrative, with a particular interest in Gothic. Her books include *Daphne du Maurier: Writing, Identity and the Gothic Imagination* (1998) and *Gothic and the Comic Turn* (2005), both co-authored with Avril Horner and published by Palgrave.

INDEX